A Current Adventure

In the Wake of Lewis & Clark

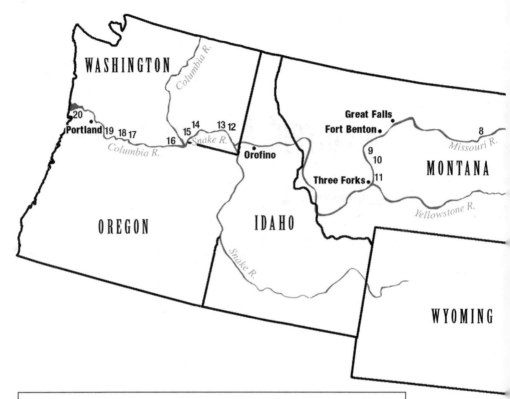

WASHINGTON

Columbia R.

20
Portland 19 18 17
16
15 14 13 12
Snake R.
Columbia R.
Orofino

Great Falls
Fort Benton
8
Missouri R.
9
10
MONTANA
Three Forks 11

OREGON

IDAHO

Snake R.

Yellowstone R.

WYOMING

1	Camp Dubois State Historical Site	11	Toston Dam
2	Gavins Point Dam	12	Lower Granite Dam
3	Fort Randall Dam	13	Little Goose Dam
4	Big Bend Dam	14	Lower Monumental Dam
5	Oahe Dam	15	Ice Harbor Dam
6	Garrison Dam	16	McNary Dam
7	Fort Union National Historic Site	17	John Day Dam
8	Fort Peck Dam	18	The Dalles Dam
9	Holter Dam	19	Bonneville Dam
10	Hauser Dam	20	Fort Clatsop National Memorial

A Current Adventure
In the Wake of Lewis & Clark

Chris Bechtold

2003 • ARNICA PUBLISHING
Choteau, Montana

Cover painting: *"View of the Bluffs near Cedar Island"* by Karl Bodmer. Courtesy of Joslyn Art Museum, Omaha, NE

Cover photograph: Chris Bechtold and Herschel on the bank of Lake Sharpe at Pierre, South Dakota, courtesy of Dorinda Daniel

Library of Congress Data Cataloging-in-Publication Data
Bechtold, Chris, 1971-
    A current adventure : in the wake of Lewis & Clark / Chris Bechtold.
    p. cm.
    ISBN 0-9728538-0-4 (pbk. : alk. paper)
    1. Lewis and Clark Expedition (1804-1806) 2. Bechtold, Chris, 1971—Journeys—West (U.S.) 3. Rivers—West (U.S.) 4. River life—West (U.S.) 5. Boats and boating—West (U.S.) 6. West (U.S.)—Description and travel. 7. West (U.S.)—History, Local.
I. Title.

F592.7.B437 2003
917.804'33—dc21   2003005911

Arnica Publishing
P. O. Box 543
Choteau, MT 59422

For Herschel, the best dog
(and friend) in the world

&

Amy and Wilbur,
My Family.

ACKNOWLEDGMENTS

MORE THAN ANY ONE PERSON, I want to thank my father, Dan Bechtold, for being there for me. He accepted my decision to follow this crazy scheme and supported me enthusiastically. I only hope I can live up to being the father he has been. Also, I want to express my deepest thanks to my mother, Phyllis Bechtold, for understanding my need to do these types of things. My wife, Amy has been supportive from day one and has put up with all the doubt, frustration, and cluttered tables from the start.

Special thanks go also to Calvin Garrett for all his help from the inception of my trip up to this day. So many folks have helped me in the creation of this book and along the trail that I don't have room enough to mention them all. Some I can rattle off: Joe and Joan Lang, Larry Reid, Dick Ivester, Chuck and Sharon Blixrud, Brian McCabe, and Hal Stearn, for suggesting I try to do some writing.

Is THERE ANY ONE OF us that has not dreamed of seeing the world as it was before our own time? I doubt it. As for me, I have always been fascinated by the thought of the West before European settlement. I like to imagine a windswept plain with looming mountains full of wildness and wonderment; a world that tested its inhabitants allowing those who passed nature's tests to survive.

Maybe that is why the stories of Lewis and Clark and the early fur trappers captivate me so. Those men entered a wilderness that set the rules. Those that passed its difficult tests survived. Those that did not were, more often than not, never heard from again. For those that did survive, the West became an alluring land of plenty: plenty game, plenty grass, plenty cold and plenty tough. The stories of these early trappers and roamers of the west are the stories that generations of Americans have grown up on.

I grew up reading about Jedidiah Smith, Jim Bridger, Hugh Glass, and countless others. But before any of these American legends set their boots on a westerly course, there was Lewis and Clark and the Corps of Discovery. Those men, the men of the Corps of Discovery, were the men that truly shaped our American destiny. Men like John Colter, and George Drouillard and roughly two dozen others were the first of European descent to traverse the continent.

What must it have been like to see all that those men saw, feel all that they felt, and endure what must surely at times have felt like an impossible journey? I had always tried to envision in my mind the land as it was when these early explorers first gazed upon it. Many a time, I have visited destinations along the Lewis and Clark Trail and stood looking over the countryside trying to piece together what the land used to look like. How the land must have looked to those men as they labored through the country.

The problem for those of us today who long to see the West as it was is that we can only try to imagine the land and the past. There is no crystal ball that allows us to look back in time and see what things used to look like. We can only look at the here and now, piecing together clues from the past to guess how it all must have looked. Too often, we use these clues in the wrong context anyway.

The journals that were written by early explorers did not have mile markers to gauge location by. No highway exits were listed so followers could take the correct exit. The men who traveled into unknown land had only the land about them to gauge their locations: a rock, a mountain, the forks of a river, or the sweep of a river bend. These were the landmarks of the early travelers.

Unfortunately, most of today's followers of the Lewis and Clark Trail travel via highway and byway, using travel guides to get them to the important places in history. They drive by important markers to gaze out over the land and compare their view to that of Lewis and Clark. I say this is unfortunate, not because travelers look from their vehicles or a scenic viewpoint, but rather because what they view is not the landscape Lewis and Clark saw.

Lewis and Clark viewed the West from the river bottoms, principally the Missouri River and the Columbia River. From the moment the men of the Corps of Discovery left the St. Louis area, they lived day to day along the Missouri River and it's tributaries or the tributaries of the Columbia River, excluding their sojourns through the Bitterroot Mountains. So, in order to see the land as Lewis and Clark had, one must look at the West from the river.

In a round about, convoluted path of circumstance and fate, that is exactly what I ended up doing. From the mouth of the Missouri River, upstream to the Three Forks of the Missouri River, I followed the same course as Lewis and Clark had along the great Missouri. Then one year later, I continued in their footsteps down the Clearwater River to the Snake River and onward towards the Pacific Ocean on the Columbia River.

I saw the land of today as Lewis and Clark had in their time—from water level. What I saw, unfortunately, was very little of the land and river that Lewis and Clark had seen. With their journals by my side,

I traveled day in and day out the same path of the Corps of Discovery. From the writings of Meriwether Lewis and William Clark, I could see in my mind the landscape they beheld, but with my own eyes I saw a world far different.

Today, very little remains of the river these men saw. Small, scattered stretches of the original river exist, far removed from one another. For the most part, the rivers have become completely different beasts. Numerous dams confine the rivers, preventing them from running unhindered to the sea. Little is left of the meandering, muddy Missouri or the cascading Columbia. Yet both rivers still retain a small vestige of wildness, allowing brief glimpses of the rivers they used to be and the rivers they may become again.

I feel lucky that I was able to see beneath the veneer of dams and channels and experience a small part of what those early explorers must have felt: wonderment, trepidation, and freedom lurking around every bend. After all, I imagine that even the early travelers must have wondered what the river was like long before they ever laid oar to the waters.

The Missouri River has always been a part of my life. Like the deep currents of the famed river, the Missouri formed me in imperceptible ways with a power unfathomable and unstoppable. The big rivers of my youth were something to just take for granted and never at the forefront of any one thought. I grew up in the small town of Godfrey, Illinois. It isn't even on the river, any river, yet it is influenced in all aspects by river culture. Just 5 or 6 miles from town, the Mississippi River flows lazily by. It is wide, muddy and deceptively powerful. Ten miles to the north, the Illinois River joins the Mississippi giving it added strength and color. Roughly ten miles west, the Missouri river joins forces with the two flows to create the Mississippi that made St. Louis famous.

Surprisingly, growing up in an area dominated by river culture, I had been out on the river a total of two times. And those times were as a guest on a family ski outing. Not exactly qualifications for an extended small craft river journey. I had never been on the water of the Missouri River.

When I left home at eighteen and moved to Montana, I frequently found myself somewhere along the Missouri. I even lived right on its banks for two years as a ranch hand on a large ranch. Yet, I had never floated the river. One might ask if that shouldn't deter a young man from traveling roughly 2,300 miles on the river that defines the western U.S.— upstream—with a dog for a traveling companion. But that, experience notwithstanding, is just what I had decided to do.

In the fall of 1997, I was working as a guide in the Bob Marshall Wilderness of Montana. The summer season had already wound down, and by this time of the year the ranch was putting up the fall hunting season camps. This involves numerous trips in and out of the mountains to haul all the needed gear for a comfortable late season camp. In between these trips, one person must stay at the camp to keep an eye on things and to keep any curious bears away. This particular year it was my turn to watch camp. This meant I had about four days alone in camp to do chores and enjoy the peace and solitude. A person can only cut so much firewood in a day and the rest of my time I spent reading. I had just received a copy of Undaunted Courage by Stephen Ambrose. I devoured the book and spent the remaining evenings alone looking into the campfire lost in thought about life on the river in 1804 and today. Had anyone ever retraced the Lewis and Clark expeditions tracks? I guessed that surely someone had. But, oh, wouldn't it be something to see the river they had. To travel through the heart of America and experience the river for the first time like so many other Americans had 150 years ago. The thought stuck in my mind and stayed there like a little pinprick.

Circumstances rolled me along like a rock on a river bottom that winter and by spring I found myself back in Godfrey, Illinois, working as a meat cutter in a specialty shop. I stuck with it for a few months and saved up some money to get me back to Montana. I had obligations with the ranch I guided for to be back at work by the end of May. So, with money in my pocket and time on my hands, I began to have recurring thoughts of the river.

It started at first with idle thoughts and a little research. This led to more questions and trips down to the river edge to watch the water flow. According to my research, I had found one other man who had traveled up the Missouri River to its source. I tracked him down and made a phone call.

This adventurer turned out to be a chiropractor from Oklahoma who had made the trip all the way up the Missouri and down the other side of the divide to Astoria. Unfortunately, I have since lost his name or I would surely give him credit for his immense undertaking. His boat was a custom-made 20 ft. jon boat and he had a support crew of 8. I talked for almost an hour, asking questions and feeling out his opinion. By the time I hung up I was thoroughly discouraged. I could never make it. Not enough experience or money. Best drive back to Montana.

I moped around for a few days mulling it over, and finally decided to hell with it, I was going to give it a try. Like Bob Dylan said, "When you got nothing, you got nothing to lose." Right on Bob! I began to look for a boat.

First, I borrowed a friend's canoe to see if it was feasible to paddle up river. It wasn't. I put the canoe in the river below an interstate bridge and loaded it up with about 300 lbs. of weight (what I estimated my gear to weigh for the trip). I paddled all day long with hardly a break until I reached a wing dike that I could not paddle around or haul the boat over. At the end of the day I was about 6 miles from where I had started and thoroughly whipped.

Wing dikes are a set of posts and board set in the riverbed to divert the current of the river towards its center. They average roughly 150 feet in length and, when the river is flowing at normal, stand out of the water about 3 feet. When canoeing, it is quite easy to paddle upstream behind the dikes, but when you try to get around them it is another story. The current rushes around the end of the dike creating a drop of about six inches in the water. This powerful surge of water is sufficient to turn the tip of a canoe and keep one person from paddling further upstream. Try as I might, I could not get any further up stream. The last few dikes I had passed, I was forced to unload the canoe and pull it over the dikes. Dangerous business in cold, deep river water on a snowy day in February. I started to give up the idea of paddling a canoe.

My next thought was to get a canoe with a square stern that I could attach a small outboard motor to power me along. This is where I fully committed to the trip. Up until this point it had been a lot of talk, but no real monetary commitment. After researching canoes for weeks, I found a used one in St. Charles, Missouri that was just what I was after.

The reasoning behind using a canoe was that I would need to be able to haul all of my equipment around the dams on the middle river by myself. By using a small outboard and canoe, I would be able to pack each separately around the dams. It was a fine idea. I needed to get going with the purchases now and get on with the trip.

Before buying the canoe, I had been down to the local boat shop and after much talk and research decided to buy a 9.9 hp Mercury outboard. I figured it would be all the power I would need and get me scooting right up the river. I bought the canoe a day or so later. Now I was set.

I picked up a few waterproof gear bags, waders, and assorted plunder for the trip. And, I was beginning to get nervous. Word of my plans was also beginning to get out. People were asking questions and my pride was on the line. I sure hoped I could do this. I had also just spent a lot of hard-earned money for equipment.

Word got out to the local radio station and newspaper, which both showed interest in covering the trip. They called asking numerous questions and when I was planning on leaving. I picked a date and held my breath.

With ten days to go, and just to be safe, I decided to take my boat and motor out for a little test spin in a friend's pond. My Dad rode along with me to the pond and we quickly threw the canoe in the water and hopped in. We sat about two inches out of the water. When I gave the motor any gas, the front of the canoe would surge upward and the back end would dip down below the water level and take on water. The more gas I gave the motor, the more water I got in the canoe. We paddled ashore and pulled the canoe out of the water. That's about as close to quitting as I came. The only thing more dangerous than a large river is a man's pride. I couldn't quit now. Nobody likes a quitter. Swallowing my fear, and the money I had spent on the canoe, I went looking for a little boat, one that a 9.9 Mercury could push up the Missouri River. I had about a week and a half before departure date to find it. I planned to take about 45 days to ascend the river and still needed to be at work on the ranch by the end of May. Time was running out.

Back to the boat shops and researching boats. This time I went with the conventional wisdom and decided on a jon boat. They are THE boat on the big rivers around Godfrey, Illinois. Good in shallow water, stable on the river and hold a lot of gear, just the boat I needed. I found what I was looking for in a 14-foot Sea Ark 48" jon boat with a modified V front. I asked the salesman if he thought it would do the job. He didn't know anything about the upper river, but he guaranteed it on the lower river. He also said he wouldn't go out in anything smaller. I bought the boat for $1,425.00.

This time I tried it out on the Illinois River on a calm day. It handled like a dream and had more room than a canoe. My dog, Herschel, would be much more comfortable. I began to get excited. With much confidence I continued my preparations. The next hurdle was how to get a 14-foot, 250-pound boat around the dams on the river. I could only manhandle a boat around so much, and I sure couldn't pick it up and carry it. Calvin Garrett, a good friend of the family, came to the rescue. With his help and design, we came up with a clamp-on wheel system that allowed us to flip the boat over and wheel it like a wheelbarrow. It wasn't light, but it was possible for me to wheel the boat for quite a ways. All systems go at this point. I was ready to begin the grand journey.

As the day of my departure approached my nervousness increased. Like I said earlier, the only thing more dangerous than the river itself was my pride. Growing up in a land loving family in the Midwest, we always subscribed to the saying, "Don't go near the water." With just a few days left to go, the question of the day was "are you still going to do it?" Hell Yes, come hell or high water. It was high water. The spring floods were coming down the river and with one day left before departure, the flood crested at St. Charles, Missouri. I was so nervous by this point that I didn't even like the thought of getting wet in the shower. I tried to keep up the tough guy image on the outside, but on the inside I was getting worried.

From what I had heard, the best time to be on the flooding river (if there was a best time) was the day after the crest of the flood. The theory being that the majority of the debris in the water will have been left on shore as the water recedes. Sounded like a good theory to me. I needed a good theory at that point.

So there I was, the night before I was to leave on my trip, packing and worrying. To make it doubly difficult, I was packing my bags so that I would have everything I needed for the entire summer and fall, in addition to all I would need for the trip. I would need to ship some bags to the ranch and plan on taking others with me. It was all very confusing. I had to plan ahead because my truck would be left in Illinois at my folk's house. So, once I got to work, all I would have would be my duffle and a boat. A whole lot of good a boat will do a cowboy on a Friday night.

I barely slept a wink that night, and before I went to sleep I made an entry in my journal as to what should be done with my stuff should I not make it. Those sorts of preparations make for light sleep and low confidence. Early the next morning I found myself at Camp Dubois in Wood River, Illinois. There is a memorial there to the Corps of Discovery. Unfortunately, it resides at the end of a small, dank road across an interstate from a chemicals plant. It does not inspire one to greatness when standing at the monument. Instead, most people tend to think about whether their cars are locked or not and wonder if they have any insect repellant.

EDITOR'S NOTE: *As of the date of publication, a new interpretive center has been erected at the site and many improvements made.*

CHAPTER 1

*"I set out at 4 oClock P.M. in the presence of many of the
neighbouring inhabitents, and proceeded on under a jentle
brease up the Missouri"*

William Clark May 14, 1804

*". . . the Mississippi was up fairly high and choppy.
plowed through the waves and finally hit the mouth of
the Missouri. My stomach was in a knot all morning."*

Chris Bechtold April 20, 1998

IT WAS A COOL SPRING MORNING as I stood at the monument with my
family looking out over the Mississippi River. The date was April 20,
1998. Notice that I didn't say it was a CALM, cool, spring morning. At
least it didn't feel that way. The Mississippi looked like it was 10 miles
across. I could have sworn that the waves were big enough to sink the
Queen Mary as I stood there. Oh well, like Bob Dylan said. The local
radio station was there as was the newspaper. I did a short interview
with both. Larry Reid, the local outdoor radio personality chattered
away into a tape recorder as I busied myself with the final details. "Yep,
gonna try to make it all the way to Montana . . . Just like Lewis and
Clark . . . a local adventurer . . ." My mind was beginning to focus and
I was ready to get going.

Along with the radio and newspaper people, my family and friends
were also there. I still do not know if they all showed up to wish me luck
or to see me one last time before I was swallowed by the river. Calvin,
Dad, and Dick Ivester, a good friend of the family, helped to unload the
boat and get it in the water. I didn't buy a trailer to go with the boat
figuring that I really wasn't going to need it. So instead of backing a
trailer down into the water like normal people, we drug the boat off of

*Camp Dubois State Historical
Monument at Wood River, Illinois*

a utility trailer that we had borrowed. I scurried about readying all of my equipment in the boat and finally proclaimed myself ready to depart. With hugs all around, I climbed into the boat with Herschel. The motor fired right up and with everyone waving good-bye and holding their breath, I backed out into the deep waters.

I was so worried, I almost twisted the throttle off of that little outboard motor on the way across the Mississippi. I never looked back. Hell, I was too worried about what was in front of me to look back. What seemed like ages probably only took a minute or two and then I turned into the mouth of the Mighty Missouri River. It was all upstream from there. I could let out a breath and relax, if only for a moment. It wasn't all that bad. I scooted along pretty good and the boat handled well. After about 6 miles or so, the knots began to loosen in my shoulders and what had seemed like a cool spring day began to warm a little. I passed by beautiful homes sitting high on the hills overlooking the river. Homes and properties I never knew existed in all the time I spent growing up in the area. Wow, I was on my way and the enormity of it grabbed hold of me. If I ever felt in my element it was when I was outside, and camping, and being on my own. Here I was, in my element at last. Oh, how good it felt, and the boat was running good. All seemed well, except that Herschel didn't look too frisky. In fact, he looked a little glassy eyed and he was drooling a lot.

After I noticed that he didn't look well, it dawned on me that he might be seasick. Great. I try to plan for every emergency and my dog gets seasick. I knelt down alongside him to see how he was doing and I realized how he felt. He was sitting next to my legs looking over the back at the wake (over the stern in boat talk) as we motored along. It doesn't take much of that view to make anyone feel a little queasy. I rearranged the boat so he could sit closer to the front and look ahead. In no time, he was feeling a little better and settled in to river life. Herschel was my sanity on the entire trip. He was something to keep me grounded, so to speak, and someone to talk to when I got tired of the drone of the motor.

We made quite a team in our river duds. I wore a pair of brown hip boots and a skier's life jacket with a cowboy hat and my fuzzy little friend had on a brown life coat that I insisted he wear. Not that he couldn't swim, just that it helped him float a little better and kept him a little drier in the rain and spray. It was just a neoprene dog vest, but I put his name on it and my brand and address. We made quite a sight. I don't think anyone ever mistook us for a local no matter where we were.

That first day on the river was quite an experience. In the 56 miles I traveled that day, I learned a lot about how the boat handled and reading the river. The smooth surface of the river could be quite deceiving. Small lines littered the brown surface of the river like the cracks on a windshield. Not all the cracks meant something. Some warned of obstacles under the water while others were nothing more than the current tracing around formations on the river floor. Boils of water sprouted constantly while along the rivers edge, whirlpools spun off the end of the dikes.

My biggest concern, after settling down, was the whirlpools. As the current rushed past the end of the dikes, it created whirlpools varying in width from 10 to 30 feet. I had heard all sorts of stories about the dangers of these whirlpools when I first began to plan the trip. Old timers would tell stories of small boats being sucked down into the pools never to be released. The old timers sure got my attention.

I avoided the whirlpools like the plague most of that first day until I became more comfortable with the boat. Finally, screwing up some courage, I edged down alongside one. Nothing happened. Later, with a bit more courage, I decided to dash across a small whirlpool. I zipped out the other side. After that I realized how stable my boat was and would use the whirlpools to slingshot me faster up the sides of the river.

Day one also gave me a little lesson on barge traffic. For one thing, I learned how to read the navigational signs on the sides of the river. The entire navigable stretch of the Missouri River is lined with mile markers and green and red navigation signboards. Green is for Port and red is starboard as you look up stream. This is fairly important information when traveling on the river. The barge traffic uses these signs to maintain their course in the deepest part of the channel which is also the part of the channel with the most current.

Knowing this, I intended to read the navigational markers and steer just opposite of them. This would keep me out of the deepest, swiftest portion of the river and out of barge traffic. Not that there was a lot of traffic at this time of the year. The majority of riverboat traffic on the Missouri takes place in the summer and fall, when water levels are more stable. There are down sides to traveling opposite of the markers. Like I said, you are out of the main travel channel and have to keep your eyes open to obstacles. More than once in that first week, I found myself grounded on sandbars.

The largest danger when traveling on the river with tugboats wasn't so much their wakes, large as they were, it was knowing that they had a limited visibility and steering capability. Motoring past St. Charles, Missouri, I zigged and zagged around 3 towboats and dredge boats as they made their way around the waterfront. With the rough water and in a small rain shower, I had to be quick in my movements to stay out in visible territory of the big boats. In time though, the barge traffic lessened as I went on and I saw very few other boats by the time I got above Kansas City, Missouri.

Let me go back to the first day. I was traveling along at a pretty good clip and really enjoying myself by the afternoon of my first day out. Beginning to become familiar with the handling of the boat and the feel of the river, I got caught up in the scenery of the country side above St. Charles.

The banks of the river had become more rural and lush. The land there is prime farm country teeming with deer and turkey. In the midst of all this peaceful thinking, my motor sputtered once, revved, and ran out of gas. Almost simultaneously, I happened to look up and a tugboat pushing eight barges appeared around the bend coming right for me. My first thought was "don't panic." Then I began to panic. I crawled up to the front of the boat and grabbed my spare jerry can of gas. Herschel looked over at me a little glassy eyed, obviously unaware of the danger we were in.

Trying not to get too shook up, I opened up the fuel tank to refuel. When I opened the jerry can I accidently sloshed fuel all over the boat while trying to pour into the fuel tank. The barges were bearing down on me at this point, so I only put enough gas in the can to get the motor started. I put the open, nearly full can of gas between my knees, put the cap on the fuel tank, and primed the motor. All the while I kept an eye on the barges. They weren't turning any or slowing down. Which goes back to that thing I said earlier about them having limited visibility and not a lot of stopping power. I pulled the rope and low and behold the motor started. I roared off to the bank. I became a tried and true believer in Mercury Outboards at that point. I also learned about how much fuel my boat uses in a day. I had used six gallons up to that point and it was mid afternoon. I figured I would use about ten gallons a day or so. That first day I went 56 miles and made camp at a little road access.

My folks were traveling along for the first four or five days to shop in the small river towns along the way and see how I was making out. I carried a cellular phone, which my mother insisted upon, and my folks carried another so we could keep in touch if there was a problem and to meet up at the end of the day. I gave them a call and told them where they could find me. When they arrived, Herschel leapt up and ran over to their mini-van. He jumped into the front seat and looked off in the distance away from the river and me. Try as I might, I couldn't even get him to look at me—or the river. I thought I had lost my traveling partner. It was obvious that he wasn't having any fun. Finally, he consented to join me when I promised we were done for the day. My folks had brought me a little dinner to celebrate the end of my first day of the journey and we had a beer and visited for a while. Then they headed back home and I began to prepare camp on my first night out.

I am not a believer in large, luxurious camps. After all, I was just going to sleep then hit the river again first thing in the morning. Camp for most nights on the river consisted of spreading my sleeping bag on a sleeping pad and throwing a canvas manty (a seven foot by seven foot tarp used to wrap up loads for pack mules) over the top of me. On rainy nights I would stake out a lean-to with another rubberized canvas tarp or just roll up in the rubberized tarp. I cooked over an open fire most every day and made coffee in the mornings on a small backpacker cook stove. It made for spartan accommodations, but I was quite comfortable with them.

That first night I rolled out my bag on the sand alongside the river, covered up with the manty, and fell fast asleep. I woke in the middle of the night to a flashlight shining in my eyes. My first thoughts were that this was it; I was to be robbed and beaten on my first leg of the journey and there wasn't a thing I could do about it. I had left my pants, underpants, and shirt down by the boat and was nestled nude, deep in a mummy sack. Not the way I had pictured myself dying. The voice behind the light seemed as startled as I was. It said, "I'm going fishing." I replied, "I'm sleeping." I couldn't think of anything else to say. The light stepped over me and proceeded down to the waters edge. Through all of this, my trusty watchdog watched.

I hardly slept a wink all night. I lay there naked in my sleeping bag, and watched as the fellow with the light set up a chair and lantern and proceeded to go fishing just a few feet down from my boat. Finally, the first hint of a glow in the East arrived and I decided to get up. The fellow down by the water had started a fire and was still sitting there in his lawn chair watching the river. When I had crept down and gotten dressed, I eased over and introduced myself. His name was Jason. We exchanged pleasantries and I offered coffee which I put on the fire to boil. There I sat on the first morning of my trip watching the sunrise with a stranger as we sipped hot coffee and listened to the turkey's gobble and the slap of beavers on the water.

Come to find out, Jason worked the evening shift at an electrical plant in Labadie, Missouri, and spends his time after work fishing in the dark and enjoying the solitude of the river. I truly think I perplexed him more than he startled me. We talked of the river and fishing and the country around us. He used his time fishing at night to think and absorb the peacefulness of the river. A tom turkey gobbled and flew across the river in front of us. He picked up his fish and as he packed up he offered one to me to take along. I declined since I had enough food for a while and didn't really feel like I needed to pack a fish along with me. It was actually a good meeting and a good omen for the rest of the trip. I never had any real problems with the people I met as I traveled the river. All were as nice and helpful as Jason. But I did learn an important lesson that first day, never to camp at a public access point. From there on out I camped at spots that were not easily accessible from land, except for one notable exception, which I will get to later.

That second day out turned out to be cold and breezy. I bundled up in my heavy wool coat and a pair of hip boots I had bought for the trip. The banks of the river already showed signs of change from the banks near St. Charles. Here the riverbanks turned to high limestone bluffs and the forest canopy hung heavy along the river edge. I saw only one other boat on the river that day; a jon boat full of fisherman. It was a 16-foot boat with a one hundred horsepower outboard. It went screaming by me. I felt a little under gunned after it went by sending a rooster tail of water in the air. I was lucky just to leave a wake with my little 9.9. Most folks along the river consider boating on the Missouri with a 9.9hp motor like going to the Sturgis Rally on a moped.

Sunrise on the lower Missouri River

I pulled into Hermann, Missouri later on that morning and walked up to a small bait shop. The sign out front proclaimed this the K and S Bait Shop. I went in and found two old-timers watching the shop and swapping stories. They offered me a cup of coffee and a bucket full of opinions and advice. Seems like there is one thing the river brings out in people and that is opinions. I hung out in the shop for about a half an hour and soaked up the heat listening. Everyone has something to say about the river. I found that most people on the lower river are somewhat afraid of the mighty Missouri. Most everything they hear about the river is usually some sort of bad news: drowning, a capsized boat, flood waters, et cetera, so there becomes this ingrained fear. I really think it is a fear bred of ignorance. The river flows right under their noses, but very few people take the time to get to know the river and enjoy it. Of course, after listening to a few bait shop stories, who wouldn't be afraid of the river. Those old-timers sure don't know anything about easing fears. They'd never make it as river counselors.

I could picture them now. "So, been fishing?" I bet I heard that a thousand times on my trip. "Not fishing? Where you heading?"

"Tough river up stream. I heard of a fellow got drowned up near Kansas City."

"Say, that your boat? Awfully small . . . "

"So and so was out on the river with a boat just like that. Fished him up down near St. Charles." Then after all the small talk, "Yep, have a good trip." Real inspiring advice.

Though, later that day I got a taste of how quickly the river can claim a person. I had decided to meet Mom and Dad at a little river town named Chamois, Missouri. From the map I carried, it looked like the last place to pull over and meet up with the folks before it got too late in the day. I figured I had to be getting close to town when I passed a large electrical plant. I could see an excavator working near the slag pile and a little creek running right by it. Pulling into the creek, I eased up the channel until I was across from the excavator. The banks of the creek were fairly steep and muddy with little vegetation. My biggest worry was grounding out the boat in the water because I couldn't see the bottom in the chocolate colored water. The boat nudged up against the bank and I stood up to step onto the bank. My foot slipped in the mud and I fell from the boat into the water. I never did touch bottom. My hand slapped down on the boat as I fell and I was able to grab hold of the edge of the boat as I went in. Only my hat stayed above the water.

I drug myself out of the water and into the boat. The cold muddy water stank of earth, sewage, and rot. I had been wearing my hip boots which were completely filled with water. The heavy wool coat I had on was now a really heavy wool coat. As cool as it was, I figured I had better put on some dry clothes immediately. I pulled over to the bank again and gingerly stepped out of the boat. Then I tied off and dug through my gear to get some warm dry clothes to put on.

When I was sufficiently clothed, I went up to talk to the excavator operator. Luckily, he hadn't seen my little show. I asked him if I was near Chamois and he pointed me up river less than a mile. I felt like a fool after I heard that. Back into the boat I went and motored up to the riverfront park in Chamois. In a short time Mom and Dad pulled in and I ate dinner with them at the café in town. They left and I slipped down into the brush and built a fire to dry my clothes and warm up to. That was the only time I fell in the water the entire trip. A year after I had finished my trip, if I got my wool coat wet it would smell like the water in that creek outside of Chamois. It was probably for the best that the dunking incident happened as soon as it did. It made me more careful about handling the boat and making sure I had my life vest on.

It wasn't until the end of the second day that I noticed a change in Herschel. He was still slobbering a little and shaking now and then. I don't think it was the seasickness the second day as much as it was just fear of the water. By evening, about the time I fell in the water, he had begun to relax a little. From that point on he was a river dog. I could tell him "Get in the boat!" and he would eagerly load up. But those first two days were as trying for him as they were for me. We had about as much river experience as a ground tied camel in the Sahara.

Herschel has been my traveling partner and best friend for quite a while. He is a one hundred percent Moo-Tee-Tee, or in other words, a M-U-T-T. I got him at the county animal shelter in Missoula, Montana when he was about 3 months old. He grew up on a cattle ranch in Wolf Creek, Montana and traveled all over western Montana with me as I worked as a seasonal for the U.S. Fish and Wildlife Service. In all my travels, Herschel has always been with me. And, just like me, he had very little experience around water. Our ideas of going to the river have always been walking down to the bank and trying not to get our feet wet. Now, Herschel was riding along with me on this outrageous trip that he had no say in. I know he wasn't too happy about it those first couple of days. But, like I said, it grew on him.

He would sit up at the front of the boat like a hood ornament in his little life vest, eyes peeled for birds and beavers. He loved to spot beaver and I truly think he believed if I let him out he could whip every one of them. I think I knew a little better and never let him out. He loved it when geese would get up in front of the boat flapping their wings, running across the water leading us away from their goslings. Once again, he believed if I would only let him out he could run them down. Not once did he ever jump out of the boat, unless I told him to. I hate to sound like a braggart, but I think he's the best dog in the world. Of one fact I am sure: he is definitely the only dog to travel up the entire length of the Missouri in the last 100 years. I guess I had better fess up. I'm pretty proud of him.

That night in Chamois was cool and wet. I didn't sleep too well as the beavers kept me awake most of the night slapping the water and bumping up against the boat. Each time I heard a bang against the boat I would worry that it had come loose and drifted away. Thinking back on it now, it was almost comical the number of knots upon knots I would fasten into the rope to hold the boat. I've spent a fair amount of time around horses and tied my boat up better than most knot picking horses. The beavers kept up their antics most of the night and a brief downpour of a shower came through. I managed to keep dry under my lean to tarp and woke up to a cool, overcast day.

My wool clothes had dried out somewhat. Not much, but enough to keep me warm. It is the magic of wool that does this. It weighs more than most other fabrics, but it has sure withstood the test of time. I put on most all the warm clothes I had and pushed off into the river. Bird life was everywhere that morning. From my first day out to the last day I pulled off the Missouri, I saw geese.

They were a constant form of entertainment for not only me, but also Herschel. The adult geese never ceased to amaze me how they would try to lure us from their goslings. They would run across the water just in front of the boat, flapping their wings, and honking as if every step might be their last. Or, if there were two adults, one would lead the way to safety followed by all the fluffy little goslings while the other adult would follow along in the rear pushing up against the young ones, hurrying them along. By far, one of my favorite tactics was when the female geese would try to hide on their nests. The closer the boat approached their nests, the lower the old hen would melt into the nest until she was a flat as a cow patty. Herschel would stand at the front of the boat and watch the old hen as we passed by, tormenting her with the fact that he knew where she was hiding.

That particular morning, the river seemed full of geese and other birds as well. Herds of Coots scurried across the water in front of us. Their little blue legs a blur as they eventually flew off. Cormorants slithered through the water like large beaked snakes, then crawled up onto stumps to hang their wings out to dry. Groups of three or four would disinterestedly watch us as we motored by, their black wings outstretched like Dracula's arms within his cape.

Great Blue Herons dotted the shore of the river around most every bend. I would run into these birds repeatedly throughout the trip, finding more than one rookery along the banks of the river. Every time I would see one of these birds with their long angular beaks and S curved necks, I would be reminded of a story a friend had told me about working in a bird rehabilitation center. The veterinarian on duty was repairing a wing on a heron and the assistant held tight to the bird as the anesthetic was being administered. With that penetrating, blank stare that only a large bird can give, the heron gave a quick peck at the eye of the vet and knocked the lens out of her glasses. It gives one some idea of the power and speed these birds have and how they have become so adept at catching fish.

CHAPTER 2

"George Drewyer & John Shields who we had sent with
the horses by land . . . gave a flattering account of the
Countrey . . . The Two Muddy rivers passing thro. & som
fine Springs & Streems"

William Clark June 2, 1804

"Day three on the river . . . Lots of bird life today, pileated
woodpecker, wood ducks, cormorants, coots, herons, and
geese . . . After passing the mouth of the Osage the river
began to smooth out."

Chris Bechtold April 22, 1998

NOT LONG OUT OF CHAMOIS, I passed what I considered the first (or last, if you look at it that way) major tributary of the Missouri. The Osage River comes into the Missouri from the south in a wide, muddy addition to the river. At the confluence of the two rivers is a sign board much like the one I remember seeing on the TV show M.A.S.H. Hand painted signs in the form of arrows were pointing either up or downstream with towns and distances scrawled across them. I could read two that stuck with me as I passed slowly by: "Belleview, NE 435 mi." Another read "Stateline, MS 750 mi." I didn't know how far I was from Great Falls, Montana, but I knew it had to be a hell of a long way.

The river began to become narrower at this point and meandered back and forth more than it had further downstream. I noticed also that the wing dikes tended to reach further out into the water. I picked up on this, like most astute river travelers, when my prop slammed against the submerged top of a pylon. With high water, the dikes were hidden just underneath the surface of the muddy water. Trying to keep out of the current as much as I could, I hugged close to the bank of the river when possible. I must have hit a dozen dikes that day. I am quite sure more than one lower unit and prop has been lost to the dikes of the Missouri.

When I hit one, the throttle arm of the outboard lept down out of my hand and the drone of the motor changed to a high-pitched whine as the prop flew up out of the water. When I really hit a dike hard, the motor caught on the ratchet settings of the prop that controlled the tiller of the motor. I knew I had hit good when that happened. Thankfully, the outboard that I was using was a new model and had a slip clutch on the prop for hard knocks. Otherwise, I don't think I could have carried enough shear pins along. By mid-day, the motor was vibrating badly and I was forced to pull over and take a look at the prop. I had bent one of the blades right at the end. Being a conscientious boater and marine engineer, I did what any other person would do in a similar situation, pulled out my Leatherman pliers and bent the blade as straight as I could. That seemed to quiet down the vibrations enough for me to keep on going.

The Missouri tends to be more sandy at this stretch than I had seen in any other areas downstream and it wasn't long before I got a taste of how deceiving the river could be. Shifting sandbars lie just beneath the surface of the water from below Jefferson City, Missouri to up above Boonesville, Missouri. When I first got into this stretch of water, I was still quite green at reading the water. I cowered at the boils of water rising everywhere across the surface. I soon learned that these boils were nothing more than the rolling action of the current as it passed over the shifting floor of the river. Riffles, V's and traces of current perplexed my inexperienced eye as I passed over the brown waters. Within a few days I had learned much about the behavior of the Missouri River. A few groundings on the sand and a few bumps on the prop helped me to pick up on the intricacies of reading the current and detecting what lay below the water's surface.

I found that If I got into the right depth of water, and at the right speed, the boat would actually ride a little higher out of the water and my speed would increase by a few miles-per-hour. So what? Big deal. Well, when your average speed is 7 mph, it makes a big difference. So I would try to squeeze out as much speed as I could and risk the chances

of grounding to gain a little speed. That day my luck wasn't very good. After a minute or so of moving along at a wonderful clip, I felt a bump on the prop and the boat skidded to a slow stop like it was caught in molasses. I had grounded out. But that wasn't the worst of it. Because I had been in the shallows so long, the boat was quite a ways from any deeper water and by stopping, the hull had lowered in the water until the boat sat quite solidly on the sand. Time to put the waders on, hop out, and pull. My first taste of pulling the boat . . . definitely not my last.

A person needs to pull a boat up a river to fully appreciate what the voyageurs who pulled the keelboats up the Missouri experienced a century ago. For the Voyageurs, cordelling was an arduous, cold, muddy task. Imagine gripping a rough rope and dragging the immense dead weight of a keelboat against the unyielding current. Just walking upstream tends to wear many people out. Now try to picture this muddy activity with the drag of a boat behind you. I really had it easy by comparison. I wore rubber hip boots, not leather moccasins and leggings. In addition, I had the luxury of a motor, so I only pulled the boat when I made a blunder. Day in and day out, the tedium of cordelling a boat against the Missouri would tax even the stoutest of men. Clark wrote of the great difficulty the men encountered pulling their boats against the river: "the current excessively rapid and dificuelt to assend great numbers of dangerous places, and the fatigue which we have to encounter is incretiatable the men in the water from morning untill night hauling the cord & boats." My main complaint about towing the boat was the disgusted look I got from Herschel when I would turn around. He seemed to disdain my efforts, no doubt quite aware of how we got into these sorts of pickles. I would come to recognize that disgusted look long before the end of the trip.

Jefferson City is the capitol of Missouri, home of a beautiful capitol building for which all the people of Missouri should be proud. The statehouse is a great stone building resembling many other state capitol buildings with stone columns and a great rotunda. Several times in my travels I have driven past the capitol building, never really giving it much thought. It has a large rotunda with Demeter, Greek goddess of agriculture, adorning the top of the building. It is a statehouse. Every state has one and all are impressive, but driving by the one in Missouri

Me and Herschel

never really gave me reason to pause. However, if you ever were to see the Missouri capitol building from the river, you will have a whole new perspective on the building itself and the body of water passing by it.

When I first rounded the bend in the river below the statehouse, I was astounded at the view that confronted me. I had not realized how close to Jefferson City I had traveled, but the view of the statehouse looming out over the river amazed me. I am sure the feeling that I experienced as I first sighted the building is exactly what it's designers had anticipated. It was at this moment that I realized how much history flowed in the waters of the Missouri River.

I began this trip with an interest in Lewis and Clark and the Corps of Discovery. I wanted to see the river as they had. Push upstream and watch the West unfold before me like it had for the men of the Corps. But along the way, I began to realize that the river captures the imagination of its travelers. It transcends time and brings the past to the present. Like the water that flows in its channel, each drop has a story to tell and a history of own, yet combined, and at any one time, they make up a moment in time on the present river. It seemed to me that was how my trip was to proceed.

At any one time I was just another traveler on the river, but at every bend, tributary, and stop I caught a glimpse of history and what helped to shape the West and the expansion of our country. The Missouri State Capitol Building sparked this thought within me. It was never intended to be viewed from behind. When it was erected there were no cars, no interstates and the main form of travel to the great western landscape was via riverboat. The capitol building was both a welcoming to those coming from the west and a marking point for those going to the west. At the time of its construction, the capitol building sat upon the true interstate of American travel, the Missouri River.

How many people looked out from the railing of a paddle wheeler at the grand old building and dreamt of what they were to see in the weeks ahead? Travel in those days was an adventure. Not like today where a traveler merely strides upon a plane with a small bag of carry on. In those days, a person had to plan ahead and plan for the unknown. You couldn't change your mind and catch the next flight home tomorrow either. You had to tough it out.

The men of the Corps of Discovery did not have travel insurance nor could they cancel reservations if something caught their eye. They were forced by nature and duty to continue. Likewise, the early fur trappers made commitments to the travels that they undertook. For the journeys that these men took could take years, or for some, lifetimes. There is something admirable to be said about this form of travel and the people who lived by it.

I motored past old Jefferson City taking in the beautiful bluffs downstream from Boonesville, Missouri. I believe the wooded bluffs below this town are the most scenic portion of the lower Missouri. I can understand why Old Daniel Boone chose this area for his final home. It has a peaceful air about it. I pulled into town in time to catch up with my folks and eat dinner with them. They headed into town after our meal and I slipped off across the river and made camp downstream from the bridge leading into Boonesville. I had made good time. It was the end of my third day on the river and I was at mile marker 197. I had hoped to average 50 miles a day.

If I continued at this pace I would be ahead of schedule (if you can say I even had a schedule). I hated to count my chickens before they hatched, though. I still had no idea what to expect further up the river.

My initial calculations were to arrive in Three Forks, Montana in 45 days. Unfortunately, this time frame allowed me no days to relax off the river. That meant I had to keep at it every day for a month and a half. After a while on the river, there became this little pinprick of momentum in the back of my head that kept me moving on. I couldn't have stopped if I had wanted to. Every day I would awake and wonder what is around the bend, what is upstream, what wonders are there to see that day? There was no real motto that kept me moving on, just the will to see new things.

That night at dinner, my Dad asked if it would be all right if he rode along with me. I thought that was a great idea. So the next morning he met me down at the river with a short lawn chair to use as his seat in the boat. We unloaded the equivalent of his weight in gear and put it in the van for Mom to haul. The boat was loaded right to its maximum for efficient speed—any more weight than what I had in it and it would not ride high enough in the water and I would lose a few miles-per-hour in speed. So it was important that I match the weight of my father when exchanging gear for him.

As we were unloading gear and getting him situated in the boat, an older gentleman passed by while taking his dog out for his morning walk. He asked how we were doing and inquired as to what we were up to. When we told him our story, his eyes lit up and he began to tell stories of his own days on the river in his youth. He told us quite a bit about the river around Boonesville and the buddies he fished and hunted with on the river. He was an old man. The last thing he told us was that all his buddies had died; he never got out on the river anymore. I wish I had offered to give him a ride. We always look back on the things we should have done, but it just seems like we are in so much of a hurry. As I look back, I know I wasn't in that much of a rush.

We finally got out in the water and after having Dad move around a little until his weight was distributed right, we were underway. We never saw another boat on the water that day and hardly any sign of another human being. It was a peaceful day on the water with just the buzz of the motor droning behind us. The bluffs that stood magnificently along the river below Boonesville were gone now. Farm land lined the banks of the river and we saw little wildlife, a total of 3 turkeys and a whitetail deer. But we didn't mind. My father, who has always been a man of action, going 100mph to keep his family taken care of, burning the candle at both ends, seemed to slowly melt into his seat. He visibly relaxed and I could tell he was enjoying himself immensely.

When I had first proposed this wild idea, I remember him saying it would be quite an adventure. He was my first supporter and I know he was secretly wishing that he had the chance in his youth to do the same. But Vietnam, a wife, family, and work obligations had taken his time. I know he would have been quite a traveler. He gets along great with everyone and he has never been afraid to try anything. He couldn't wait for my trip to begin, just so he could have an excuse to come along for a while. My father sat ahead of me in his short lawn chair soaking in the scenery and trying to leave the rest of the world behind. The river is good at helping one to do that.

We made 66 miles on April 23rd , my fourth day, and came to rest for the night at the waterside town of Miami. Miami, Missouri has nothing in common with its namesake in Florida other than they both have waterfront property. Dad and I had a beer that night sitting on chairs carved from the stumps of cottonwood trees in the town park. Mom took a picture of us both sitting there drinking beer with our sunglasses on. I titled the picture Miami Vice. I think we both looked a lot better than Don Johnson. Lord knows we were just as dangerous!

My folks took off to find a motel in a town close by and I settled down to write a little in my journal and watch the sun set across the river. It was a crimson sunset and I took a photo of myself sitting on the bank with the sun setting across the river. What a beautiful evening.

I was just settling down and getting ready to crawl into my sleeping bag when a beat up old Chevy van pulled up and parked not thirty yards away. An older fellow in a v-neck t-shirt and jeans got out and pulled a five gallon bucket and a fishing rod from the van. He waved hello and walked around a little cove of water that abutted the park. There was less than a half hour of daylight left so I just sat down on my sleeping bag and read a book that I had brought along.

I glanced up as the old fellow baited his hook and lobbed the line with a yellow bobber attached out into the cove. He reached down into his bucket before he sat on it and pulled out a Busch beer. I smiled and nodded when he looked over at me and he raised his beer in greeting. Just moments later I noticed a beaver swimming down the river side of the point that separated the cove from the river. The beaver dipped under the water and rounded the point. When it surfaced again, it was less than ten feet from the old man's bobber. It immediately went back under the water with a large slap of its tail. The old man jumped up excitedly and began to reel in his line.

As soon as he could get all his line in, he cast out again in the spot where the beaver was last seen. I watched this a little puzzled with it all and set down my book to see what would happen next. The beaver surfaced again in the little cove and again went quickly under. The old man reeled in his line and cast out to where the beaver disappeared under the water. By this time he had set down his beer and was standing anxiously holding his rod. The beaver surfaced moments later and the process repeated itself. This continued until it was too dark to see well.

The old man finally reeled in his line, gathered up his bucket and walked over to me. "Did you see that big old catfish?" he asked. "Well, uh . . . " I stammered. I thought the man was joking. But the look on his face told me he was dead serious. I was stumped. Should I tell the old guy he's been fishing for a beaver? "You know, I'm not sure, but I think that was a beaver you were seeing." "Nope, that was one of those big old river catfish. I been coming down here for a week trying to catch him. Shows up every night at the same time. I'll get him eventually. Just got to get the right bait." The old man couldn't possibly be serious I thought. But he was.

"Well, uh . . . you know . . ." and about that time I could see the beaver surface in the little bit of light reflected off the water. I pointed out at the beaver and told the old man. "There he is, and I really think it's a beaver." The old man stared out at the V shaped cut in the water and, as he was watching, the old beaver crawled right up on the bank with a stick in his mouth and began to gnaw on it.

"I sure think that's a beaver you been casting at." I said. "I watched him come down around the point as you were sitting over there."

"Well, I'll be damned" the old man said. "I been fishing for that son-of-bitch for a week. And it's a damned beaver. Never seen one of those things before . . . Well, shit. Want a beer?" He offered me a beer and we talked for a while.

The old fellow had just moved up to Missouri from Florida a couple weeks before. Since he had been here, he had been coming down to the river in the evenings hoping to catch his first catfish. Obviously, he hadn't had any luck. But he sure liked living in Missouri and really enjoyed being so close to the river. He said he couldn't believe how cheap land was there in Missouri and that Florida land prices were going through the roof. The more he talked, the more I couldn't help but believe that the old fellow may have been taken in a land scam. I could picture him seeing an ad for land on the edge of Miami at an unbelievable low price. I guess he just didn't realize it was Miami, Missouri and not Florida. I drank my beer with the old guy and we told a few stories. He bid me good luck in the night and drove off in his old van. I slipped down into my sleeping bag smiling to myself about the beaver-catfish and life in downtown Miami, Missouri. I couldn't help but think of that song that always used to play at the beginning of TV show "Miami Vice." You meet all kinds on the river.

CHAPTER 3

"It is worthey of observation to mention that our Party has been much healthier on the Voyage than parties of the same number is in any other Situation"

William Clark July 20, 1804

"A golden day. Warm and sunny. Got a little bit of sun on my face and hands. It's a warm tranquil evening here."

Chris Bechtold May 23 1998

LIFE ON THE RIVER IS LIKE NO OTHER LIFESTYLE THAT I CAN IMAGINE. It is at once monotonous and yet ever-changing. Like the river itself, everything is the same at first glance and yet is new and wholly unique unto itself. Looking out over the water, the great Missouri seems as static as a highway of pavement, but on closer inspection one begins to notice the swirl and eddy of the current, the pull of gravity on this massive body of water. A quick glance at the water leaves one with the impression of a muddy swill but look closer and you will see debris of small leaves swirling by, perhaps lost from some tree hundreds of miles upstream or bits of stick maybe cut by a beaver or muskrat.

The whole river is a study in imperceptible change and that is how life on the river progresses. It is an imperceptible transformation. The strength of the river slowly wraps itself around a person, passing on the vigor and health of all the world upstream. By the time I had left Miami, I had noticed a slowing in myself. The anxious feeling in my gut had loosened and I was able to listen to the river. The soft gurgles at night lulled me instead of filling my dreams with nervous wonderings. I began to develop an eye for the current in the river. Notice small nuances that revealed the rivers course and hidden obstacles under the surface.

None of this happened overnight though. It happened in river time, slowly and imperceptibly.

I was getting my river education. It took less time than any schooling I had ever had, yet I learned more about myself in those days than I ever could have in any institution. The old Missouri River scoured away all the outer shell of me and revealed the core of myself that I needed to find.

I left Miami early on the morning of April 24th, basking in the morning sunrise. Day five dawned cool and clear. Coots ran hurriedly in front of the boat and geese ducked and dodged trying to decoy me away from their young as I motored up river. I was in farm country this morning and mist rose from the fields along the river. I saw deer strolling along the field edges and turkey bobbing along the brushy draws leading to the river. The river itself felt more frisky and playful. Sand bars became more frequent and I was forced to pay close attention to the navigational markers and the tale of the current.

I was scooting along at a fairly good pace that lovely morning, trying to get the most out of my motor and riding the edge of the sand bar, when I misjudged and ended up aground in the middle of the river. When I finally came to a grating halt, it was well over 50 yards to the bank of the river, and much farther in the other direction. Yet, I was aground in 5 inches of water. I stepped out of the boat and wrestled the craft until I was able to get it afloat again. Herschel sat in the boat and stared disgustedly out at me, perturbed in the loss of momentum. It was such a funny sight looking at him sitting in the boat all alone in the middle of the river that I had to take a photo of him. He didn't even smile.

At 8:30 or so in the morning, I pulled into the little river town of Waverly, Missouri. It is a typical little river town with a small grain elevator, park, and older houses nestled atop the hills by the river. I noticed this morning that almost all towns have a sign or marker of some sort to tie themselves to the Lewis and Clark Expedition. Waverly was no different with a marker at the riverside park stating that the Corps of Discovery camped just upstream on June 17th, 1804 to "make oars, & repair our cable & toe rope &c. &c.". It is our great American Saga that ties together all who live along the trail of those great explorers.

My folks were waiting for me in Waverly that morning and Dad was up for another ride in the boat. So Mom and I exchanged gear for Dad and I pulled out into the river with my father. Our plan was to meet up with Mom in Lexington, Missouri. This short trip up the river turned out to be a true turning "point" in my Dad's life.

We hadn't been out on the river long before nature called and Dad asked if I could pull over for a moment. I pulled in to a brushy spot along the shore and Dad hopped out of the boat and I tossed him a roll of TP. Quite a few minutes later he returned to the boat a bit ashen looking. He gingerly stepped into the boat and returned my roll of TP, most of which had been used up. Now, I'm not the most sensitive person in the world and what most bothered me was the fact that most of my TP had been used up in one stop. I immediately began to give Dad grief on how wasteful he had been with a most important commodity.

When I had finished my little tirade, he told me he had had a little "accident." I wasn't sure if I wanted to hear more or not, but he filled me in. When he had slipped out into the brush, he had found a nice little opening that the beavers had made with a fallen log handily situated for gripping while he took care of his business. He nestled himself in and when he was ready to stand up, the log had broken and Dad had fallen down backwards and landed most expertly upon a sharpened stob left by a beaver. He said he didn't stay there long. No sooner than he hit bottom on the little spear and he was up again. So, most of my TP was used in a medical sense.

Well, when he had told me this, I couldn't help but laugh. Of course, it wasn't much of a laughing matter to my Dad. If you ask him, he'll tell you that no matter how smooth the surface of the water looks, it can be an awfully rough ride under those circumstances. I'll give my Dad credit though; he toughed it out for the day and rode with me all the way to Fort Osage, Kansas.

We kept our date with Mom, too and had lunch with her at Lexington, Missouri. She was about as sensitive to Dad's situation as I was and could not keep from laughing. It proved to be a serious wound in the end (pardon the pun) and I still to this day cannot think about or relate the story without chuckling. Like my Dad said, the odds of that happening are like throwing a washer out of an airplane and it landing around that beaver stick.

In Lexington, Mom had talked to someone from the local newspaper and I was interviewed on the banks of the river on the how's and whys of my trip. My Mom did like any Mother would and played PR person anytime she could. I was just as happy to keep to myself and just enjoy the trip. I always hoped in the back of my mind though that someone would want to sponsor me and chip in a little to defray the costs. No luck. From Lexington we set our sights for Ft. Osage, Kansas.

The river widened at this point from what it had been and I noticed that it seemed a bit shallower also. Dad was still with me, though he seemed to be a little uncomfortable. The wind had come up and the surface was getting choppy. Not the best of conditions for traveling with a perforated posterior. We passed a large power plant on the South side of the river and shortly thereafter pulled into Fort Osage in the late afternoon. Stepping from the boat onto the shore at the fort was like stepping back in time.

In an amazing event of coincidence, I had arrived at Fort Osage during a rendezvous reenactment. Bustling all about the old log walls of the fort were people in breeches, leather and period garb from the early 1800s. What a setting for a follower of Lewis and Clark to step into.

Fort Osage is a historically accurate reproduction of the original fort established by William Clark in 1808 on a site picked by the expedition. It remained an important trading post until 1826 when it was abandoned by the military. After it's abandonment, the fort served as ground zero of the mileage records for the Santa Fe Trail. The fort is tucked cozily on a hill overlooking the Missouri and a small grove of shade trees. Consisting of 3 buildings, the fort is made entirely of hardwood logs just as the original was over 150 years ago. The interior of the building remains consistent in theme and there are rooms supplied as they would have been at the height of the fur trade business which the fort supplied.

Early trade goods line the lower level of the fort's storerooms and a fur press can be seen in one of the rooms. A fur press is a screw-type contraption that compresses a stack of pelts into bale form which can then be bound together for ease of transport further down the river. In addition to the trade room, the displays revealed the spartan conditions of the enlisted men's quarters which were comprised of no more than a rope bed and table. Reviewing the meager daily necessities of the quarters made me realize how pampered all of us are today.

The rendezvous was just getting started when I arrived and many of the participants had just begun to set up. I stuck out in the crowd for more than one reason. Not only was I not attired in period garb, but I also did not fit in with the average tourist. Looking like a team roping trout fisherman with my hip boots, wool coat and cowboy hat, I strolled around the grounds.

It wasn't long before I had struck up a conversation with some of the re-enactors. Jay, Mike, Jim, and Ward kept up a conversation with me while setting up tents and arranging trade goods for display. All were clad in leggings, breeches, or wool and all had a myriad of stories and questions for a fellow history buff and river rat. They invited me to camp near the fort and to come visit them later in the evening for stories around the campfire and the evening festivities. Even more hospitably, they offered me use of the fort showers so that I could get cleaned up. I took that as a hint and kindly used the facilities.

After getting cleaned up, I visited for a while more with the guys and retired to my boat to set up a camp. I wanted to sleep close to the river so I could keep an eye on my boat. It was a good thing I did. That evening I learned where the high school hangout was for the kids around Fort Osage, Kansas.

A dirt two-track led down to the river below the fort and ended at a fishing spot where a creek dumped into the river. This is where I pulled my boat in to keep it out of the current of the main river and to provide some shelter in case the wind came up. The sky looked overcast and I was not sure if it would rain or not. I had barely gotten into my sleeping bag that night when the first of the teen-age partiers arrived. By midnight I was camped in the middle of a full-fledged party. I attribute the partying to the time of year. You must remember that it was towards the end of April and a Saturday night. The seniors were making memories.

Trying to ignore the ruckus going on above me and remain inconspicuous, I kept to my bag and attempted sleep. But my luck did not hold, and before long, one of the kids came strolling down to the waters edge and discovered me below the cut bank. "Hey, there's a dude sleeping down here!" He yelled. I'm sure this teen-ager is destined to go on and become a nuclear physicist in his later years. He was a real Einstein. I informed him that I was TRYING to sleep and I would appreciate it if he went back to the party and moved on. This of course brought more lookers and I was forced to get up and tell the kids I was camping and would like it if they moved their party on down the riverbank. Herschel helped me out the entire time by sleeping close to me and growling whenever he heard anyone approach.

Lucky for me they took my advice, but I remained wary and slept with one eye open the remainder of the night. I had no choice with the sound of cars, stereos, and motorcycles all night long. This was my last attempt at sleeping anywhere near a vehicle access in the Midwest. It did end up sprinkling a little that night, but by that time, I was too tired to care. I broke camp early the next morning and got out on the river. I still regret not heading up to the fort to say good-bye, but it would have been too early to roust anyone up and I was ready to get going by that point. The overwhelming pull to see new ground lured me onward.

April 25th turned out to be a beautiful day; in fact, it turned out to be a hot day. The temperature reached 84 degrees on my sixth day of the voyage, too hot for someone figuring on encountering snow on the upper Missouri. That morning thunderclouds scooted along the horizon to the north, increasing the wind a little later on in the day. Off to my left, I passed another river mile marker. I now had traveled 337 miles up the Missouri. I still had a long ways to go.

My mind drifted as I motored along that morning thinking of the guys I had met the night before and all the sights I had already encountered on this relatively short stretch of my trip. I also kept my eye out for sign of Kansas City. I was due to pass through the renowned river city some time that morning and had heard some ghastly stories last night about what to look for in the river.

It seems there had been a rash of murders in the city that spring and the bodies were being dumped into the river. The fellows at the fort had told me this and said I should be aware in case I saw something unusual. That's not the sort of thing I wanted to hear or the sort of thing I wanted to find in the water. Nevertheless, I couldn't keep my mind off the subject. So, as I was traveling up the river, I couldn't help but notice everything I saw swirling in eddies. With a start, I spied a garish white body floating in a whirlpool on the south side of the river.

I eased back on the throttle and tentatively edged in closer to take a look. I really didn't want to find a body. I knew enough to know that bodies found in the river take on a most ghoulish form. "Oh my God" I thought, the bloated form looked to have blond features and kept bobbing disfiguratively in the water. I edged closer and gave a sigh of relief. The shape was the body of an unfortunate yellow Labrador retriever. I backed the boat away and started out into the main current vowing to myself not to watch the shore too closely until I got above Kansas City.

It didn't take long to know I was getting close to the city. I could smell Kansas City long before I could see it. It smelled of an awful mix of sewage, oil and barbecue sauce. Unique, I thought, but a terrible smell. Kansas City was a true disappointment to me on my journey. I know that the city has a wonderful little park along the Kansas River, but no riverside park was visible along the Missouri riverbank. Instead I saw the most industrialized riverfront since leaving St. Louis. In fact, it may have even more industry along its shores than St. Louis. Across the river from the loading docks, mills, and grain elevators are a string of riverboat casinos blaring their rows of lights to the shore. In my opinion, the only thing worse than a riverboat casino is one that doesn't even sit on the river. The ones along Kansas City fit this bill. They are nothing more than barges with casinos sitting upon them floating in a stagnant moat of water.

The gaudy "riverboat" facades have been embraced by many river towns all along both the Missouri and the Mississippi Rivers. In my opinion, these towns have sold their souls to the devil in the name of downtown improvement. It is true that much tax revenue is generated by the boats and it does funnel into downtown coffers to revitalize the downtown areas, but at a loss to the historic and cultural flavor of the towns. Are casinos, with their garish lights and Disneyland facades, the saviors of river towns? I don't think so.

But enough about the casinos. I saw many of them on my trip up river. I won't go on any more tangents and bore you with my opinion of them. Kansas City was not the first town where I encountered them and it was not to be my last. Most of them were in the Midwestern states and I never saw any past Sioux City, Iowa.

After passing the mouth of the Kansas River, the wind picked up substantially and the swells developed small white caps. It made for rough traveling in my little boat, but I was making good time and there was little current at that point. Off to my left, I passed the famed Fort Leavenworth, Kansas, home to all the bad boys in the military. At one time, this fort played an important role in providing cavalry to patrol the overland trails across the plains. I kept on until I reached the town of Leavenworth, Kansas and pulled in when I saw my Dad waving me in from the shore.

He had found a microbrewery in the town and we walked over to have a beer and relax. I needed it after the rough water I had encountered down near Kansas City. Dad looked like he could use one, too. Since his accident, he had developed a fever and a headache and he really didn't look too good. We relaxed on the patio of the brewery enjoying our beer and the sunny afternoon. Unlike Kansas City, Leavenworth has a wonderful little riverside park with a lot of character. It is a nice little town.

After our beer, Dad and I decided to meet up again at Atchinson, Kansas. We parted and I went down to the water and hopped into the "Teddy Roosevelt" which was the name I gave my boat when I first took it out on the Missouri. I chose that name because not only did it commemorate a President that did much to preserve some of our Western lands and who lived along the Little Missouri River, but because it was a Rough Rider too! Hence, I began to call the little green boat "Teddy." I reached Atchinson with plenty of daylight left and sunburns on the tops of my feet from going barefoot in the boat. Mom and Dad were down by the river to wave me in again and we went into town for pizza and beer. We joked quite a bit at Dad's expense. It was hard not to, but all joking aside, he wasn't looking too good. Mom had brought along a little antibiotic just in case someone got sick. Dad started taking it. It turned out to be a good thing he did.

When we split up after dinner, I took the boat across the river and, finding a small sandy beach across from the mouth of a creek on the Atchinson side of the river, pitched camp. I had learned my lesson well about sleeping at easily accessible areas. The creek that was across the river from me turned out to be Independence Creek and was named by Lewis and Clark. At this spot they had celebrated the fourth of July in 1803, the twenty-seventh birthday of our nation with a "a discharge of one shot from our Bow piece." Like them, I had a warm evening full of mosquitoes. Doubtless, I felt the uncertainty of my own journey like many of the men on that great journey did.

CHAPTER 4

*"As the Creek has no name and this day is the 4th of July
we name this Indepedance Creek"*

Sergeant Charles Floyd July 4, 1804

*"The Corps. Celebrated the 4th of July just a mile from here.
Or maybe here for that matter . . . Must have been a nice
place to celebrate."*

Chris Bechtold April 25, 1998

LIKE THE CORPS OF DISCOVERY, I was noting changes in the river at this point. Lewis and Clark had seen their first beaver of the trip in this area. This was attributed to heavy trapping along most of the lower river. Here, only 400 or so miles up the river, I could detect a perceptibly narrower and cleaner river. Not clean enough that I would bathe in the water yet, but cleaner. With the river becoming so much smaller than at it's mouth, it was a wonder that towboat traffic was able to navigate these upper reaches at all. I must give the towboat pilots credit for the difficult job they face traveling the upper end of the navigable portions of the Missouri.

After settling down to read through the journals of Lewis and Clark awhile, I finally let curiosity get the best of me. I hopped into the boat with Herschel and we zipped across the river to investigate Independence Creek. I wanted to know what the little tributary looked like at the location where the men of the Corps had spent Independence Day. I traveled about three quarters of a mile up the little creek to get a feel for it. It is straighter now. Probably the bank is much more steep than it was 200 years ago. Just a typical muddy little mid-western creek. A good spot to fish, no doubt, but for the most part unassuming. I'll bet it was a nice spot to celebrate.

I camped that night at mile marker 437. I was making great time so far and hoped that my luck would hold out as far as river conditions were concerned. I was still naïve enough to think that I could continue on at this pace. Time would set me straight. I enjoyed another beautiful morning on the river full of wildlife and soothing scenery; a light mist hung above the smooth water. The countryside consisted of a wide fertile flood plain bordered by steep wooded hills. At St. Joseph, Missouri I pulled over and visited with my folks. The St. Joseph riverfront has a park that sits underneath the interstate. I must say that rivers never go OVER a town, a distinct advantage of river travel. All those cars were speeding right past a town that played an important part in the history of the West.

Home of the Pony Express in 1860 and departing point for many a western traveler, St. Joseph still maintains some of its historical spirit. Many a stage coach and river boat traveler passed along the streets of this famed little town. I longed to wander the old town quarters and learn more about the Wild West days of this little burg. But it was early, before most of the businesses opened up, so I passed on. The river was calling to me anyhow and I felt the urge to keep going. I continued on to White Cloud, Kansas passing deer, turkey and beaver along the way.

There, I pulled in at a small riverfront park containing a picnic table and unobtrusive little granite marker noting that the Corps of Discovery had camped here in 1803. I dug out my copy of the journals to see what they had to say about the area. Mom and Dad soon pulled in to see how things were going. According to the journals, Clark had climbed a high hill near here and taken in the surrounding area. He noted the fertile soil and how rich the land looked. We hopped in the car and drove to the top of the only high hill around. We gazed eastward over an immense fertile river bottom. The entire area, as far as the eye could see, was farmland.

At the top of the hill, a series of stone monuments marked the observation point. This spot at the top of the hill is known as four state overlook. From here a person is able to see four separate states: Missouri, Kansas, Iowa, and Nebraska. That doesn't happen too often in the predominately flat Midwest. I took good measure of the river below us. It lay like a brown ribbon trimmed with the green of new leaf growth. The land on either side a stitched together patchwork of corn and bean fields.

My rough riding little boat, "Teddy Roosevelt," made good time from White Cloud. There was little current and the weather was cooperating for the most part. I had agreed to meet up with my folks again at Rulo, Nebraska. It looked like a much bigger dot on the map than it actually was. I met my folks at the bridge and we decided to have dinner at the only restaurant in town. We feasted on true river fare, fried catfish. Rulo made up for its small size with the ample portions of the dinner.

It was near Rulo that Lewis and Clark gave one of their men 100 lashes for falling asleep while on guard duty. At that time, such an offense could possibly be punished by death. I didn't have to worry about that, thank goodness. The Corps main concern was that hostile Indians might attack them. While Rulo is on the Sauk and Fox Indian Reservation, it is hardly a place one need worry about attack now-a-days. My big concern was having eaten too much.

Leaving my folks behind and promising to meet up with them sometime in the morning, I pushed off into the river to find a suitable campsite. About 12 miles above Rulo I found it. The weather was looking threatening so I stretched the rubberized lean-to tarp over my sleeping bag just in case. My campsite was just below Indian Cave State Park which is a beautiful little stretch of river. Large oak and cottonwood trees crowd the rivers edge along sandstone outcroppings.

Sunset on the lower Missouri River

It never did rain that night, though the wind blew hard. I spent the evening, before going to sleep, writing and reading nestled up to a small campfire. The carefree peacefulness of my camp lay in sharp contrast to the anxiety Lewis and Clark felt having not encountered any natives up to this point.

I had officially left Missouri at this point in my trip. From here on I would be traveling in Nebraska and Iowa for a while. I enjoyed the time spent in Missouri. The state has many well-kept conservation areas and an abundance of wildlife. Missouri had treated me well; now I only hoped the other states would do the same.

Before I really got going though, I had to stop in at Indian Cave State Park. The Cave was a little overrated, mostly just a large sandstone outcropping. Unfortunately, it looked as if everyone and their brother had carved their name in the rocks about there. I hate to see that. Today, many places along the river have been defaced by scores of grafitti artists. I guess some folks feel so important they need to leave their mark everywhere they go. A raccoon ran along the shore after I pulled out of the State park, oblivious to the noise of my motor. The wind continued to blow this morning and through most of the day. The rough chop of the water beat the boat all day long making for a bone-jarring day on the river. The "Teddy Roosevelt" was living up to its name. With the overcast skies and the combination of wind and spray, I had to bundle up in my heavy clothes to stay warm. After what seemed like a long ride, I pulled into the old river town of Brownsville, Nebraska established 1853.

The town of Brownsville would be hard to pass up for any river traveler. It wears its association with the river proudly. In the small riverfront area there is a park with a restored paddle wheeler. Small historic signs dot the park telling the visitor the unique history of this and that. I wandered about the park for a bit getting warm and soaking up the atmosphere. While I was approaching the boat to check on my gear, I was hailed over by an older man standing next to a modern reproduction of a steamboat.

He asked what I had been up to and offered me a coffee. I didn't hesitate to take the coffee or tell him what I had been up to. It turned out the man was the pilot for the riverboat, thus explaining the pilots hat he wore. He gave small tours of the river from Brownsville to Omaha.

I could tell from his smile he was enjoying the talk. Like all river men I ran into, he too wished he could see the entire Missouri. I think it calls seductively to many folks who live along its shores, tempting them to see all it has to offer.

After finishing my coffee, I thanked the man and started up the hill to check out the Brownsville historic district. The main drag looked as if it had never left the late 1800's. Small antique stores nestled into one hundred year old restored buildings lined both sides of the street. Looking in the windows I could see paraphernalia from the last century expertly arranged and restored, all for sale.

My folks had met up with me by this time and I joined them in browsing the shops that were open for business. It being the off season, most of the merchants were more than happy to visit with us and Mom made a few deals on small items before we headed back toward the river. As I pushed off, I looked back over at the park noting a sign that mentioned once again that Lewis and Clark had camped here on July 19th, 1804. It had become a given by this point that they had.

I agreed to meet up with the folks at Nebraska City, Nebraska. On my way, I killed the motor to refuel at a calmer part of the river. Along the banks were a row of summer houses and at one a couple was doing some work outside. The fellow walked out and asked how the fishing was on the river. I told him that I wasn't fishing, but traveling upstream to Nebraska City. He looked over my boat and motor and gave his opinion of the whole ordeal. "You'll never make it with that little motor you got," he said. I thanked him for his advice and before starting the motor, I told him I had started in Illinois. I never gave him time to reply, just sat down after starting the motor and sped off. Like I mentioned earlier, everyone has an opinion on the river.

I began to notice a pattern during my travels when I pulled into Nebraska City. It seemed that towns alternated in their relation to the river. One town would open its arms to the river with a small park or memorial and the next would have its back to the water as it was ashamed of it. Nebraska City had turned its back. The riverfront was an industrialized docking area with no room for small boats. I pulled in when I saw my folks waving from shore. We slipped off through the town and got dinner together. Dad still was not looking too good.

After dinner we wandered about the town for a little while taking in the sights and enjoying evening in a small town. While the town may not have had much for a recreational riverfront, it did sport a lot of history. In 1872, Julius Morton convinced the Nebraska State Legislature to set aside a day to plant trees. Thus, Arbor Day got its start in Nebraska City. I wasn't the first person to head west from here. A short ways up river from there, I pulled in for the night across from Weeping Woman Creek. Before pulling in, I had spotted a man along shore doing yard work and asked as to my whereabouts. He informed me of the name of the creek and that it was also a starting point for the Mormon Trail for the west side of the Missouri. From this point many a pilgrim traveled in search of the promised land, known today as Utah.

I was a short ways below the mouth of the Platte River according to my maps and I could smell the West ahead. I hunkered down for the night thinking of all those who had started out for parts unknown from this area. The famous Platte River lay just ahead and I couldn't wait to see this river that I had read about in so many books. To me, each day was becoming more and more exciting as I left the "East" behind. The river continued to get shallower and I expected to see a change in it after I got above Omaha.

I had noted that I was seeing more cormorants at this point in my trip and not as many coots and ducks as I did downstream. Deer and other wildlife sightings were down as well. I assumed I must be getting closer to Omaha. I had old friends that lived there and I had given them a call that day to let them know I would be coming up river and planned to visit. I looked forward to seeing familiar faces.

I woke up the next morning to a cold, steady rain. I dressed in the shelter of my little lean-to trying not to get any wetter than necessary. The dampness seemed to permeate everything I owned. By the time I had broke camp, mud was smeared over all my gear. I guess the bright side is that it was raining hard enough to wash all the mud off everything. It kept coming down all that morning, at times hard enough to reduce visibility to only the width of the river. I was thoroughly soaked and a bit chilled too. The temperature hovered around 45 degrees. When I finally passed the mouth of the Platte, I could barely make out the distant banks of the river. Shortly afterwards I saw headlights flashing at me from the West side of the river. My folks had come down to a small park in Bellevue, Nebraska, to wait for me. When they suggested a hot breakfast downtown, I couldn't say no.

We picked out a little diner on the main street that looked like the local coffee hangout. When I walked in, I got the out-of-town stare. I've traveled enough that it doesn't bother me as much as it used to. All the old-timers turned their heads and not so subtly looked me over from head to toe, then went back to their coffees and conversation. I must have been quite a sight in my waders and cowboy hat, looking more like I had been swimming in the river than boating on it. By the time we finished our breakfast, I felt as if I had melted into the booth of that little café. The warm air and good food hit me like a truck and I had to drag myself back outside into the rain. My Dad joked with me about the weather and Mom did her motherly duties, fussing over how I needed to be careful and stay warm. I told them I would let them know when I hit Omaha and we would all meet up with my friends, the Langs.

Dad's condition from the beaver accident seemed to have worsened and he still had a fever. Since my folks only planned to spend the first week with me to see how I would get along, they decided it was time to turn around. Dad also decided that there wasn't enough pride in the world to put up with the discomfort he was feeling and he wanted to see a doctor. Not just any doctor either; he wanted to see the family doctor he could trust. In his words, it was a sensitive wound and not something to be exposed to any old clinic doctor.

It continued to rain steadily all my way through Omaha. Like Kansas City, I could smell the town before I ever saw it. The water smelled of sewage just below the city. I passed barges and grain terminals that loomed out over the water's surface. On the Iowa side, casino lights flittered through the rain. It made for a dismal sight as I wound my way up river in the rain. When I had passed the main part of the city, I spied a marina off to my left and pulled in. It would have been a hard spot to miss. The marina was located right next to a naval museum containing a submarine and ships. Needless to say, I didn't expect to see a submarine on this trip.

I pulled into the marina and tied off on the docks. The marina was one of those large affairs with an armada of new pleasure boats and houseboats. At this time of the year, especially on a rainy day, the place looked abandoned. Finding a pay phone I called up my folks on their cell phone and gave them my location, then called the Lang's and filled them in on where I was. I hunkered down under a picnic shelter and waited out of the weather.

The whole area had a strange feel to it. I was nearing the outskirts of town where smaller wooded areas constituted the main portion of the river's edge. A wet quiet pervaded the area with the distant sounds of traffic in the background. Looking around, boats sulked in their moors with not even the slap of waves to wake them, and in the foreground, behind the boats in dry dock, rested the remnants of a naval fleet.

To say a ship and submarine looked out of place was an understatement. Props from larger ships and anchors were also on display along with a half-track and a howitzer. The sign on the gate proclaimed the area Freedom Park. I was to find out later that the ship, the USS Hazard, and submarine, USS Marlin, came up river on barges from the Gulf. What a sight to behold, a submarine riding piggyback on a river barge. Then they were settled on their pedestals ashore, their only hope of floating again being an immense river flood.

All my thoughts scattered as the Langs pulled up in their SUV. Joe and Joan Lang had been good friends of mine since I was 19 years old. At that time, I was working for the United States Fish and Wildlife Service on a bear research project on the U.S.-Canadian border. Joe was the U.S. Customs agent at a remote port that served as our social center and main port of entry to the U.S. The Langs, along with the Canadian Inspector, Ron Fontana, served as our surrogate family in the seasons we spent in the field.

When Joe finally retired from INS, he and Joan moved back to Omaha where Joe had been stationed with the U.S. Air Force and retired a colonel. It was sure good to see old friends, especially on a damp, dreary day. Joan jumped out and gave me a hello hug while Joe hung back; then jumped in with a hearty handshake. Joan immediately began to berate me on being crazy and being careful then told me she thought it wonderful that I was embarking on this grand adventure.

I had just begun to fill them in on the last week's adventures when my folks pulled in. Mom was worried about me, as usual, and had picked up a cooler full of good food for a picnic lunch. We unpacked everything under the picnic shelter and had a cool picnic. Everyone had a lot of catching up to do, and, of course, Dad shared his traumatic beaver story with the Langs amid shock, disbelief, and laughter. We couldn't help but laugh. But it was quite apparent that Dad was still not feeling well.

When lunch was over it was time for me to say my good-byes to my folks. I hated to see them go. This river get-away had been a much-needed relief for us all. Mom had thoroughly enjoyed her chance to snoop through the small river town shops garnering ideas for her own gift shop, while Dad was able to take a break from the hectic pace he had set for himself working two jobs and doing so much more on the side. I could see a lot of the stress and tension from everyday life had melted off of them in the short week we spent along the river. But it was time to go. Dad sorely needed to see a doctor and they had business concerns to tend to back home.

Besides, I was ready for the real adventure to begin. My comfort level with the river was rising. I no longer felt that apprehensiveness that pervaded my every pore at the beginning of the trip. Now, I looked forward to each day's adventures and trials. It was time to cut the cord and sink or swim (so to speak) on my own. It is a hard thing to describe, but I felt the need to make the trip as independently as I could from this point on. How else was I to know the river and experience it fully if not on my own? So, we all hugged and I repeatedly assured my folks I would be OK while they repeatedly admonished me to "be careful" and we said our Good-bye.

I was to learn a few days later, while checking in, how serious my Dad's wound really was. They had driven non-stop back home to Godfrey, Illinois and the next day, Dad went to the family doctor, a solemn, quiet-spoken man that handles all his cases with care and professionalism. He listened to Dad's story and by the end of the telling Dad said even the doctor was smiling. Also, according to Dad, you reach a point in your suffering where you don't care who sees what or how much, as long as the problem gets fixed. He dropped his drawers and the doctor didn't have to look long before telling dad he needed a surgeon. Pick one, he told Dad; so once again he picked a friend of the family. Mom went along to the next exam and as the surgeon probed the wound, her eyes widened as he commented, "Dan, this is quite an impressive wound," then followed with, "You wouldn't mind if I shared this with a few of my colleagues would you?" Without missing a beat, Dad answered, "Hell no, just fix it."

When asked how far the stick had penetrated, Dad had guessed about and inch or two. In fact, the stick had gone six inches into him and had created a serious infection. He had gotten to medical attention just in time. It took an extensive course of antibiotics and surgery to get him fixed up. Now, when re-telling stories of my trip up the river, Dad always has his own story to tell. All of us who love him dearly pepper him with beaver related gifts during the holidays and on his birthday. According to him, it took a stick in the ass for him to get his priorities straight. Soon after returning from the river trip with Mom and me, he turned in his resignation for a job he had held for 29 years, vowing to relax and enjoy life more.

CHAPTER 5

"Mad up a Small preasent for those people in perpotion to their Consiquence . . . We gave them a Cannister of Powder and a Bottle of Whiskey . . . The Situation of our last Camp Councile Bluff . . . appears to be a verry proper place for a Trading establishment & fortification"

William Clark August 3, 1804

"It was a long day and a long night of visiting . . . at Council Bluffs . . . Trying to drink up all my beer and reduce weight."

Chris Bechtold April 28, 1998

AFTER MY FOLKS HAD TAKEN OFF, the Langs gave me a full tour of the Omaha area, including a side trip over to Council Bluffs, Iowa to view the monument to Lewis and Clark that sits atop the bluffs overlooking the Missouri. No one knows the exact location that the Corps parlayed with the Indians in 1803, so the site was erected in a suitable spot that represents the most likely location. There was no one around when we pulled into the monument parking lot. I had Joan take a few pictures of me at the monument and we looked out over the river. Visibility was low that day, but we could still see a good portion of the area. The sounds of the interstate carried up to us from below. Today, the highway sits between the bluffs and the river. So one must look out over a river of traffic to see the stately old Missouri. What a far cry my journey proved to be from Lewis and Clark's. However, this area was the place where the Expedition had their first beneficial encounter with the natives; my first encounter proved beneficial as well.

I spent the night with the Langs and partook of their hot shower and warm bed. It was my first night inside since the start of my trip and

I felt a little guilty about not sleeping out like I had intended to, but I could not refuse the Lang's hospitality and caved in like a cheap tent. It felt great. We had a wonderful dinner and afterward Joe took me downstairs to his computer to show me a map program he had just gotten. I was glad he had it. I had no detailed maps for North Dakota and the maps I did have of the Nebraska-South Dakota state line were not too good. In this respect, I proceeded in a similar fashion to Lewis and Clark, relying on primitive maps from the locals. Joe couldn't wait to help and printed as many maps as he could. Some of them later proved to be quite helpful.

The next morning after a solid, hot breakfast, the Langs dropped me off at the marina and bid me farewell. I paid the marina guard ten dollars for watching my boat for the night and pulled out of the marina in a light drizzle. Before leaving, my Dad had insisted that I take with me some of the good beer he brought along. I didn't protest too staunchly even though I knew the extra weight would affect the boats performance. Add to the beer all the food my Mom insisted that I take and the weight of my provisions increased substantially. I was to pay for all the extra weight that day.

Up until that day I had been averaging over seventy miles a day with an average speed of roughly nine to ten miles-per-hour. That may not seem like much, but if I kept at it would take me the needed seventy miles during the daylight hours and still give me the time I needed to find and set up a camp. When the average speed decreased by just a mere three miles-per-hour, it had a marked affect on the outcome of my day's progress.

After pulling out of the marina in Omaha, I could tell I was not making good time. I began to calculate my speed by looking at my watch and the mile markers posted along the rivers edge. I was only making five miles-per-hour, and that was skirting along the riverbanks out of the main current. I would have to get rid of some of the weight.

My tenth night on the river, April 29th, I camped at mile marker 639 up river from Omaha. Having never achieved the speed necessary to bring the hull out of the water that day I knew I had but one choice. There was only one thing I could do to reduce the amount of weight I had been carrying. I had to drink all the beer. I set up the tarp and made a little lean-to in the woods and got a large fire going to dry out my sodden woolens and warm myself. Then I set about drinking beer. Oooh, it was good. Dad had given me some pretty good stuff. I had Newcastle Brown Ale, Samuel Smith Stout and Guinness, and I had a lot of it. My father never does anything small. I kept at it pretty steady, staring into the fire, writing, and thinking. Herschel kept me company for the night, talking and telling me a few river stories of his own. At least I think he did. To tell the truth, the whole night was a bit of a blur.

I woke up late the next morning with a headache and a case of beer still left. I sure didn't feel like having any more. In order to reduce weight, I decided to high-grade my gear and ship the unneeded equipment to the ranch in Montana. I wished I were traveling back down the river, in which case I could have cached my unwanted items just as the Corps of Discovery had. Even though I really couldn't stomach the thought of drinking any more beer for a while, I still could not bear to throw out good beer. I stashed a few six packs of Newcastle in the duffle bag I was sending to Montana. I planned on finding a UPS shipping spot at the next town and sending it off.

According to my calculations, I expected the next town to be Onawa, Iowa on the east side of the river. Imagine my surprise when the next town I came upon was Blair, Nebraska, on the west side of the Missouri. The extra weight I was packing had made a bigger impact on my speed than I had thought. I pulled into the bank and tied up under the bridge leading into town. Hoisting my duffle with what I deemed non-essential gear (and beer), I trudged up hill into town. I hiked about two miles or so before I found a business that had a UPS pickup point. There, I boxed up my duffle and paid to have it sent to the ranch in Montana. While talking to the man behind the counter, we worked out a trade of beer for a ride back to the river. It cost me two six packs. When I got back to the boat, I dumped out a couple of containers of drinking water I had been carrying in a last ditch effort to reduce weight and took off.

Luckily, all my efforts were not in vain. When I pulled out of Blair, I was once again averaging ten miles-per-hour instead of the five when I pulled into town. Now I was back on track and my spirits were high. The rain that had been falling for the last few days ceased and the sun was shining once again. I sat back in the boat and basked in the sun and my sense of freedom. It was exhilarating. In the middle of my life's grand adventure with the entire Missouri river stretched out before me, I reveled in the day. My only deadline was still at least a month away and ahead lay unknown land. I relished every moment of it.

I passed the Little Sioux River at 10:30 that morning and shortly thereafter noted a subtle change in the waters. The river had a cleaner, fresher smell to it. The dank, sewage odors were gone and I could faintly detect what I believed to be the smell of lake water. It could well have been my imagination, but everything seemed fresher to me after the rains had stopped. In addition to the fresher look and smell of the water, the river seemed to be narrowing down even more. The river channel itself changed at this point also. It became lined with riprap and pylons, so that it no longer resembled a river, but an immense channel, entirely man-made. Gone were the little inlets and eddies with their sand and mud beaches and gone also was the wildlife that I came to expect in these sanctuaries. The old Missouri River looked caged and bound. I couldn't wait to get out of this section of river. It reminded me of a imprisoned, wild grizzly bear. All the wildness had been stolen from it.

Before I had ever departed on this trip, I had written to the Lewis and Clark Trail Heritage Foundation to receive any information I could on points of interest along the trail. I kept the brochures I received in the bottom of my medicine sack (named for all the "medicine" i.e. camera, wallet, matches, et cetera, that I carried and not for any pharmaceuticals) and used them as a reference guide on where to stop along my trip. According to one of my brochures, outside of Onawa, Iowa there was a state park that had a replica of the keelboat and pirogues that Lewis and Clark used on their journey up the Missouri. I decided I had to see these boats.

I pulled over to the bank at the Decatur-Onawa Bridge and tied up the boat. With quick steps, Herschel and I started hoofing it to the state park that housed the keelboat. Unbelievably, the keelboat and pirogues are kept at an oxbow lake that was once on the original river channel. The park is located where The Corps actually had camped and the river had been moved. It took me a while to comprehend all of this.

I had been wearing my warm clothes due to the morning weather and had not changed after the sun emerged to warm things up. I also looked a little river worn, by this point, with mud caked pants and my old cowboy hat. Herschel and I hiked along the two-lane highway on our way to the park and I tried to hitch a ride for us whenever a vehicle passed by. We weren't having too much luck and I am sure Herschel thought it was because he was hitchhiking with a human being. Finally, a pick-up truck slowed down and pulled over. I ran up to the truck and the fellow driving asked where I was heading. When I told him the state park to look at the keelboat, his eyes lit up. In a lucky bit of coincidence, similar to Lewis and Clark's fortunes, he had been one of the builders of the replica keelboat and knew the park and park ranger intimately. I couldn't have been luckier.

Leonard Burgess was my driver's name. He was a large man with a friendly demeanor and typical Mid-Western bib overalls. Not only had he been one of the builders of the keelboat, but his wife was also an organizer of the local Lewis and Clark festival held in the area every year. Leonard quizzed me on my adventures so far and filled me in on the background of the replica keelboat and pirogues. He also told me how and when the river had been diverted to its present day location. Before the advent of the dams on the Missouri, the river had been a shallow, fast moving, shifting river. After the dams were erected; the river became much more sedate and predictable, therefore, encouraging more riverboat traffic on the lower river. To better accommodate the barge traffic and to also get bigger barges to grain terminals as far up as Sioux City, Iowa, the Army Corps of Engineers (a totally different corps than that of Discovery) had dug a new channel to straighten out the river and maintain a deeper channel. This explained the riprap banks I had noted downriver and the pylons which lined the shores. The bridge that I had tied up under was actually built before there was ever any water flowing under it.

In a twist of fate, the original campsite of the Corps of Discovery ended up being located five miles from the river. At least there was water at the park. Nothing would seem more out of place than a boat commemorating river explorers with no water in sight. Since I was traveling so early in the season, the boats that I had come to see were not even out of winter storage. But, luckily for me, I was riding with Leonard. He introduced me to the park ranger and after an enjoyable visit, I was allowed to climb around on the replica keelboat inside its winter shed.

I believe what impressed me more than any other thing was the shear size of the keelboat. I knew that it had to be large in order to carry the vast amounts of supplies the Corps used on their voyage; however, I was totally unprepared for the immensity of the boat before me. I felt as if I were ascending the Missouri in a bathtub after looking at Lewis and Clarks' boat. The keelboat in Onawa, built between the years 1985 and 1990, was constructed entirely of oak planking and built to the same specifications as the original boat. Its total length was fifty-five feet. Crawling around on the boat, I tried to imagine the amount of work it took to drag this monster up the river, fighting for every inch. I began to truly appreciate the strength, both physically and of character, that it took to wrestle against the current of the mighty Missouri.

After my curiosity had been satisfied, I climbed down off the keelboat and emerged into the sunlight outside the barn. A replica of the white pirogue sat on a trailer against the back of the park office. This boat was bigger than I imagined also, being twenty-seven feet long. Unlike the keelboat which had roughly the same shape and outline of a modern oil tanker, the pirogue had the lines of a squat, fat, little sail boat. It also looked much easier to maneuver in the water than the keelboat. Again, this smaller boat of the expedition made my fourteen-foot boat look like a toy. No matter how hard things were to get for me, I would remember the size of these two boats and think how easy I really had it.

After visiting for a while more with the park ranger and Leonard, I finally conceded that I needed to get going again. Leonard gave me a ride back to the river and dropped me off at the bridge. Before he left, he had asked if I had any matches. That's like asking the Pope if he's Catholic. Of course I did. Leonard told me I probably didn't have enough, and then proceeded to give me about fifty small boxes of wooden matches. He told me he had bought a case of them at an auction and I had better take some to remember Onawa and maybe even to start a fire. I thanked him and watched him turn around and drive off towards town once again. Leonard's matches lasted not only until the end of my trip, but for a good two years afterwards. And he was right, every time I used one I thought of him and Onawa, Iowa.

As I was taking inventory of my gasoline and stowing things away in preparation for pushing off, an old fisherman sitting upon a bucket hailed me from down the beach. I walked on down to say "Hello" and visit. As usual, the older fellow asked if I had been catching any fish. I told him I wasn't fishing and got the standard surprised response. After telling him of my journey, we commenced to visiting. The old man first felt that he needed to warn me of the dangers of the river. Not the least of which was the alligator that he had seen earlier in the week. I tried not to act too surprised and told him I would definitely keep my eyes open for alligators, though in the back of my mind, I thought it quite preposterous that there would be any alligators in Iowa.

The old man told me that just a few days ago he had been fishing in this exact spot and an alligator had swam right by. He didn't think it was too safe to be wading out in the water if I didn't have to. I assured him I would sure be careful and tried to change the subject to some

River Camp near Atchison, Kansas

other topic besides alligators. We then proceeded to talk of the generosity of people along the river, weather, and fishing. These topics we agreed upon and after awhile, I again mentioned that daylight was burning and that I had better be going. He wished me luck and plopped back down upon his five-gallon bucket perch. "Good luck and watch out for alligators!" He cried as I walked down the beach. I waved back and pushed off into the current.

My gasoline supply was short so I decided to cross the river and get gas in Decatur, Nebraska before I started any further up river. I hiked up the hill with my two six gallon gas cans and filled up at the closest gas station. On the way back down to the river, a pick up pulled over in front of me and a fellow offered a ride back to the river. I accepted and we visited on my way back to the boat. By this time, I really did need to get going. I stowed my gas on board and started the motor, easing back into the river, then turned the throttle to full and sped away. When I looked over to the Iowa shore, my old fisherman was there waving. I gave a big wave and a laugh, thinking about alligators and all the nice people in this part of the world. In the short time I had spent in this little area, I had met only kind faces.

I motored on taking in the sights and smells of the river. The water held a fresh, clean scent that day and I relished the green countryside. I believe all the kindness I had just experienced had made everything seem brighter and better. On the Nebraska side of the river I passed Blackbird Hill, named in honor of Blackbird, a Sioux chief who was buried there. Lewis and Clark had written of this gravesite and had even hiked up to it to pay respects to this chief. Thinking of this reminded me that I was now on the Omaha/Winnebago Indian Reservation. It is easy in today's world to forget that there are reservations in the Midwest. Coming from Montana, I tend to dwell on today's reservations as being large open western spaces and forget the smaller, more fertile reservations located in the eastern part of the country.

That night I found a quiet stretch of river on the Nebraska side and pitched camp. The sky was mostly clear, but I put up my tarp just in case. I had been wet enough in the last few days and didn't want to get soaked again. With a fire going, I reclined against a log and listened to voices trailing across the water from the far side of the river. It was a truly peaceful evening that had followed a wonderful day of travel. I wrote in my journal and thought of all the kind people I had met that day. My adventure had begun and it was everything I wanted it to be. Two deer fed in the brush by camp. I finished my dinner and slept soundly, the end of a perfect day.

The next day dawned with a beautiful sunrise. A clear sky emerged above a fine mist which burned off in the morning sun. Beavers slapped the water up and down stream from camp as I made my morning fire and boiled coffee. When I finally got out on the water, I counted five of the little critters around the camp area. My serene morning slowly dissipated as I kept crawling up stream. My thoughts ran back in history thinking of beaver and the pull of this furry gold that brought men up the Missouri in search of pelts. It was just downstream a few days from here that Lewis and Clark saw their first beaver on the Missouri. During the early 1800s the river had been trapped out in the lower Midwest. By the mid-1800s the rest of the Missouri followed suit. How strange that we as a culture tend to destroy the things we most covet. I had left on this trip to see the Missouri that Lewis and Clark had seen, the river that I had read about in the journals of trappers and river men. Around me though, all I saw was a channelized river that would be unrecognizable to those that had ascended it in the past.

I began to think that I would never see the "true" river, the Missouri of old, but I later was to find out that it is still out there, it just takes some searching. Small stretches are hidden all along its course that harken back to the old days when the Missouri ran wild. My thoughts on all of this were shattered by the smell of sewage. I was approaching Sioux City, Iowa and the smell of the water had pulled me out of my reverie. On my left I soon passed the culprit: a large pipe disgorging black, foul smelling ooze into the river. I should have photographed this disgrace, but I would not have known where to go with it anyhow. Soon afterward, I could make out something I had hoped to see which was the Sergeant Floyd Memorial on the Iowa side of the river. I made a beeline for the sandstone obelisk and tied up the boat to a tree below the monument. Herschel and I jumped out and scrambled up the bank to be stopped by a frightening obstacle for a man and dog—an interstate highway.

CHAPTER 6

"He was buried with the Honors of War, much lamented. A seedar post with (his) name was fixed at the head of his grave . . .After paying all the honor to our Deceased brother we camped in the Mouth of Floyds River . . . "

William Clark August 20, 1804

"I saw the Sergeant Floyd Memorial. Tied up the boat and went to see it . . . It's a nice Monument"

Chris Bechtold May 1, 1998

I STOOD BEHIND THE CHAIN LINK FENCE designed to keep people from doing just what I was contemplating doing and looked for a break in traffic. None came. Herschel and I walked up and down the fence looking for a gap in the fence so we could cross through. We finally found a spot that we could crawl under and after getting through found ourselves standing on the edge of the highway. Cars and trucks roared by a few feet away. I worried that Herschel might mistake one of my movements for a command to go and step in front of traffic. I gave a firm command for him to stay close and watched for a break in the traffic.

Finally, there was a lull in the southbound lane and we rushed across the pavement to stand along the concrete divider. I helped Herschel over and we were faced with the northbound lanes to navigate. Again, a break came and we rushed across. Another fence to cross, a set of railroad tracks and finally a grass hillside where I could finally exhale and relax. I had been worried sick that something might happen to Herschel during our crossing. I did not want this place to end up being the final resting place for my dog as well as Sergeant Floyd.

The monument stared down from above us as we worked our way up the hill. I glanced up to see a school kid looking over the stone wall as we climbed. I am sure they had a lot of questions for their teachers after watching Herschel and I cross the interstate and climb up to the pavement. Soon there were grade-schooler's asking to pat Hershel as I wandered about the memorial. He made a show of tolerating all the strange hands petting him. I am sure it was not as uncomfortable as he made it look.

When the school kids left, Herschel and I enjoyed the memorial by ourselves. The memorial is a fitting tribute to a member of the Corps of Discovery. It stands towering above the Missouri and takes in the view of all the surrounding country. I am sure old Private Floyd never would have imagined his final resting place to be so majestic. As I took a few photos of the memorial and the surroundings, a gentleman approached from the parking lot to read the plaque at the base of the obelisk. I asked if he would mind taking my photo with Herschel and he agreed. We soon began visiting and I told him of my trip. He became quite interested and it turned out that he too was from Montana and following the Lewis and Clark Trail. He immediately invited me over to his motor home and introduced me to his wife.

The kind folks offered me cookies and coffee and we swapped stories about the Trail and the differences between our experiences. The couple had already traveled the western half of the Trail from the continental divide to the Pacific. They were now in the process of following the eastern half. They filled me in on what to expect as I traveled further west and wished me much luck. They had already been to St. Louis and were now on their way home. I thanked them for their hospitality and they said they would leave greetings for me along the way at the different waypoints. They kept their word too. When I reached Fort Randall Dam, one of the employees at the visitor center said a couple from Montana had mentioned I would be coming and to say "Hello." Taking their leave, I headed back towards the river.

With brave hearts, Herschel and I descended the hill and faced the interstate once again. Funny, but getting back to the river seemed to me much more dangerous than being out on it. We made it and headed up stream through Sioux City, Iowa. The weather was fairly warm as I passed through the town, and I saw quite a number of people on their lunch breaks strolling along the riverfront park. Work was being done on a new marina and the whole riverfront area had a fresh, prosperous look about it. I never stopped, but kept on until I saw a large marina on the edge of town. It was a pleasure to see a city embracing the river rather than turning it's back on it.

The pumps were locked up and I wandered around until I found someone to help me fuel up. A young fellow, about my age, in shorts and a muscle shirt walked me back over to the fuel area. While talking to the guy at the pump, I asked how far until I got to Yankton. He looked me over and asked what I was up to. After telling him, he told me that I would never get through the shallows between here and Yankton and that I would probably need to portage or drag the boat the rest of the way. After fueling up, I thanked him for his optimistic outlook and continued on, concerned about what lay ahead and if I could make it.

The man at the pumps was right; the river was very shallow and sandy. Not knowing any better, I continued on threading my way through the shallows trying to discern the right channel. Several times I had to back out of areas that were not deep enough to allow the boat through. It was a study in continuous diligence, and I could not take my eyes off the river or risk missing some telltale clue as to the nature of the channel. At most, the river seemed three quarters of a mile wide and at its deepest two feet. I grounded out several times in the ensuing hours. By evening, I could see a thunderstorm approaching and knew I needed to get off the water. I just had to find the right spot to get off the river.

The difficulty was in finding a spot deep enough for me to get to shore. I finally found a spot above the mouth of the Vermillion River and camped on the South Dakota side of the Missouri. Welcome to South Dakota, the sixth state on my voyage, but I had little time to celebrate. I hastily erected a tarp and had no sooner gotten situated than it began to rain steadily. I squatted down and built a smoky little fire to eat and read by.

Earlier that day, I had seen a sign at the waters edge that gave mileages to different points along the river. At that point, I was 785 miles from my starting point. The disheartening part was that I was, maybe, only a third of the way to the end of my trip. Fort Peck, which was listed on the sign, was 988 miles. I sat under my soggy tarp and thought about all of this. But it was still early in the trip and I couldn't let those daunting mileages keep me down for long. I read in the journals and soon was dreaming of the "spirit mound" that Lewis and Clark had seen in this vicinity and the vast numbers of buffalo they had observed on their hike to this mysterious hill.

Clark wrote, "Capt. Lewis & Myself concluded to go and see the Mound which was Viewed with Such turror by all the different Nations in this quarter." The mystery of the hill was the vast amounts of bird that circled continually around the hill. Meriwether Lewis determined the reason for all the birds was not the so-called spirits flitting about restlessly, but the huge numbers of insects to be found around the mound, thus drawing in the birds to a ready food source. I imagined the hill in my mind, since in all the drizzle and rain, I could not see very far. I doubted I would get to see the hill at all, but in my mind I could easily envision it, surrounded by a sea of buffalo undulating on the plains. A strange new world was unfolding before the men of the Expedition. I am sure I was feeling something similar to all those along on that great voyage; yes, I had finally reached the West.

I awoke the next morning to strong, cold winds and driving rain. I didn't even bother to get up, just rolled over and started a small fire. I laid by the fire and read until 9:00. Finally, I dragged myself from my sleeping bag and sat up to drink coffee and watch the weather. The rain began to let up and I was able to pack up and get on the water about 10:30.

Although the rain had let up, the wind had not. It made finding the channel in the hard chop of the waves all the more difficult and I repeatedly hit bottom. The waves in the shallow water felt much rougher than they looked. Sitting in the boat was like riding a metal snow saucer down a rock pile. The Teddy Roosevelt was living up to its name. In the chop and the spray, I rounded the bend and ahead of me lay the town of Yankton, South Dakota. I pulled in at the docks in front of the city's riverfront park.

I must have made quite a sight stepping out of my boat on that windy, cold day. I pulled two empty gas cans from the boat and started walking across the grass towards the parking lot, main street in the background. I was still wearing my hip boots and wool coat. I passed in front of the only vehicle in the parking lot and as I walked toward the town, a middle-aged woman sitting inside lowered her window to ask what I was up to.

I told her my story. She looked me over closely and asked, "Really?" "Yes," I responded, but she still did not believe me. I assured her once more that I was really traveling up the entire Missouri River. She leaned forward in her vehicle and peered down at my boat. Finally, after much scrutiny, she agreed to give me a ride up town to get some gas. On the short drive to the station and back she kept on about how unbelievable it was that someone would do a trip like mine. I think I completely flabbergasted her. When she dropped me off at the boat, I promised that I would send her a card at the end of the trip to let her know that I made it OK. I kept my promise. In fact, from that point on I tried to get the address of everyone who helped me in any way and send them a card at the end of my trip, letting them know I had made it.

From Yankton, it was a short trip to the Gavins Point Dam, the first dam I was to encounter on my trip. I was anxious to arrive for many reasons. For one, I thought that a switch from going against a current to lake waters would make for easier traveling and better time. Also, I was ready to see how well I would do at getting around these obstacles that I knew I would encounter many more times in the coming weeks. And finally, I was ready for a change of scenery and ready to experience something new. I sure got what I was looking for.

When I first graduated from college, I took a job on a large cattle ranch in Wolf Creek, Montana which was roughly half way between Helena and Great Falls. The ranch was on approximately 8,000 acres of deeded land and had leases equaling at least that much, all of which was bounded by the Missouri River on the east side of the property. My house on the ranch looked out over Holter Dam and the reservoir that backed up behind it. I came to take the dam and the river for granted living there and looking out upon them every day. Having never seen any other dams on the Missouri River, I came to believe that all of them were most likely similar.

Holter Dam is a small electric generating dam. It houses two turbines and is 1,326 feet long and 120 feet high. Many a time I had walked down around the dam to fish. If the fish weren't biting in the lake, then they might be biting in the river. It was a small jaunt, taking no time at all. My conception of dams on the Missouri River was based on my knowledge of Holter Dam. I was damned wrong.

When I rounded the corner from Yankton and first looked upon the Gavins Point Dam, my jaw almost hit the bottom of the boat. In front of me was something of incredible size. I had expected a small cement dam similar in size and design to Holter and the others on the upper Missouri. What I encountered was an earthen dam of immense proportions. The dam is 8,700 feet long and 74 feet high. I knew I was about to make a drastic change in plans.

Before leaving on the trip, Calvin Garrett and I had worked together to come up with a system to clamp a set of wheels onto the boat so it could be wheeled like a wheelbarrow around the dams. Calvin had welded two brackets with ball bearing wheels which attached to the gunnels of the boat. By flipping the boat over and holding the front end, I could wheel the boat like an upside down wheelbarrow and, using the wheels as the balance point, lift very little weight. All of my plans for portaging the dams relied on my being able to carry or wheel my equipment and supplies around the dams in several short trips. I had not anticipated wheeling anything two miles, or carrying a motor and bags of gear that far.

I pulled in at the boat ramp docks below the dam and tied up. Surveying the situation, I decided to walk up to the Army Corps of Engineers office and see what I could do. I had heard that the Corps might ferry a boat around since the dam interfered with a navigable river. I walked into the main office and inquired if this policy was indeed true. It was not. I asked if they knew of any way that I could get a ride around the dam. They did not. I walked down to the boat and did the only thing left to do. I sat down on the docks and begged folks for a ride around the dam as they came in off the water. It worked.

I sat on the docks and as boats came in at the end of the day I asked the people aboard if they could give my boat and me ride around the dam on their boat trailers. At first, most folks only shook their heads and looked at me a little funny, but then a family from Nebraska came in. They heard my story and looked me over carefully before saying that they would give me a lift. The father helped me load my boat on their trailer and towed me around to the upper side of the dam. Meanwhile, the mother and children kept watch on their own boat. I thanked him profusely for taking the time and offered to pay him. The man, a high school principal, wouldn't take anything and instead wished me good luck on my journey. I took down his address and told him I would write when I made it at the end of the river. When the truck pulled out of sight, I took the boat across the cove along the eastern side of Lewis and Clark Reservoir, looking for a campsite for the night. The waters were rough and choppy, although the sun was out and it had warmed considerably since morning.

I camped in a break between the high white bluffs that lined the eastern side of the lake. The small cove I pulled into had a pebble beach and the bluffs on each side provided shelter from the winds that were blowing across the lake. I made camp and sat happily by the fire content with how easily I had portaged the first dam on my trip. It was not through any merits of my own, but rather through the goodness of others that I was to get around all the dams of the Missouri. I was learning that the success of my trip relied more upon the help and kindness of others than my own strengths. Like Lewis and Clark before me, I would have to trust in the goodness of the native peoples to help me through.

I watched the sun set over the waters of the lake, turning the white bluffs to a magnificent opalescent scarlet. I read my journals that night and imagined others before me watching the sun set upon these same ancient bluffs. I spent the remaining hours of my thirteenth day on the river wondering if those before me felt as fulfilled and satisfied as I did.

I awoke the next morning to a sublime sunrise. Scarlet colors danced off the water, pasting themselves to the bluffs overlooking the lake. I hurried to get on the water hoping to miss any waves that might start when the wind came up. Lewis and Clark Lake is only 37 miles long and it took very little time to cover the distance that morning, though I must admit, the water was still a little rougher than I thought it would be. I set a course for the end of the lake and soaked up the sunrise and clear morning scenery.

My peaceful thoughts were shattered when I reached the end of the lake and drove the boat up onto a sandbar. Ahead of me, still roughly

200 yards distant, was a wall of reeds. I pulled on my waders and stepped out of the boat to survey the situation. Walking about in the ankle deep water, I concluded that I had no choice but to drag the boat.

I made a loop in the lead rope and settled it over my shoulders to begin the drudgery of pulling my boat. Herschel sat eagerly up in the front of the boat to cheer me on, giving me a helpful smile every time I looked back or stopped to rest. I eventually reached the reeds and then was forced to determine the correct channel I needed to get through the maze. Trying first one channel, then another, alternating between riding and pulling the boat, I finally found a channel that seemed to go somewhere. I followed its serpentine course until I found myself at a small boat launch outside of Springfield, South Dakota.

With a sigh of achievement, we pulled in. Herschel hopped from the boat and I lugged a pair of empty gas cans from the boat. With both cans, I started up the hill towards town. I hadn't gone far when a truck pulled over and offered me a ride. A nice fellow ran me up the hill to the closest gas station and then took me back to the docks and wished me well. I knew I still had a ways to go in the reeds and wasted no time in filling the tanks in the boat and preparing to leave. While doing this, an old bird of a fellow walked down from the parking lot and asked what I was up to.

I told him my story and how I planned to ascend the entire Missouri River to Montana. He listened, then like every other crusty old fellow I had run into, he gave me his opinion. I am glad they call it "two cents worth" although I believe it over priced. The old man told me to give it up, that I would never make it out of the reeds and even if I did, that little motor I had wouldn't make it up the river. I told him I'd just have to find that out for myself and climbed in the boat.

Nothing makes me more determined than being told I can't do something. After listening to that old man, I figured I would die out there in the reeds, lost and starving before I would come to shore begging for help. Lucky for me, I had no trouble at all back tracking through the channels and finding a way through the reeds. I believe I had already made it through the tough stuff before I got to the boat launch.

The trick to finding the correct channel was to follow openings with the most current and stay close to the reeds. I found that the sand accumulated on the off side of the channels sometimes almost reaching across the entire width of the openings. But by staying in close to the reeds, touching them sometimes even, I could keep the prop in deep enough water and continue to make progress. Standing up on the bow of the boat, I looked for openings in the vegetation and slowly worked my way through the maze of openings. Finally, I reached open water and saw ahead of me huge pillars stretching across the river. Construction crews were building a new bridge across the river. Seeing all the activity, I knew I had escaped the labyrinth of reeds.

Just up stream from the new bridge, I passed the mouth of the Niobrara River. If nothing else, I just like to say the name, Niobrara. It sounds like a river full of character. When I passed the mouth, I knew instantly where all that sand and silt that had stacked up downstream was coming from. As I passed the junction of the rivers, the water turned from a creamy coffee color to a deep emerald green. The two rivers remained separated for a time, like someone had drawn a line through the water, then mixed slowly together taking on the hue of the Niobrara.

After passing the mouth of the Niobrara, the surface of the river calmed to a glass-like appearance. I tightened the tiller of the motor down, letting it hold the course of the boat. It was still early in the trip and I hadn't bent the prop enough by pulling the boat to affect the pull on the motor. Later on in the trip, I had to keep a hand on the tiller at all times just to keep from turning into the banks, but that is a story for later. With a course set, I climbed up to the front of the boat. I stood on the bow of the little craft, like a hood ornament on a used Cadillac, looking out over the river ahead of me. I was puffed up and full of the river and myself. I'll tell you, there is no feeling like that freedom I was feeling that morning. I was to feel it time and again along the trip. This swelling sense of freedom, wildness, and open skies makes for an addicting elixir. I hope I never tire of the drink.

Shortly thereafter, I pulled over on the Nebraska side of the river at the small town of Verdel, Nebraska. Verdel consists of an assortment of small river cabins and trailers and one bait shop/ general store. I pulled in, tied up, and walked up to the bait shop to use the phone to call friends and family and let them know of my progress. After using the phone (there was no pay phone, so I was kindly offered the shop phone to use), I visited with the owners of the shop and told them of my adventure. Joe and Carol Pischel are farmers outside of Niobrara, Nebraska. In the summer, they ran this little bait shop along the river, keeping locals and tourist up-to-date on how the fish were biting and where.

Carol is a kindhearted, mid-western woman who reminded me of my grandmother. After visiting awhile and telling her my story, she insisted that I sit down with them for lunch. I have to admit, I was in a hurry to reach the next dam, but not that much of a hurry. I went out back of the bait shop and met Joe, a big man whose gruffness belied his friendliness. I could tell he truly loved the river. While we talked, Joe cleaned fresh morel mushrooms in a bowl and Carol busied herself in the kitchen fixing lunch. We feasted on fried chicken, fresh morels and onion rings. It was delicious. Finally, I confessed that I had to get going. Carol walked with me down to the docks, visiting with two other women we passed on our walk.

Before I left, I ended up getting my photo taken with the ladies and Carol. I promised I would write to let them know how I made out and Carol promised that she would write about me in the Verdel Newsletter which she contributes to on a regular basis. She kept her word too; somewhere in my scrapbook is a cutout with the details of my brief, but not forgotten visit to Verdel, Nebraska.

Shortly after returning to the river, I reached the Fort Randall Dam, behind which lies Lake Francis Case. I found that the dams were growing as I headed up river. My first impression of Gavins Point Dam left me amazed. Fort Randall Dam totally astounded me with its size. The dam dwarfed the previous dam down river. Instead of a length measured in feet, the earthen dam here is measured in miles, holding behind it a lake 107 miles long. Having had such good success at the last dam, and not really having any other choice, I tied up at the boat launch and began to ask folks for a ride around the dam. Again, I had only wait about an hour before Dave Fairchild and his family pulled in. Dave and his son agreed to give me a lift around the dam while his wife kept watch on their boat. Not only did he give me a lift around, but also, he pulled in at a gas station so I could fill my tanks easily before getting out on the water. Disregarding their own schedules, these people took time from their lives to help a total stranger get up the river. I could

Fort Randall Dam

never have completed my journey without the help and support of the kind folks along the river. I promised to write as I left and raced out across the glassy surface of Lake Francis Case. Evening was quickly approaching and I wanted to find a good camp spot for the night.

I found one not far from the dam on the west side of the lake. A small cove protected a rocky shelf along the shore. After unloading my gear, I sat down by a cozy fire to relax and enjoy the setting sun. The peacefulness of water lapping on the rocks soon had me feeling senti-mental. I wrote a long entry in my journal that night rejoicing in the solitude of the river and the kindness of all the folks I had thus met.

My supplies dwindled rapidly in the previous weeks leaving me with few appetizing choices for dinner. Rummaging through my grub box, I found a pizza mix stashed in the bottom. Why I packed a pizza mix I will never know. I do know that it is very difficult to make a homemade pizza over a campfire with only one pot. After a futile attempt to prepare the meal, I ended up mixing all the ingredients together and warming the pot of yeasty mush over the fire. My culinary skills had hit rock bottom. A beer rounded out the evening. By this time, I must admit,

I was getting meat hungry. Herbivory is not my strong point, and I desperately was craving a big steak. I had started off the trip with a case of beef jerky, but I did not want to eat it all so early in the trip. Even with rationing, I had little left by this time, it being so easy to eat a piece of jerky rather than stop to fix a meal. But my cravings were insistent and I planned to find a steak as soon as possible.

Not only were my food supplies beginning to run short, but my personal hygiene situation was none too good either. The water in the lower river did not exactly invite one to swim and bathe. In fact, the water had a dirty film to it that I found very difficult to remove from anything that became wet. The lower unit of my motor had developed a dingy gray / brown film on it that I could not scrub off, and I noticed that my sunglasses would not easily wipe clean if water droplets dried on the lens. Using a filter did not help. The muddy water clogged the filter before I ever purified enough to use. Needless to say, I didn't feel I would get too clean by bathing in the river water. In fact, I never even washed my face with river water until I got above Sioux City.

However, the waters of Lake Francis Case had the dark, deep green hue of lake water and I felt that the time was ripe (pardon the pun) for me to jump in the lake and clean up a bit. With the sun setting on a beautiful prairie night, I jumped into water that was deceptively colder than it appeared and cleansed myself. The remaining hours of the evening I spent lounging about my small fire listening to the mingling sounds of the lake and the prairie. The silence was so complete that voices at docks almost two miles away could be faintly heard carrying over the water. Small splashes punctuated the night as I lay in my bag gazing at the stars and listening to the pop and crackle of the last embers of my fire.

The lady I had met at Yankton had asked if I ever got lonely being on the river by myself. No, even so much time alone didn't make me lonely. If anything, I enjoyed the days of solitude. I found that on the river one never has to be alone. On any day I could work my way to shore and find someone to visit with, but I seldom felt the need. I stayed content just to let the days pass as they will. I enjoyed the company of Herschel and the occasional visits of folks I met along the river. No, I never felt lonely. I have only ever felt loneliness while being in a crowd.

I woke to a rosy, silent morning with only the sounds of birds and the occasional splash of a fish to disturb the glowing calm. After hot coffee over the fire, I pushed off into the lake. The boat skipped along over the water at a brisk clip, using little fuel, the wake from the boat slicing a drawn out V behind the boat. I saw my first mule deer that morning and observed small coniferous trees growing in the draws, a sure sign I was now out West. What most caught my attention that morning was the geology I noticed along the shores of the lake. Long layers of grayish shale appeared in the shoreline strata. Amongst those layers, I began to notice round granite stones like those to be found in the rivers further west. Intermingled in the layers of shale and round stones, a conglomerate formation was visible that looked similar to the formations I had seen along the Rocky Mountain Front. All the geological change that I saw around me emphasized my complete lack of knowledge in the field of geology. With no field guide or background, I could only guess at the ancient history of the river and the land around it.

By 11:00 that morning I had other things to think about. The sky had darkened to the West and the glossy surface of the water slowly began to crack and roll. In no time, the waves had increased enough that I was forced to keep the boat close to the West shore in an effort to stay out of the brunt of the wind. I hugged the shore for protection, hoping to find a spot to pull in and set up camp, but no openings were to be found. I was left with no choice; the lake swung to the west leaving me no shelter from the full force of the winds. I had to either turn around and backtrack several miles, or cross the width of the lake to seek shallower water on the far side. Like most guys, I hate to lose ground, so I set my sights on the far shore and quartered across.

The waves by this time were high enough that the boat was taking on splashes of water with each slamming wave. The "Teddy Roosevelt" was now charging up the waves like a true Rough Rider and fully living up to its name. Herschel had maneuvered in between my legs for shelter and comfort and I was just trying to hold the whole outfit together and not go down with the ship. I made it across over two thirds of the distance only to find that sand bars extended almost a hundred yards from the eastern shore.

The shallowness of the water made it impossible to get the boat in to the shore and accentuated the severity of the waves. I tried to find that fine line between just enough and not enough water, but with the waves throwing us about, I was having a hard time of it. Waves started to roll into the boat one after another and I was thrown into shallow enough water that the prop couldn't turn. There was no time to debate what to do, so I raised the prop, jumped out of the boat, turned the bow toward shore and pulled the boat on shore and out of reach of the waves. Around me there was nothing but rolling grassland as far as I could see. The wind whipped across the lake sending a fine mist intermingled with sand from the shore.

I had no choice but to find a place to get out of the wind and make camp. Traveling on was out of the question. With Herschel trailing along behind, I started walking the shore looking for any sort of shelter from the wind and rain that I was sure would follow. The prognosis for finding a good camp looked pretty bleak as I searched the rolling prairie to the east. I decided to locate under a scrubby cedar tree in a draw that afforded scant shelter from the wind.

I hauled gear up the beach from the boat and hiked it over to my spartan camp. With the wind howling about me, I fashioned a crude lean-to under the tree and stuffed my sleeping bag back into it. It was 1:00 in the afternoon. With nothing else to do but wait on the weather to change or darkness, I crawled under my shelter and listened to the wind. My firewood situation looked bleak, so I was forced to use the small dead branches from under the tree and any other dry brush I could scrounge up from the bottom of the draw. I decided to search for as much firewood as I could find and try to get my clothes dried out. With this task accomplished, I again hunkered down under my shelter and pulled out a book to kill time. My stomach growling, I kindled a small fire to cook over. Boredom was beginning to set in and the wind had not let up, even though the sun was shining. It made for a dull evening sitting below my little shelter listening to the wind howl.

In my search for a suitable camp, I had found a few old farm implements, most likely all that was left from an old homesteader shack that must have been in the area. I also found a 4 x 4 whitetail skull that I carried back to the boat to keep for a souvenir. It was near this spot that

John Colter saw and killed the Expedition's first Mule Deer. From a high spot on one of the hills behind camp, I had noticed a river coming in from the west. While lying in camp, I deduced it was the White River. According to my map, if the wind would lie, I should be in Chamberlain, South Dakota soon. Darkness came and I closed my eyes to sleep.

In the middle of the night, I woke up to what sounded like two bobcats fighting in a burlap sack not three feet from where my head lay. With a start, I woke and rolled away from the commotion and right through the middle of the campfire ashes. In the scramble to find my flashlight, I managed to get hung up in the lower branches of the cedar tree and tangle myself up in my sleeping bag. I found my light and turned it on to find Herschel covered with cedar needles and a blank look on his face like he had been hit between the eyes with a two by four. He was drooling and rocking in place. At that moment I realized what had happened and it didn't take long to realize it. Herschel had gotten into a fight with a camp-raiding skunk and had taken a direct spray in the face.

I rolled back away from him and got into my bag. Feeling totally rejected, he tried to snuggle down in the bag with me. I kept telling him to go away and the more I talked, the harder he tried to find comfort in the sleeping bag with me. He finally gave up and we both passed a fitful night trying to get a breath of fresh air to sleep by.

Morning came slowly with a stench of skunk heavy in the air. While fixing coffee, five whitetail bucks walked by our little camp not twenty-five feet away. I think the smell of skunk was so overpowering that not even the deer could detect our true odor. The wind had stopped and the morning was cold and clear. I bundled up and we hit the water as soon as we could, trying to get in some miles in case the day turned blustery again.

A few miles below Chamberlain I spotted something ahead in the water. Three deer were swimming across the reservoir towards the west side. I pulled in close to get a picture and noticed how scared the doe was. Thinking better of it, I backed the boat away and shut off the motor hoping it would let the deer calm down and make it safely to shore. When all three reached shore, they shook themselves off and bounded up the hills out of sight. The image of all three swimming across that wide stretch of water sticks with me even now. The river at that point is roughly a half-mile wide.

I reached Chamberlain before 9:00 in the morning on May 5th. Having time before the marina opened, I strolled the streets in search of a donut. I found one at the bakery and bought a cup of coffee to warm up with. Chamberlain, South Dakota is a mid-sized town located on the East side of Lake Francis Case. Interstate 90 stretches along the south boundary giving the town an abnormal number of hotels for its size.

Fishing and bird hunting seem to be the dominant form of tourism in Chamberlain. In fact, I think it is the major past time for most anyone in the Dakotas. Every time I met someone along the river, they would ask me how the fishing was. When I told them I wasn't fishing, people would look at me like I was some sort of leper. Not fishing! Heresy. I strolled into a small antique shop along Main Street to warm up a little and look around. The store had all sorts of knick-knacks that I am sure I could not live without if I were traveling via truck. But since I was putting along in a boat, I was relegated to the role of looking only.

I got to visiting with the shop owner, Barry, who showed immediate interest in my trip. Turns out Barry and Jason—the guy in the back room—were both biologists and also big fans of the Lewis and Clark Expedition. We visited for at least an hour that morning about antiques, history, the river, biology, on and on. While we were visiting, they called the local paper which sent down a reporter to do a little column on my passing through town. The reporter showed up and asked whose dog was on the porch. When I answered he was mine, the guys insisted I let him in. I had forgotten about the skunk incident. Not to worry, we were all well reminded the moment Herschel strode through the door. Herschel did a quick U-turn as I escorted him back out to the porch.

After asking Barry and Jason about what I might expect to run into further up river, I decided it was time I got going. I arranged to meet with the reporter down at the marina in about a half and hour, then said my good-byes. Before I left town, though, I had to get that steak that had been on my mind. At the local grocery store I bought the biggest roast in the case and stowed it away in my bag. At the marina I stocked up on two-cycle oil, stowed my meat, and motored across the cove to meet up with the reporter who took a quick photo of Herschel and me in the boat. Then, I was off.

The most important information I gleaned from the guys at the antique store was to watch out for submerged trees upstream from Chamberlain. When the reservoir had been built between 1946 and 1954, all the trees that lined the river were submerged still standing. Since that time, many a boat has collided with underwater limbs in the changing water levels of the reservoir. I heeded the warning, using their advice to keep an eye on the terrain to follow the original river channel. In no time I found myself at the next hurdle of the trip, Fort Thompson Dam, above which lie Lake Sharpe.

Big Bend Dam was completed in 1963. After completion, Lake Sharpe filled behind the dam creating a reservoir eighty miles in length. The dam itself is similar in size to Gavins Point Dam being only 10,570 feet in length and 95 feet high. Even though this dam is considered one of the smaller earthen dams on the Missouri, it still impressed me with its size.

My luck continued to get better, day after day, dam after dam. I only asked two people before I had a ride over the dam. It took less than an hour from the time I pulled in until I was back on the water above the dam. The water lay as smooth as silk on Lake Sharpe, and it was not long before I came to a feature of the river I had read about in many journals, Lewis and Clarks being the first to mention it. It was the Grand Detour, or The Big Bend of the Missouri. The Grand Detour is a curve of the river that circles almost entirely back upon itself. In thirty miles of river channel, the river only gains a mile of lateral distance. It is truly the Big Bend.

Whitetail Deer swimming across Lake Francis Case

CHAPTER 7

"proceeded on to the Gouge of this Great bend and
Brackfast, . . . we Sent a man to Measure the Distance
across the gouge, he made it 2000yds., The distance around
is 30 Mls . . . above and below the bend is a butifull
inclined Plain, in which there is great numbers of
Buffalow, Elk & Goats"
William Clark September 21, 1804

"Passed the Grand Detour. A curve in the river 30 miles
around, but only 1 mile across. Seemed like it took a long
ways to get a little ways."
Chris Bechtold May 5, 1998

CLARK HAD WRITTEN ABOUT THIS SPOT and how they had hiked over a
low saddle between two hills to wait for the boat which took the greater
part of the day to reach the captains. I looked up at this low saddle and
spotted a small tree outlined in the middle of it. A few hours later I
looked off to my left seeing the same little tree. I would love to see an
aerial picture of this bend in the Missouri. I imagine it to look like an
enormous horseshoe.

I located a campsite that night on a high cut bank looking over the
waters of Lake Sharpe. It was a beautiful spot. There was grassland as
far as the eye could see. I picked the spot so I could soak up the scenery and also because it afforded an immense view to the east so I could
watch the sun rise in the morning. My special treat that night was rump
roast. I started a fire and cut a hunk the size of two fists off of the roast.
Skewering it on a stick, I roasted it over the fire, eating the sizzling outer
crust as it cooked. If you have never eaten a hunk of meat this way, I
firmly suggest you try it. The outer layer cooks to a delicious crispness

while the inner part stays juicy and tender. My mouth waters thinking of it even now.

As I read the Journals that night, I thought back upon all that I had seen that day: deer swimming across the lake, snakes, beaver, lots of geese. It all seemed pale in comparison to the vast herds of game The Corps encountered. Clark wrote on the 23rd of September, 1804, "I walked on Shore & observed Buffalow in great Herds at a distance." I sat on my overlook in the peace of the evening and tried to imagine great herds of buffalo, elk and antelope. It is so easy to get caught up in the romance of it all.

Yet, I had to keep reminding myself how different all that I saw looked from that which Corps of Discovery saw. From where I sat, hardly a tree could be seen to the far horizon. I noticed in the Journals how the Expedition burned cottonwood for firewood. Since the advent of the dams, the riparian zones of the river in this area no longer existed. It had become a world of grass, sky and water. Though, I must admit, the sky and water both appeared quite clear. I fell asleep to the whisper of grass in the wind.

The next day I arrived in Pierre, South Dakota, location of the Bad River which Lewis and Clark called the Teton River. Nowadays I don't believe the area could ever live up to a name like that. The captains named the river after the Teton Sioux. This tribe provided much trouble for the Expedition. It was with much luck and bravado that the Expedition was able to pass by this band of Sioux and continue on their voyage. I had nothing but good experiences in the state capitol of South Dakota. The morning winds were light that day and I had no trouble reaching Pierre by 9:30 in the morning. What most impressed me upon my arrival was the beautiful, downtown riverfront park. It is the type of park that most towns along the river probably wish they had, full of large cottonwoods, benches and picnic tables. I tied up and walked into the downtown area where I found the Chamber of Commerce. There I received a map of the city and information on what to do and how to find it. The State Historical Museum immediately appealed to me, so with Herschel in tow, I started hoofing up the hill to the museum, located behind the South Dakota State Capitol Building.

Like Missouri, the Capitol Building of South Dakota, built in 1910, faces the river, another reminder of the important role the Missouri River played in shaping the destiny of the state. My hike proved to be a little longer than I had anticipated, but I was making good time and needed to enjoy the day a little more. Upon reaching the museum, I drifted through the displays, then found myself in the Gift Shop and Book Store. Mother's Day was not too far away, so I picked out a gift for Mom and a book for myself.

The ladies working at the Gift Shop got to visiting with me and after hearing what I was up to, decided to call the local paper. One thing led to another and I ended up getting a ride down to the local newspaper office which was not far from where I tied up the boat. There I met another kind woman who insisted on taking Herschel's and my picture with the boat. I told the lady I had a few more errands to do and I would meet her at the park. I made a few phone calls, mailed Mom's gift, and went back to the river, only to find a teenage kid stepping out of my boat with the whitetail skull I had found below Chamberlain. I hollered and grabbed the kid who insisted he was only looking. Yeah, right. I guess, like Lewis and Clark, I had to keep an eye on my gear and boat around the Teton River. This was the only incident of thievery that I experienced on the entire trip.

I met Dorinda Daniels from the paper, who moments later took my photo with Herschel for a small article. She promised to mail me a copy once the story ran. She kept her word and I received it at the end of my trip. From Pierre, it is only a short distance to the next dam I needed to get across, Oahe Dam. However, the wind had picked up considerably by the time I left town and I felt things were going to be nasty on the lake.

Once again, I had to beg a ride around the dam. I had tied up at a small marina, but there were few people on the water with the wind blowing like it was. With no luck there, I decided to walk over to the Corps of Engineers office and see if I could get any help from them. For the most part, they couldn't really help me, but one of the guys in the office was just getting off work and said he thought he could help. He called the owners of the marina where I was tied up and told them my story, asking if they could give me a hand. When he hung up, he told me it was all taken care of.

I hopped into his truck and by the time he dropped me off at the marina, the owners already had a trailer hooked up and backed down into the water. To thank the man who helped me at the Corp office, I gave him the 4x4 whitetail skull I had found, which he had been admiring. Then I was off with the marina owner to get around the dam.

Lake Oahe by far eclipsed any of the reservoirs I had encountered further down river. The Dam itself looked like something from a science fiction movie and the reservoir behind it dwarfed anything I had seen so far. The buildings that housed the turbines were cylindrical shaped affairs and had the appearance of large silver grain elevators. The constant hum emanating from the dam gave everything an ominous feel. I didn't waste time on the scenery below the dam. I wanted to see the reservoir itself. Lake Oahe is two hundred thirty miles long and has more shoreline, 2,250 miles, than the entire western United States coastline.

When the marina owner dropped me off at the boat ramp, the wind was howling across the lake, kicking up white-capped waves that made my stomach churn just looking at them. From the looks of things, I didn't see any suitable camping spots in sight so I opted to skirt the coastline in hopes of finding a good campsite for the evening. I only made it about four miles before the waves got to be too much for my little craft, and I was forced to pull over on a small gravelly beach.

I nosed the boat up on the gravel, but the waves crashed in behind me with such force that they washed over the back of the boat and immediately filled it with water. Pieces of gear floated or sank depending on their location in the waterproof bags I had packed. All in all, I had a real mess, but I was just glad to be off the water and on solid ground. It had been a harrowing four miles just to reach this point.

The trick to maneuvering the boat in high wind and waves is to keep the bow, or front, of the boat facing into the brunt of the waves. Any deviation of this causes the waves to slap the boat from the side and ship water over the gunnels, endangering the boat. The whole process sounds easier than it really is. With a Jon boat like mine, there is no V shaped hull to help slice through the waves and reduce the amount of beating the boat gets from each individual wave. The blunt nose of my boat heaved up with each wave and slammed down on the following. This continuous beating was not only hard on the riders, but also hard on the structure of the boat. It could be very dangerous if the driver did not stay totally focused on the waves and direction of the wind. At this point in my voyage, I felt like I was finally getting a handle on how the boat reacted to high waves and wind. Later on, I would find out how little I really knew.

For the moment, my boat lay full of water and gear. The waves continued to surge in behind the boat pushing it further up onto the beach with each lapping wave. I climbed from the boat and pulled it completely out of the water to make sure the waves didn't pull it back into the reservoir during the night. After emptying all of my gear out of the boat, I found a small willow tree with a sand dune against it to block the wind and set up camp. I was whipped from the stress of fighting the wind. Hunkering down on the lee side of my tarp, I started a fire and pulled out a book to read. There was nothing to do but wait.

The next morning, May 7th, 1998, dawned cold and windy. My gear was still wet and the boat held a few inches of water in the bottom of it, so I had work to do before I could get started for the day. I built up the fire and put a pot of coffee on before I set about drying out my gear. First, I had to completely empty the boat; that entailed taking off the motor and flipping the boat over on its side. I used the boat as a shield against the wind and a heat reflector for the fire, which I built up. Around the fire, I strung gear that had gotten wet using sticks and string. I felt like Robinson Crusoe after the shipwreck with all my plunder strewn about and the boat flipped over. But my efforts paid off, and in a couple hours, "our Instruments, Medicine, merchandize provision &c, were perfectly dried, repacked and put on board," to quote Captain Lewis.

The winds had not let up and neither had the waves, but I decided I wasn't getting anywhere just sitting around, so I pushed off to see what kind of distance I could make before it got too rough to continue. That may, or may not, have been a good idea. Before we left, Herschel had chased a beaver off into the water and got thoroughly soaked. He paid for it the rest of the day. The winds blew hard with only a peek at the sun around noon. I found out later that the temperature hung around the thirty-eight degree mark most of the day. I know for sure that it was cold in the boat.

In fact, the coldest part of me was my feet. They stayed in constant contact with the cold metal on the bottom of the boat. With the water temperature being so low, the cold traveled right through the metal bottom of the boat into my feet. I soon learned to put my feet up on a piece of gear. I also made sure Herschel stayed off the bottom of the boat and lay on the gear to keep from getting chilled. It helped for him to wear his neoprene life vest in the boat to keep warm. We both fought the cold wind all day.

For the most part, the land around us was totally barren save for grass. With the exception of the beaver in the morning and a few birds, we saw hardly any sign of life and nary a tree. I'll bet the school kids in this section of the world climb aboard a bus once a year for a trip just to see a tree. There was nothing but wind, waves, grass, and sky from horizon to horizon. Finally, around late afternoon, the little State Park of West Whitlock showed up, and I pulled in to warm up and see what to expect further upstream (if stream could be used to define what I traveled upon). I refrain from using times at this point because I had crossed from the Central to Mountain Time Zones at the Oahe Dam. But since the time zone line followed the river, the time could change depending on which side of the river I was on.

The first thing that caught my eye as I pulled into West Whitlock was the replica of an Arikara earth lodge on the point of the cove. Having read the Journals every night, I had just read Lewis and Clark's description of these same sort of lodges. It made a wonderful connection to the past to see the lodge sitting on this promontory overlooking the water. Bringing the boat about, I hopped ashore with Herschel to investigate the lodge.

The lodge itself was constructed entirely of earth and poles. Shaped somewhat like an earthen igloo, it had an entrance arch and a smoke hole in the center of the lodge. What surprised me when I entered was how warm the interior of the lodge was. No wind could blow through the earthen walls which helped to maintain a steady temperature. Envy swept over me and I even contemplated sleeping in the lodge, for it looked much cozier than the conditions under which I had been camping. But since I was in a state park, I knew I would only get in trouble doing so. I walked around the park with Herschel to warm up, then hopped back in the boat and motored over to a group of buildings with a gas pump nearby.

This was the local bait shop and convenience store for the park. When I walked in the warm air threatened to melt me. I felt instantly tired. Deciding on splurging a little, I ordered a frozen pizza from the cooler and a cup of coffee. There wasn't much talking to be done, so I just enjoyed a hot meal and coffee soaking up the warmth of the building. Looking at my watch, I decided I had better get going. I filled up on gas with little comment and headed out. While leaving, I spotted a historical marker that caught my interest.

The marker argued the point that the Mississippi should in fact be called a tributary of the Missouri rather than the other way around. It based its arguments on the total distance of the Missouri (which the sign declared was 3,100 miles) and the fact that the Missouri drained a larger sum of area. Having become fond of the Missouri, I agreed with the sign. I left West Whitlock feeling a little overwhelmed and possibly a bit proud that I had undertaken my journey on the great Missouri and not the little old Mississippi.

I pulled out of the cove, racing along on choppy water until I found a good spot to spend the night. Cold and wind had taken a toll on Herschel and me both as we huddled over a fire at the little campsite. According to the map, our location lay a few miles north of West Whitlock. It didn't take long for Herschel to fall fast asleep near the fire while I read the Journals and filled out my own entry of the days' events. Hopefully, tomorrow would be a warmer day.

The next day dawned cold, but clear, with light winds. I got on the water early and like to froze in the cool air that settled over the water. I had to remind myself that this far north, the ice had not been off the water long, and the air still held the chill of winter. Bundled up in all the warm clothes I had, I motored up the reservoir hoping that, by the end of the day, I would make it to North Dakota.

I had hardly been on the water any time at all before I made a wrong turn. Now it may sound funny, but many people had asked me if I worried about getting lost. I answered by saying, "Why worry, as long as I was heading upstream, I know I'm going the right way." HA! Did I ever prove myself wrong. I managed to make a wrong turn below

Mobridge, South Dakota and went about a mile up the Moreau River. That was the only time on the entire trip that I went up the wrong channel. Serves me right, though, just to keep me honest.

Back on the Missouri, the wind picked up shortly thereafter, and I rounded a large bend to see Mobridge, South Dakota ahead on my right. To my left, according to some brochures I had picked up, was a monument to Sitting Bull, medicine man of the Sioux, and Sacagawea, Lewis and Clark's famous guide. I could not pass up so important a place. I pulled in to take a look. The monuments lay atop a lonely grass hill overlooking the great bend in the river by Mobridge. A wide, glistening ribbon of water trails off to the North and South from the spot. With the wind blowing and the sun still low in the sky, the place had a lonely, desolate feel to it. I climbed up the steep hill to the monuments, expecting to see a more elaborate memorial than what actually stood there. Instead, I found a large stone statue to commemorate Sitting Bull. At the base of the monument, small cloth offerings lay scattered around amid sweet grass bundles.

I felt moved seeing that others still came to the gravesite to remember this great leader. Somehow the loneliness of the place felt right. Maybe this high desolate overlook was the most fitting place for a great man who had suffered so many wrongs and died at the hands of his own people. I can say that the place certainly affected me somehow. I felt very meek standing before this stone memorial to the great Sioux leader. Now, I could put a place to the image of Sitting Bull.

Further back on the hill from Sitting Bull's grave stood a smaller stone tablet that described the probable demise of Sacagawea. The memorial told of how Sacagawea most likely had passed away upstream at an old fort that Manuel Lisa had erected near the North Dakota/South Dakota line. Her remains were not cataloged or listed in any formal burial and so we will never know exactly where she was laid to rest. Most likely, it was along the great Missouri just upstream from this point. She supposedly passed away from the "putrid fever." We will never know what happened to this famed woman. The small stone that I stood looking upon marked, as close as anything, her final place on earth. Today, with the bicentennial approaching, the mystery of Sacagawea's final resting place still remains.

I spent a few moments sitting on the hill contemplating all that history had done for these two beings memorialized behind me. One fought for what he believed in and ended up being killed by his own people at the mouth of the Cheyenne River just visible in the distance. The other lived a short life of obscure importance only to die unknown in wild lands far from her birthplace. How strange life could be.

With the melancholy of the monuments settling upon me, my thoughts lingered on how the land had changed. Every evening I read the Journals of Lewis and Clark to anticipate what to see and what to look for in the coming day. Every day what struck me most was not how much our images of the river resembled each other, but how much they differed. Most people like to look at the Missouri River and think that what they see in front of them is the same as what all the participants in history saw. In this fantasy, they believe the only thing to change is the date. Well, it is not true.

The river is a tamed beast, a wild animal that has been haltered and broke to do man's work for him. It still has that wildness to it, but it is an undercurrent that one has to look for. I love the river because it can still be wild, not because it has been tamed.

When I traveled on the waters of Lake Oahe, I considered that what I saw was the stage upon which much of history took place: Sitting Bull's life, the death of Sacagawea, the expeditions of the fur trappers. I had to pinch myself to remember that all of this grand drama took place below me, under the waters that I so blithely traveled upon.

The trees that stood silently along the river, witness to so much, are buried beneath everything that is so visible today. We cannot even read the accounts of those that traveled before us without realizing that all they saw will never be visible to us. It is a vanished world in many ways. The world changes, but in most places we can stand upon the land that shaped our history. Only on the Missouri River, the river that shaped who we are as Americans, is our history lost forever, never to be trodden on again by those seeking to see what our forefathers saw.

This sad realization hung over my every move as I traveled the final legs of my trip upon the reservoirs of the Dakotas. I had taken this journey to see what Lewis and Clark had seen, to follow in their footsteps like I had in their overland travels in Montana, only to find that hundreds of miles of the grand journey could only be read as fiction, unreachable for myself and anyone else.

I left the hill saddened by my thoughts. Here I was, retracing the grand western expedition, and I was hung up on technicalities. I tried to rouse myself out of my funk and look on the bright side. This was still one heck of a fun journey. I still had the sense of adventure. I crossed over to Mobridge and got a cup of coffee to go. When I hit the water again, my gloomy funk had lifted. Nothing like a cup of coffee to set the morning on track again.

CHAPTER 8

"I saw some rafts on the S.S. near which, an Indian woman was scaffeled in the Indian form of Deposing their Dead and fallen down . . . Saw several buffalow lodged in the drift wood which had been drouned"

William Clark April 20, 1805

"as I did walk along I saw lots of bone fragments. I suppose them to be buffalo or cattle. Who knows? All are very old . . . The bones litter the beaches."

Chris Bechtold May 8, 1998

FROM MY LIMITED MAP—a few sheets of paper that Joe Lang had printed out for me in Nebraska—I knew that there wasn't much for towns ahead of me. Puttering along on the wide-open waters of Lake Oahe, I kept my eyes on the shoreline, looking for anything that would catch my eye and relieve the monotony of grass, sky and water.

The one thing that I desperately wanted to find on my trip was a bison skull. I knew people that were lucky enough to find these treasures from the past, but I considered the feat purely luck, like finding a needle in a haystack. Nevertheless, I kept my eyes peeled all the way from Yankton, South Dakota to Three Forks, Montana, trying to spot one of the hidden treasures. I found just enough bones to keep my attention held the entire trip. Just above Yankton I found my first bison tooth. From then on, I found teeth, jaws, possible pieces of skull and a myriad of assorted bones.

It got to the point that I always kept my eye on the far shore trying to determine what areas were most likely to hold bones. I got pretty good at it. By looking at the lay of the land, I found that large flats along bends were good bone holding areas, as well as tight bends with high sediment layers. I also kept my eye out for open silty beaches and assorted areas that might hold "treasures." You could say looking for bison bones was my hobby while traveling the river.

At any rate, I always kept my eye out for anything of interest as I motored along. Not long after leaving Mobridge, I spotted what I hoped to be a partial bison skull along the banks. I pulled over only to find I was fooled once again by an overly active imagination. However, not far down the beach, I stumbled upon a long layer of bones in the cut bank of the river. The bones virtually shined in the dark dirt of the bank after it had crumbled toward the river. I never could tell if those particular bones were cattle or bison. They looked very old at any rate. My little bone fetish got even more interesting later in the day.

Shortly after putting back into the water, I spotted a back eddy on the west shore that looked like a good bone spot and also a good place for Herschel and me to stretch our legs. I pulled in and while wandering along, perused the gravel for anything of interest. I guess you could say I am an inland beachcomber. I noticed a few small bones, vertebrae and ribs lying in the gravel, but didn't give them much thought. I saw deer bones frequently and was not interested in them. After all, I wanted to find a bison skull.

However, one bone piece caught my eye. It was a thin, concave bone that roughly resembled something belonging to a fish. I could see a suture point along one edge of the bone and a half circular opening along the other edge. The bone was strange enough that I put it in my pocket and kept looking around. In no time, I found another bone that looked just like the first. I pulled the first out of my pocket and compared it to the one I had just picked up. They looked similar. When I fitted the suture points together, the top portion of a human skull stared at me from the palm of my hand. I suddenly realized that those were not deer bones I had seen earlier. I collected all the bones I could find and ended up with some jawbones, a pelvis, femur, et cetera. Not knowing what to do, I placed all the bones together in my cooler so I would not lose them and planned to drop them off at the next Corp of Engineers office I passed.

My curiosity ran wild at this point. From my nearest guess, I figured I had the pieces from two different skeletons. One I guessed to be a child and the other, judging from its size, a small adult. I based my guesses by comparing the femur length with my own, and on the size of the jaws. Both were decidedly smaller than mine.

Where had they come from and who could they be? I thought about this as I puttered along. To the west I had been traveling alongside Reservation lands since passing the mouth of the Cheyenne River. The lands that I was now passing to the West comprised the Standing Rock Indian Reservation. No doubt, the skeletons could belong to Native Americans, or maybe the skeletons could be those of early homesteaders or travelers. I never would find out.

I believe that no matter who they were, the remains most likely were buried in lands covered by the reservoir and over time washed onto the beach. I suppose that whoever the unfortunate souls were, I will never know. I hope the remains found a final resting place whoever and wherever they may be. Before I got back into the boat, I did find an old license plate from 1930, a pitchfork, and a wrench. Possibly all of the items came from an old homestead site buried underwater close by. Who will ever know?

A short time later, I came upon another area that looked like it might hold bones. I couldn't resist the temptation and went ashore to look around. This time I found what I knew to be bison bones. Long layers of the bones littered the shoreline for at least one hundred fifty yards. I wandered down the shoreline pulling apart clods of dirt looking for a perfect bison skull, but to no avail. I did find several partial skulls, but nothing that was in good of condition. I eventually had to give up the search and climbed up on the bank to investigate a small pile of stones that caught my attention.

What looked to be a pile of stones turned out to be a shrine of sorts. Shaped like a small tipi, the shrine was constructed entirely of stones with a small sheep wire fence surrounding it. To the north was a similar construction of stones that appeared to be another shrine or alter. I walked the short distance over to the structures to investigate more fully. Both structures stood completely alone upon a vast, grassy plain bordering the Missouri. The two of them gave a lonely, eerie appearance

*Buffalo Bones along
the Missouri River*

to the desolate landscape. I looked in the four directions and could see
no other sign of man. Upon further investigation, I found that the tipi
shaped mound was actually a monument to a Catholic priest that had
lived on the reservation from 1876 to 1896. The tipi shaped shrine
stood about 12 feet tall and roughly 8 feet wide at the base. The monument held a variety of Indian and Catholic symbols and was written
upon in Latin. I did not write down the name of the priest, or any other
pertinent information about him. The second stone structure was shaped
like a small igloo of stone, roughly 12 feet in diameter. Upon entering
it, one went down into the ground to a tiny alter in the back that looked
to have held candles at one time. Old signs of smoke covered the ceiling
of the shrine. I felt as if I had intruded upon something that did not
concern me and left the area as soon as I could. I am not a religious
man, but I do respect the beliefs of others, and I felt that the shrine and
monument that I had just looked at were meant for those who believe

and was not for outsiders. I respected that feeling, leaving as soon as I could. I felt like an outsider. I returned to the boat thinking how much the cultures of the river have changed over the last two centuries, from a native nomadic prairie existence to a more settled European farm culture.

Shortly after I started up river, I crossed over the North Dakota state line. It was a little after 5:00 in the evening and the water lay ahead of me like a sheet of glass. I pulled into the small reservation town of Fort Yates, North Dakota. The sense of being an outsider enveloped me at once as I crawled from the boat. Two little Indian girls, dressed in dingy shorts and soiled tops, sat upon the rip-rapped bank staring down at me. They looked to be about seven years old. I waved hello, but they seemed to not even acknowledge my existence. I proceeded to unload my fuel cans and smiled up at the girls from time to time hoping to get a response, but they continued to stare blankly at me.

To my surprise, I began to feel intimidated by these little girls that watched my every move. Here I was on a grand adventure, a solo traveler on the great Missouri, and two little girls were making me feel uncomfortable. With Herschel at my side, I clambered up the bank and hiked off through the little town in search of a gas station. If I thought I had felt out of place in towns before, this one made me feel like a traveler from another country altogether. The streets were littered with wrappers, cans and bottles. Plastic bags slowly tumbled across the streets in the slight breeze. I walked along looking for some sort of Main Street, but there seemed to be no business area. Only boarded up establishments and run down houses. The windows of the buildings were boarded or covered with bars. I finally detected a buzz of activity down the street and headed towards it. It was the gas station I had been looking for.

I felt an untold number of eyes watching me as I walked along towards the station. The town reminded me of the reservations back in Montana, but it seemed so much more desolate and decrepit. Hopelessness pervaded everything I saw. I filled up my cans and paid at the door of the station. No one even asked what I was up to. The men around the station watched my every move without comment. I thanked the station attendant and started back to the river lugging my cans. That feeling of intrusion settled down upon me. I was not a part of this area and never would be. I hustled back to the boat and filled up the tank. The depression that wafted around the little town dissipated as I pulled out toward the center of the lake. I can't fully describe the feeling of alienation that I had in Fort Yates. It was a feeling of guilt, I suppose, for being able to leave the town and move on, when it looked like the residents had no chance of escape.

In the calm of evening, I made good time and decided to make camp on an isolated beach about five miles upstream from Fort Yates. A large tangle of driftwood covered the gravelly beach, which looked like it might provide some shelter from wind if the weather turned. Storm clouds nosed over the Northern horizon threatening to blow in some weather, but the air still felt calm along the shore of the lake. I debated setting up the tarp and making a lean-to, but the driftwood did not make a good anchor for the tarp. So I just spread the tarp over me as I settled into my bag for the night and hoped that the rain I could smell on the wind would pass by or be light.

Maybe it was the weather, the cold wind with a hint of rain in it, or maybe it was only my imagination, but I could not get to sleep that night. Maybe the human skeletons I had found earlier that day were disturbed. I can at least try to blame my lack of sleep on supernatural phenomena. But I really think the reason I at first did not trail off to sleep was my brooding premonition that the rain was not going to skirt around me, and it was not going to be a light rain. I was right.

Somewhere in the middle of the night the winds gathered force and with the winds came rain, at times large sheets of it. It pelted down upon my measly tarp throughout the night. I was lucky for the most part. It never fully drenched my bag, but it did seep in undetected. At first, I noticed my feet were a little cold, then one hip, then a shoulder. Before I knew it, I lay damp and shivering under my tarp, clinging onto the edges of it to keep out ever more inclement weather. When I woke in the morning, my bag was dotted with sodden spots. The rain still continued to drizzle intermittently. I suppose the skeletons were going to make me pay for disturbing their slumber upon the banks of the river. I skipped the coffee and fire that morning and packed up as quickly as I could. I read later in the journals of Patrick Gass that the Expedition's stay in this area had been similar to my own. Gass wrote in 1804, "We had a disagreeable night of sleet and hail." I missed the hail part, but the sleet was soon to follow.

The movement of packing up camp warmed me a little; besides there was not a piece of dry wood to be found on the beach. The driftwood had soaked up all the moisture in the air like sponges, rendering it unburnable. I figured the best thing for me to do was to get moving and warm up as I went. I might find someplace to settle into later and build a fire to dry out. Maybe.

Soon after leaving my sodden camp, I passed through a reed infested area at the end of Lake Oahe. From that point on, I traveled upon a relic remnant of the Missouri River. The channel meandered back and forth like a giant serpent. Hidden sand bars lurked under the rain-pocked surface of the water and the main channel slipped from side to side of the river. On the banks of the river, giant cottonwoods watched over the water, beneath which stood open stands of grass. I could almost imagine the area two hundred years ago looking much like it does now.

Despite this feeling of traveling on the "original" river, I ran into increasing numbers of people. I was surprised at the number of boats I began to see on the river. I passed more people fishing in that small stretch leading to Bismarck than I had encountered upon the whole of Lake Oahe. With almost every boat I passed, the same question was shouted over the water, "Catching any?" I soon learned it was easier to shake my head "no" than to divulge my true intentions for being on the river. It seemed as if every person in North Dakota was out fishing. Indeed, I firmly believe that there is no one in the state who does not fish. Later, when I finally crossed the state line into Montana, I felt relieved when I no longer had to answer that familiar inquiry, "Catching any?"

When passing a group of boats that almost blocked the river, I had to ask what all the commotion was about. It was then that I learned the reason for all of the anglers. It turned out that I had run smack into a weekend fishing derby. At least now I didn't feel so out of sorts when asked if I was catching anything.

The closer I got to Bismarck, the colder and more steadily the rain fell. By the time I reached Bismarck my teeth were chattering and I was soaked to the bone. I spied a marina as I approached a bridge and decided

I was going to go in and have a good hot drink. I needed it. The usual scenario unfolded as I walked through the door in my hip boots and wool coat. A hush fell over the guys at the bar as they turned to size me up. I tried to ignore the stares and ordered a whiskey and coffee from the bar. I nearly melted when the hot liquid hit my belly.

While sitting at the bar and soaking up the warmth and whiskey, two young guys came in and set down beside me. They said hello and asked if I had been fishing. One thing led to another and I found out that one of the guys was working at becoming a professional fisherman. That sure piqued my interest. I don't think I have ever heard of anyone who had chosen that as a career before, not to mention in North Dakota. But hey, here I was without a job, traveling upriver in the rain. Different strokes for different folks.

As I got up to leave, so did the two guys that I had talked to. I went out to get my gas cans and get them filled when the fellows saw me hauling my cans. They pulled over, and told me to hop in and they would take me to a filling station in town that had cheaper fuel than the marina. Not only did the guys give me a lift to the station and back, but they also bought my fuel for me. I thanked them both profusely as they dropped me back off at the marina. I hope I see that guy some day on one of those television fishing shows. I guess that would be the top of the mountain for a professional fisherman.

If I had thought the rain had been miserable up to Bismarck, I hadn't seen anything yet. When I pulled out of the marina, the skies opened up and the rain came down in a heavy, steady deluge. Cold water soaked the wool coat I wore and even Herschel sat in the front of the boat shivering in his life vest. I knew I had to find a place to camp and warm up soon. The problem was in finding a place I could make camp. As I motored past the banks of Bismarck, I was amazed at the number of affluent homes I saw lining the banks of the river. One after another they pressed upon the edge of the water. In the condition I was in, I needed a few particular things to make a serviceable camp. For one thing, I needed a way to get out of the rain and a place that was dry to lie down. I needed a place to make a large fire that had adequate sources of dry wood close at hand. I wasn't finding anything like this passing all the new homes along the river, and I was getting colder all the time.

Herschel, my faithful and wet friend

Finally, I passed from the areas of development. The river soon became crowded with trees and brush along its banks. I was shivering uncontrollably by this point and knew that I had to find shelter quick. The temperature was cold enough for me to see my breath, even motoring along in the boat. I spied a large old cottonwood on the South side of the river where the bank had caved in under the roots. It looked to be holding on tenaciously to the soil while half of its roots hung out over a little bar of gravel. I jumped from the boat and sized up the old tree. I hoped it would hang on for a few days longer because I planned to sleep under that overhang of roots.

Pulling my axe from the boat, I chopped all the loose roots that hung down below the bank. I piled these up to be used for firewood since they were all dry. Then using the back of my axe, I dug a shelf further in under the base of the tree and hollowed out a little shelf for my sleeping bag to lay. Below this and about two feet towards the river, I dug out another shelf that I planned to build a fire upon. Then, I hauled my wet sleeping bag up under the roots and laid it out upon the dirt shelf I had dug. Gathering all the dry and semi-dry wood I could,

I made a small fire on the second shelf and arranged the extra wood so it could dry by the fire and be in reach of my sleeping bag.

I undressed and hung my wet clothes around from the chopped off roots over head and snuggled down into my damp bag. Herschel curled up at my feet in a muddy ball. I don't believe I have ever been so happy to get out of the rain before. I made dinner that night and never once left my sleeping bag. By the time I woke in the morning, my bag and clothes had dried out almost completely. I had been awfully lucky to stumble upon such a cozy spot for camp. It didn't look like much, but Herschel and I were very thankful for the old tree. We slept well that night.

The next day was Mother's Day. I was glad that my mother hadn't seen the conditions I had been out in the day before. I doubt she would have rested as peacefully as I did. Of course, I doubt she would have slept under an old cottonwood that was ready to fall into the river either. I made a note to myself to remember to call my Mom and let her know I was all right and wish her a good day. I was also wishing myself a good day, too. Turned out I should have wished a little harder.

As I broke camp that morning, a tom turkey and some geese held a debate as to whether the rain would continue or not. The muffled sounds of gobbling and honking bounced across the water in the damp, foggy air. With little idea of what lay ahead, I started out in the fog of the morning. I proved to be quite lucky that morning. The river continued in its braided fashion with sandbars and channel weaving back and forth. In the fog, with visibility of less the one hundred feet, I strained to keep the boat off the sand bars. To make things even more challenging, the rain commenced about an hour after I left and came down in buckets. Most of my sleeping bag and underclothes had received a chance to dry out, and my pants were even a bit dry, but with the latest deluge, all the clothes I was wearing became soaked once again.

Luckily, though, I was able to get most of the dry clothes and sleeping bag wrapped up and stashed in my waterproof sacks. With the weather like it was, I could only hope for a good camp that night and another chance to dry out the warm clothes I was wearing. As it was, I only grounded out once in the stretch of river from Bismarck to Washburn. I ended up dragging the boat a short ways and was able to continue on until a break in the fog showed the town of Washburn, North Dakota on my right. By that time I was ready to get a hot meal and get out of the rain.

The next day and with Herschel by my side, I slogged up the hill to the North Dakota Lewis and Clark Interpretive Center in Washburn. The Center sat in a large open field a quarter mile back from the river and looked out over the river bottom. I went inside and found that I was the only visitor in the place. A young volunteer by the name of Brian was working that slow day. I introduced myself and stated my purpose of the visit. After a short visit with Brian, he offered to fix a pot of coffee and took my soaked coat in the back to dry by a heater. The warm air in the center and the hospitality soothed my chilled outlook.

The Interpretive Center itself is a new affair, built with thought and taste in 1997. Inside are well put together exhibits on the types of material the Corps of Discovery carried with them and the obstacles they encountered up to their arrival at Fort Mandan. I wandered about for over an

Fort Mandan re-creation

hour soaking up the warmth and information equally. My favorite part of the museum was the reproduction dug out canoes. Anyone who has spent any time in a canoe or small boat needs to take a good look at these one and a half ton, thirty-three foot behemoths. They stagger the mind in their massiveness and length. The fact that the Corps dragged, paddled, and wrestled those unwieldy craft upstream was a feat in itself. The weight of those boats, when fully loaded, is unimaginable. I stood in awe of the canoes thinking of the difficulties I had encountered so far myself. At that moment, I was able to truly appreciate the incredible sacrifices the men of the Corps made to complete their journey. To ascend the Mighty Missouri on its own terms with these crafts is a feat that is unachievable today.

Of course, I read the Journals the night before and caught up with all that those men had done and endured while staying at Fort Mandan. I was now ready to see the Fort itself. After finishing my tour of the Center, Brian took me back to a café in town. I thanked him for his hospitality and got directions on how to find the reproduction of the Fort. The rain had subsided by this time and I detected a glimmer of sunshine to the West. I crossed my fingers and hoped this was the case. Back at the boat, I needed to unload all my gear and pour the water out. I had put ashore in high water and the water had receded enough to leave the boat high and dry, but full of rainwater. After putting things back together, it was short hop upstream to Fort Mandan. I tied off on the bank and with Herschel in tow investigated the grounds.

To my surprise, the Fort was much smaller than I anticipated. A palisade of logs constituted the outer wall of the quarters, shaped in the form of a triangle. Inside, I noted how small the rooms themselves were. I imagine most people would think how terrible it must have been to be in such small quarters. After the weather I had endured the last few days, I imagine the men of the Corps were quite happy with the cozy quarters and no doubt were tickled just to have a roof over their heads.

I took my time perusing the grounds of the Fort and looking in each nook and cranny. During the tourist season, the grounds are manned with informational tours presented to visitors. Obviously, I was not there at the tourist time of year, so I contented myself with reading the copy of the Journals I had brought with me while sitting in the quarters of the men and perusing the brochures I had picked up at the Interpretive Center.

I tried to imagine life in the fort as it must have been for the men. Cold days and nights spent inside the small rooms telling stories and mending gear, the speculation of what tomorrow might bring and the day after. No doubt the men talked often of their escapades in the Mandan village across the river, or they spent long nights debating what the "shining mountains" that lay ahead of them would be like. Like the men of the Corps, I sat in those small quarters and wondered what the future would bring for me, too.

Since there wasn't another person around, I had Herschel pose for pictures a few times inside the fort to get a feeling for the size of the quarters, then I went back down to the rivers edge to gaze across the water. Looking out over the low fields, I tried to imagine covered with earthen dwellings similar to the ones I had seen further downstream near Whitcomb. This lonesome area that I looked upon had at one time been a major population center and the center of trade between the Western and Eastern tribes. Nothing is left that even hints at the importance this area once played in the exploration and settling of the West. I sometimes wonder if we think too highly of ourselves nowadays. How arrogant we are as a society that we leave our indelible mark upon the land and do so little, whereas, the great contributions of history so quickly revert to dust.

CHAPTER 9

"This little fleet altho' not quite so respectable as those of
Columbus or Capt. Cook, were still viewed by us with as
much pleasure as those deservedly famed adventurers . . .
these little vessels contained every article by which we were
to expect to subsist . . . enterta(in)ing as I do, the most
confident hope of succeeding in a voyage shich had formed
a darling project of mine for the last ten years,"

Meriwether Lewis April 7, 1805

"Hard to believe that Lewis and Clark took (the dugouts)
up the river . . . (this) gives a person a whole new respect
for the Corps of Discovery and the hardships they faced . . .
I had to unload the boat, drain it, and drag it back to
water . . . when it stopped raining . . . From there I
headed up river."

Chris Bechtold May 10 1998

THE SUN PEEKED THROUGH THE CLOUDS in a few isolated spots to shine
a shaft of sunlight down on the prairie to the West. I broke my reverie
at the fort and got going on the river. I wanted to see the spot where
the great artist Karl Bodmer had painted the immense Hidatsa village
along the river. The mouth of the Knife River was not only mentioned
in the Journals, but also in many other works chronicling the exploration
of the West. Somewhere, somehow, I missed the historic Knife Indian
Village at the mouth of the Knife River. I must have passed on the off
side of an island and—great adventurer that I was—I missed the whole
river; so much for technology making one a better traveler.

Instead of seeing the mouth of the Knife which I was looking for
to get my bearings, I came upon the Fort Garrison Dam. The second
to the last of the great earthen dams I would have to cross on the Missouri

and the fifth largest earthen dam in the world. Behind this massive dam lay the waters of Lake Sakakawea, the largest reservoir I was to encounter on my voyage. The lake is 178 miles long and contains one third of the total water stored by all the dams on the lower river. It is six miles wide at its widest point and holds enough water to cover the state of North Dakota with six inches of water. I would soon learn that Lake Sakakawea, named after Lewis and Clark's famed guide, was a force to be reckoned with. Using my standard portage procedure, I pulled in at the boat dock and waited for someone to show up and give me a ride.

My knack for quickly obtaining a ride did not hold out. I had to wait for over seven and a half hours before I was lucky enough to get a ride. I had not taken into account the lack of people who would be out on such a nasty day, and the fact that the fishing derby was downstream by Bismarck. It made for a long lonely wait. I used my time to read, write, and generally catch up on some rest that I had not gotten in the last few soggy days. I finally got a ride around the dam with an older fellow who was kind enough to help me out. I traveled a very short distance and set up camp for the night.

A large Corps of Engineers office is located above the dam alongside Lake Sakakawea. In the morning, I planned to locate a staff archeologist and turn over the skeletal remains I had been packing with me since I crossed over the North Dakota line. I felt that maybe if I returned the remains, it would improve my luck a little, or at least improve the weather. All the cold and rain soured my mood and I needed a few good days to get me back on track and optimistic about the river ahead. I settled down to a simple meal of couscous.

My supplies had dwindled considerably in the previous week, and I desperately needed to replenish some items. Not to mention the fact that I was getting sick and tired of eating plain couscous night after night. The meal is simple and efficient for camping, but has the consistency of gruel. Hoping to improve my larder, I slipped off along the waters edge in hopes of finding a duck or goose to fill my pot for the night. I never had considered it before, but my belly was telling me that was a good idea. I had a rifle with me, more as a security measure than anything, so I took it for a walk along the lakeshore. Every day I had been seeing wildlife of some sort. Waterfowl seemed to follow me everywhere I went, but they must have known my evil intentions that night, for I could not find a bird to save my life. I settled for more couscous and decided maybe it was a sign that I should not be looking for dinner out of season. Herschel was not so sure he agreed.

I slept in the next morning, having a difficult time crawling out of my warm sleeping bag. The air was cool and crisp, but at least the sun was shining. After enjoying a lazy breakfast and sipping coffee alongside the fire, I packed up and motored across the bay to a small set of docks close to the Corps office.

The Corps of Engineers office at Lake Sakakawea is a beautiful brick building that looks like it would be equally at home on a large Southern plantation. The grounds surrounding the building were well tended with lush green grass and sturdy trees nestled close to the building for shade. I entered the main doors and looked over the list of offices printed on the wall. Locating the chief archeologist, I headed upstairs. I had my little lunch cooler filled with bones tucked under my arm when I knocked on the door and entered the office.

The archeologist was sitting with his feet up on his desk, Jimi Hendricks music wafting from the small radio in the room. I wore an old wool sweater and grimy, mud caked pants and boots. The Archeologist looked over at me with his Hawaiian shirt and sandals. He asked how he could help me. I explained how I had found some human skeletons and thought I should turn them in. He looked over at me like I couldn't possibly know what human bones looked like. "What makes you think they're human?" he asked derisively. I sure didn't like his tone or his air of superiority. So, as I pulled out each of the bones in the cooler I named it by the correct anatomical label (i.e. tibia, mandible, femur, et cetera.) and laid them all on the table.

At this the fellow hopped up and took notice. Yep, he could see I had some human skeletons. Did I know it was against the law to pick up human remains? No, I didn't. But I explained that I thought it best to bring them in to an archeologist rather than leave them in the gravel. Well, he reiterated how I had been wrong to pick up the bones, then asked me to pinpoint on the map where exactly the bones came from. I showed him on the map that hung on the wall. I could tell that neither one of us was much impressed with the other. Before I left, he told me that I shouldn't pick up any more human remains if I found them, but should carefully mark them and call him so he could come and investigate. I made up my mind right there that if I did happen to find any more remains, I would make a point of notifying any archeologist but him. With that, I left the office and decided that was enough government bureaucracy for the week, and I would try not to deal with the government any more if I could avoid it.

Back on the water, I started along the south shore of the lake and pulled in to the marina located above the dam. I was the only customer of the day, and probably the only one for the week the way things were looking. It seemed as if all of Lake Sakakawea still lay dormant from the winter. According to the man who filled my tanks at the marina, the last of the ice had melted off only a few short weeks before. While talking with the guy at the fuel tanks, he looked over at my ears and asked how long I had been on the water. About three weeks I figured. He said my ears looked pretty well fried from the sun and gave me some sun block for them. In truth, my ears had been bothering me for some time. They felt like two pieces of bacon attached to the side of my head. When sleeping at night, they would sometimes crack open and bleed. I had managed to severely sunburn them even though I had worn a wide brimmed hat every day. All the damage was due to glare off the water. I thanked the fellow for the sun block and asked what to expect on the lake.

His parting advice was to heed the wind as much as possible and stay close to shore, two bits of advice that I did not need to be reminded about. After crossing the large reservoirs below, I had a healthy respect for big water, and Lake Sakakawea is big water. When I pulled out of the marina, I could look towards the northwest and not see the horizon. This would be by far the largest body of water I crossed. I began to get a small lump of concern (it might have been called fear, but I didn't want to sound scared!). I hugged the shore all that morning trying to work up the courage and the reasoning for crossing over the wide-open expanse.

Lake Sakakawea proved to have many tricks up her sleeve for me. The first is what they call the Van Hook Arm. The Arm is in actuality a very wide, deep bay that looks just like the main channel of the lake.

Many people mistake it for the main river, in fact, because it is wider than the actual channel of the Missouri. Before reaching the Van Hook Arm, one must also keep his eye out for the mouth of the Little Missouri. It extends to the Southwest between high grassy hills and looks like a most inviting little river. As much as I wanted to go explore that area, I decided to take advantage of the good traveling conditions and try to cross as much of the Lake as I could while the water was relatively calm. I hated to pass by the chance to see some of president Teddy Roosevelt's stomping ground.

One of the most interesting things I noticed that morning were the long seams of coal that lined the banks of the reservoir. I had read the Journals and knew that Captain Lewis had noted the amount of easily available coal that could be found along the river banks: "the coal appears to be of better quality; I exposed a specimen of it to the fire and found that it birnt tolerably well." But I never expected to see so much coal along the lake. The wind eventually picked up enough that I was forced off the water and retreated to a secluded cove just below the mouth of the little Missouri. I took this opportunity to try out the coal and see how well it burned. The Corps of Discovery had been pleased with its quality, I thought I would try it out myself.

In truth it was a good thing there was so much coal, because there sure wasn't much wood about. I gathered some small twigs of brush that I found growing in a little coulee feeding into the cove and went back to the beach to build a fire. It took a little while to get the fire hot enough for the coal to ignite, but once it did, I had a hot even burning fire that was a pleasure to cook over. Putting a pot of coffee on the fire, I leaned back and enjoyed the warmth.

A few hours later the wind laid down enough that I thought I could proceed. The sky had become overcast and the air noticeably cooler. The water had calmed enough that I thought I should at least try to gain a few more miles. I passed the mouth of the Little Missouri and swung west into the main channel of the Missouri, past the Van Hook Arm. A small, little voice in the back of my head made me wonder if I had made the right decision. I still had no maps of the area, and was traveling solely on the advice of the man at the marina. The waves continued to slowly increase so I decided to pull over for the night. The problem was that now that I had turned into the main channel, there was no place for me to pull over. The banks of the reservoir were high black cliffs with no place to escape the brunt of the weather that now seemed to threaten a storm. After some amount of worrying and fighting the waves, I found a small split in the cliffs that held a muddy beach littered with beaver cuttings. It looked like it would make an acceptable camp. I gladly pulled in and thanked my lucky stars for shelter from the wind and waves that had been pummeling me on the open expanses.

I had been on Lake Sakakawea one day and already I could not wait to get this lake behind me. Little did I know that the lake had just begun to toy with me. Unaware of what was to come, I settled in to a comfortable evening and warm, steady coal fire. After dinner, I climbed up the steep hills above camp to the cliff tops bordering the lake. Oh, the sight that rewarded me for my climb. I stood upon a peninsula of land with the main channel of the Missouri on my left, the valley of the Little Missouri back and to my right, and the Van Hook Arm directly ahead of me. I felt as if I stood at the point of creation.

The setting sun filtered down through the scattered clouds to make pools of diamond studded water dance in the evening light. Dark scattered clouds whisked by over the slate gray water. In between the

Overlook of Lake Sakakawea

water and sky, a great sea of green grass could be seen in the distance. I could not pull myself away from the enchanting sight. Sitting on my perch in the buffeting wind, I watched the water until the light finally surrendered to darkness, leaving a butter cream moon to light my way back to camp.

This land was beginning to feel a lot like Montana, and oh, how I yearned to get back to that great state. I knew the most remote stretch of river would be in Montana; the White Cliffs Area. I was ready to see this section of country that I read so much about, and there is nothing so beautiful as springtime in Montana.

At the moment, though, springtime still felt like it was weeks away. I woke in the morning to heavy dew that bordered on frost. Bundled up in my woolens and long johns, I started up the narrow stretch of lake below New Town, North Dakota. I was passing through the lands of the Fort Berthold Indian Reservation. Of course, I had not realized that until later on in the morning when I pulled into New Town.

Dressed in my warmest clothes, I was still chilled to the bone. The cold air hung just above the water's surface. In addition, the cold seeped through the metal bottom of the boat into my feet. Herschel sat forward in the boat on the gear to keep from getting chilled, although I doubt he could get too cold in that heavy fur coat that he has. Not long after we set upon the water, Herschel jumped to attention looking off toward the left bank. To my surprise, there standing on the shore, was a small group of bison. I felt as if I had stepped back into time. I never expected to see bison on my trip, especially in the open breaks along the river. I am sure it was a sight that many a river traveler one hundred and fifty years ago took completely for granted. But, for me, it was a once in a lifetime experience to catch a group of buffalo watering in the morning's first light, not a sign of humanity around. It was breathtakingly beautiful.

I slowed the boat while Herschel and I sat transfixed. The group of nine cows and calves watered, then rushed back up the steep broken clay banks. They disappeared quickly up through the breaks in the cliffs. My final sight of them was a lone cow and calf on a point as the sunlight bounced off their heavy coats. I had killed the motor when I first spied them. After they disappeared, I sat quietly in the water watching where they ran, stunned by my brief trip back in time. So the Missouri is not without the bison. Here in this far corner of North Dakota, the bison still range upon the grasslands of the great Missouri River. Somehow that little bit of knowledge is like knowing that the pyramids still stand along the Nile. It means that in a small part of the world, things have returned to the way they were and should be. I started the motor deep in thought and headed to New Town, North Dakota.

At the bait shop in New Town, I learned all about the bison I had seen. They belong to the Fort Berthold Indian Reservation which keeps a small herd. I jawed with the man at the bait shop and got the latest scoop on what to expect further up the lake. Sitting there, I ate the breakfast of champions: bag of potato chips, coffee, and Danish. My food supplies were dwindling quickly. I was down to couscous, pancake mix and coffee. Still, I had no desire to walk all the way to town and buy groceries, so I satisfied my hunger at the bait shop, bought fuel and headed out on the water again. I called home before I left to check in and let everyone know I was still OK and moving right along. To my surprise, my Mom informed me that Dad and Calvin Garrett had loaded up the minivan and were on their way to meet up with me as we spoke.

It seems that Dad had recuperated sufficiently from his "beaver wound" and was disappointed he had missed out on his few days of riding in the boat. He hated to miss an adventure and planned to surprise me at some point along the river. My first thought was that Dad's infection had affected his thinking. But, after a moment, I got excited to see a familiar face again. I had really been enjoying my solitude and freedom on the river, but a few days with Calvin and Dad would be fun. Besides, I knew they would have a ball following along and riding with me from time to time. I told Mom that if she talked to them later today, to tell them I would get to Williston, North Dakota by nightfall and I would leave my cell phone on for a few hours that evening so I could get in touch with them. I planned to get food when I got to Williston which I figured was attainable.

Lake Sakakawea was not going to let me off the hook so quickly. I had no sooner passed from sight of New Town than the wind came up with a vengeance. Small waves that were rough in and of themselves, soon became almost unnavigable. In a short time, I was forced off the water onto a windswept grassy flat. The boat had been beaten severely in the wind and waves by the time I reached shore. With little to break the full force of the wind, it had blown directly into the bow of the boat. I could not turn to quarter the wind for fear of capsizing in the high waves. The front of the boat would rear up only to be caught by the wind and be pushed even further into the air. Then, the forward momentum of the motor and weight would slap the boat back down and onto the next wave. It felt like I was riding a bone crushing bull. I held tightly to the tiller of the motor with one hand and with the other I gripped the under lip of the bench I sat upon. Poor old Herschel hunkered down between my legs. If I had not lashed most of my gear to the bottom of the boat, I am sure it would have been thrown into the lake. With conditions like this to contend with I was happy to find a spot to pull over and wait out the wind.

"the banks of the river are steep . . . the bed seems to be composed of mud altogether."

Meriwether Lewis April 22, 1805

"Ran into marsh and then silt. A great flat bed of it."

Chris Bechtold May 12 1998

BY MID AFTERNOON THE WIND HAD LAID ENOUGH that I felt I could make it to where the lake turned south, thereby getting out of the teeth of the West wind. My plan worked, and after turning south, I hugged the west shore for protection until I reached Lewis and Clark State Park. There I fueled up and inquired how far to Williston. The young park ranger said it was only about 20 miles and I shouldn't have any problems. I think I must have asked the wrong person. Because I ran into one of the biggest problems of my entire trip.

About ten miles from the state park, I encountered a wall of reeds across the end of the lake. I had seen this type of thing before at Lake Lewis and Clark back in Nebraska and was dreading the maze I knew I would soon encounter. The main channel of the river seemed to be flowing in from the southwest side of the lake. Skirting along in this deeper water, I scanned the reeds ahead looking for an opening or some telltale sign of flowing water coming from the wall of vegetation. So far, I couldn't see anything. When I approached the reeds, a small break in the vegetation opened up and I skimmed into it. I knew that the water level was dropping from the high-pitched whine of the motor. I had very little water under the boat, but I hoped to find a break in the shallows ahead that would put me in a deeper channel and guide me through the reeds. No Luck. About that time the prop touched bottom.

Spurting mud and water in the air behind me, the boat slid to a standstill in the muddy water. Well, time to get out and pull, same as I had done back by Springfield, South Dakota. I put on my waders and stepped out of the boat. Instantly I knew something was different. As my leg went over the side of the boat it never touched solid footing. I pulled my leg back into the boat. The water color was that of coffee with cream in it and I could not see bottom. With the spare oar that I carried, I leaned over the gunnels of the boat and probed for the channel bottom. I never touched anything solid. It looked like I had "run aground" in a thick silty soup. It was too thick to paddle and too thin to get out and stand in. I was in a real pickle now.

At first, I tried the motor again. No luck. The little Mercruiser would whine and pitch mud and slop six feet in the air behind me, but it couldn't budge the boat. It only succeeded in wallowing out a little spot in the mud where the prop was. Next I tried to push my way back to deeper water with the oar. Leaning over the side of the boat, I hadn't the leverage or strength to move the boat. Herschel looked over at me with a somber look upon his face. He realized we were in a fix. I sat back down in the boat and thought this might be a good time to use that little cell phone my folks had given me for emergencies.

I pulled out the cell phone and tried Dad's cell phone number. By golly, he picked it up right away. "How are things going?" he answered. "Not too good," I replied. And I proceeded to fill him in on my predicament. I asked where he was. He had just come through Glendive, Montana and planned to be up my way in a few hours. I told him I might be a little late getting into Williston, but that I would keep him informed of progress. Wow, talk about coincidence. Earlier that morning, I had been out on the river on my own with no need for any aid. But the moment I got in a pickle, who should happen to be around, almost 1,500 miles from home, than my Dad. Who'd a thunk it?

Meanwhile, I was still stuck in the mud. On top of being stuck, there wasn't a sign of life in any direction. I truly was out there all alone. I prodded in the silt and rocked the boat, trying anything to free it up. Still no luck. I decided at this point to try another tactic. With my waders on I slid over the front of the boat and hung onto the bow. This caused the rear of the boat to raise up a little bit and bring a wider amount of the bottom in contact with the water. By kicking my feet and hanging over the front of the boat, I could move a few inches at a time. I kept at it, with Herschel standing on the bow urging me on. Gradually, I moved the boat back to water deep enough that the motor could pull me free. When I climbed back in the boat I was soaked in sweat and covered in stinky mud, but I was floating free. I backed the boat out into deeper water and let it sit there while I stood on the bow and looked over the situation.

I detected another little inlet in the reeds and eased over towards it. I was gun-shy of getting stuck now and proceeded with the utmost caution. When I got to the reeds, I could see there was no way through. I did this for the rest of the day. Easing in and out of openings trying to find a way through the tangle of reeds ahead of me. At one point, I got close enough that I could see the grain elevators and water tower of Williston, but still I could not get through. I kept in contact with Dad every hour or so. Finally, I told him to meet me at Lewis and Clark State Park. For the first time on my trip, I was forced to go backwards. I hated it. I hated to give up. It wasn't the river that was beating me; it was the reservoir, the siltation, the damned dams.

I sped on back to Lewis and Clark State Park. It was nearing dark by the time I got into the dock area. Not a soul was around. I pulled up at the dock and unloaded the boat. Just as I finished, Dad and Calvin rolled up to the boat ramp. I was sure glad to see them.

They had been on the road since the morning before. Their trip had been a spur of the moment thing for the both of them. After Dad had recuperated sufficiently from his beaver ordeal, he had moped about the house wishing he could see the river and be on the adventure until Mom finally told him to just "Go, damnit!" He didn't waste any time. He called up Calvin who is always ready for any kind of adventure. The next morning they loaded up and set off for Montana.

While I greeted Dad and Calvin, telling them of the difficulties I had encountered at the end of the lake, another boat pulled into the marina. It kind of surprised me to see that someone else had been out on the water. When the fellow pulled in alongside us and started visiting, I told him of the problems I had faced finding the channel at the end of the lake. After listening intently, the man told me that he had made it through the reeds the previous year while fishing the river from Williston, and proceeded to explain to me the course he had taken to get through. I took careful notes and decided to try again in the morning.

Dad, Calvin and I went into town for the night to have a beer and dinner to celebrate their arrival. Afterwards, they took me back to the launch and said they would meet up with me in the morning to try it again. They proceeded to head back into town to find a motel room and I sacked out by the boat. Early the next morning they pulled in with a steaming cup of coffee and a hot meal, starting the morning out on the right note.

I decided to reduce the weight in the boat as much as I could to make it sit higher in the water. So we unloaded all the unnecessary items and gear. Herschel opted to ride along with Dad for the day. Then I took off. The man at the boat ramp had told me to stick close by the east shore of the lake and follow along the high banks on that side. I tried every trick I could and followed every conceivable flow of water that I saw coming through the reeds with no luck. I never even got as far up the river as I had the day before. I backtracked through the maze and tried one last time to see if I could get through in the opening I had made the most progress in the day before, but to no avail. Defeated, I called up Dad and Calvin and told them I couldn't make it.

When I turned around and got out of the reeds, the wind had picked up and the waves were rolling with whitecaps. I had ten miles to go and no weight in the front of the boat. It was a long ten miles. The boat lept off every wave, bow in the air, then slapped the wave ahead of it. The pounding of the waves upon the boat threatened to shake my teeth loose. Some of the waves were large enough to toss the boat completely out of the water. When this happened, the motor would make a high pitched whine while exposed to the air, then the front of the boat would slam down into the waves with a tremendous crash. I had a death grip on the tiller. My little Rough Rider threatened to pitch me overboard.

Dad and Calvin returned to the park and waited nervously for any sign of me. They said they could not believe a boat could even be out on the water, not to mention one the size of mine. Calvin walked the protective dike along the marina looking out over the lake for sign of my approach while Dad paced back and forth by the van. Calvin later said he could hear the boat pounding the waves long before he ever caught sight of me over the whitecaps. I eventually made it into the marina and to safety. My arm muscles felt like jelly from clenching to hold onto the boat. I decided that I needed to portage around the reeds.

I told Dad and Calvin of my plans, and we all jumped into the van and drove into Williston, North Dakota to find a truck to rent or borrow. One of the dealerships in town had pick up trucks for rent so we went in and pleaded our case to rent one. After the man that owned the lot heard my story, he offered a little Dodge Dakota for no charge. I don't think he will ever know how much I appreciated that gesture. I had made it so far without having to miss a single mile of river and it tore me up to have to go around this section. But it could not be helped. It had been a low water year and it was still early, before the major spring run off. There just wasn't enough water to make it through.

Back we went to the marina in our little pickup. We unloaded all the gear into the van and threw the boat and motor in the pickup. When we pulled the boat out of the water, we noticed that the front end of the boat had been caved in a couple of inches from the force of the waves earlier that morning. That is an indication of the size and severity of the waves I had been fighting.

We took the boat through Williston and dropped it off at the boat launch at the edge of town. The man at the truck rental spot had notified the newspaper of my trip and scheduled a little interview before I got going. I answered a few quick questions, but I was in no mood for an interview. I still was a little miffed I had to miss roughly seven miles of river. When the interview was over I hustled into the boat and told Dad and Calvin I would meet them at Fort Union.

CHAPTER 11

*"I determined to encamp on the bank of the Yellow stone
river . . . the whol face of the country was covered with
herds of Buffaloe, Elk & Antelopes; deer are also abundant"*
William Clark April 25, 1805

"much pleased at having arrived at this long wished for spot"
Meriwether Lewis April 26, 1805

"And I passed the famed mouth of the Yellowstone River."
Chris Bechtold May 13, 1998

As I was growing up, I had often read about the famed confluence of
the Yellowstone and Missouri Rivers. It seemed like some magical place.
The meeting place of mountain men, and the great tribes of the plains,
in a land of rolling prairie with many undistinguishable landmarks, it
was THE definitive mark on the land; a place that any wandering soul
could find, where Lewis and Clark, the first explorers in the country,
had chosen for a meeting spot in 1806. Many a traveler had passed
through this famous spot. Hence, it was also the chosen spot for trade.
It was where Fort Union was established in 1828 to garner as much
trade as is could from the Yellowstone and the Upper Missouri. In my
mind, I had imagined this fabled area to ooze with history and the
ambiance of the old west.

Instead of the mystical spot I had pictured in my mind, the Mouth
of the Yellowstone is in fact, like any other river mouth I had passed in
the previous one thousand or so miles, maybe a little muddier. While
it did not look to be home of the spirits of all the mountain men of the
past, it did look to be home of all the paddle fishermen of the present.

As I motored past the muddy confluence of the two famed rivers, a crowd of people eyed me suspiciously. All of them were in pursuit of the prized Missouri River Paddlefish.

These fish are a throwback to earlier times. They resemble a very large catfish with an enormous proboscis. Their large snout is what they derive their name from because it resembles a paddle. They are bottom-feeding fish whose main diet is composed of microscopic plankton stirred up off the rivers' bottom. Considering the turbidity of the muddy water, and the fact that they do not eat anything that humans could use for bait, it makes fishing for them seem a bit challenging to say the least. But that doesn't slow down some folks. From what I could see as I motored by, Paddle fisherman are a different crowd.

The banks were lined with mud covered pickup trucks, old campers and folks in lawn chairs. The lawn chair folks looked as if they were there only for spectating. For to fish for Paddlefish, you have got to be standing along the bank. The standard tackle consists of a long stiff ocean type rod and reel with a large weighted treble hook at the end of the line. The fisherman launches the hook out into the river then jerks and reels, jerks and reels, jerks and reels until the hook is brought in and the process repeated. The trick is to snag a paddlefish, anywhere, anyhow, and get it hauled up to shore and landed. I guess I am just not cut out for this type of fishing. At least I would want bait on the hook, if only to make me feel good.

Shortly after passing the mouth of the Yellowstone, I pulled in to Fort Union, at one time, the largest and most famous trading post on the Missouri. During the height of the fur trade in the 1830s, the Fort saw many famous personages pass through its front gates. Today, the Fort has been restored to its original grandeur and is run by the National Park Service. I could not pass up the opportunity to visit the grand old stopping off point of early river travelers.

What I found most striking, from the moment I nosed my boat into the bank, is how much the original river channel has changed in the 160 years since the Fort was in business. Many original oil paintings still exist, from such famous painters as Karl Bodmer and others, that showed the Fort in its entire splendor. According to these paintings and historic records, we know that the Fort stood just yards away from the Missouri river bank. When I nosed my boat into shore, I still had over one hundred yards or more to reach the front gates. This just re-iterates the fact that the Mighty Missouri is always changing.

I climbed from the boat with Herschel in tow to tour the sights of the Fort. Dad and Calvin were already inside; I could see their van in the parking lot. The Fort is constructed in the shape of an enormous square. Two of the corners have fortified lookouts upon them and are connected by walls that stand at least 15 feet high. The most eye-catching part is the trade house. The building would be grand on any scale, but located here on the upper Missouri, almost 2,000 miles away from any thing closely resembling it, it is entirely captivating in presence.

The main trade house is where all the business that shaped the destiny of the Upper Missouri river took place in the early 1800s. Here is where Alexander McKenzie laid out his plans to conduct trade upon the Yellowstone and Missouri; where great chiefs of the upper Missouri came for trade and treaties; and where folks like James Audubon, Karl Bodmer, Prince Maximillian, Jim Bridger and the like came for supplies, luxuries, and respite from the rigors of the wilder-ness. The history literally oozed from the walls of the Fort. If only the place could talk. This is the feeling I got just being inside the walls, which were nothing but reconstructions, as was the whole Fort. I tell you, the history of Fort Union is the history of the Upper Missouri during the mountain man days.

Dad and Calvin met up with me and together we all toured the grounds. Inside the main trade house, we read exhibits, studied arti-facts and tried to imagine what life was like in the great hub of trade activity. Unfortunately, my stay at the Fort was cut short. While inside, I told Herschel to wait outside on the porch which he always does faithfully, but for some reason, a young kid with a tour group had come over to Herschel and for reasons unbeknownst to me, Herschel bit him. I could not believe it. I suppose there is more to it. Never before, or since, has Herschel done that to anyone. It was nothing more than a nip, but the rangers came and told us about it, so we decided to leave. But there is more to it. I camped that night under a bridge leading into Culbertson, Montana. (Yeah, Montana!) while there, the sheriff tracked down Dad and issued me a ticket for Hershel.

So, Herschel's one trip to Fort Union ended in a federal ticket for failure to have a leash for $25.00. What a memory.

On the other hand, I had finally made it to Montana. It seemed like I was almost home, almost to the end of the line. But, our delusional happiness was short lived. It only took a glance at the map to realize we hade at least another 500 or so miles of river ahead of us. Nonetheless, it sure felt good to be back on Montana soil, or water, as it was.

All in all, it had been an eventful day for Herschel and I. From our start on the silt flats of Lake Sakakawea to our eventual end of the day under a bridge outside of Culbertson, we had made a bundle of memories for one day. The wind had picked up by evening and threatened rain. To avoid a soggy night under the tarp, which just might have blown away with the power of the Montana winds, I had huddled up under the bridge and enjoyed a dry, blustery night. I felt fortunate that my difficulties and memories did not include being chased by a grizzly bear. I concluded from the Journals that Meriwether Lewis had a close encounter with a large bruin near this same spot.

I went to sleep that night a bit frustrated with all that had happened. I hated to admit that I had to portage a part of the river. It took away from all that I was trying to do. But it could not be helped. The river was low, I was on a schedule, and there was really no way around the flats at this time of year. Maybe if I had come through later in the spring and hit the higher water with spring runoff, I could have made it. No doubt, I am sure I could have made it, but that was not the case. Besides, if I had come any later, I would not have been able to use a motor to navigate upstream through the Wild and Scenic portion of the river, due to restrictions imposed by the Bureau of Land Management. I had to salve myself with these thoughts as I lay under the bridge. I was also a bit perturbed about the whole dog incident at Fort Union. Not that I was miffed with Herschel. I knew him well enough to know he doesn't bite anyone, but I was miffed at the kid who must have taunted him to do it. All these thoughts floated about in my head as I listened to the wind howl under the concrete. I could only hope things would get better.

I was home in Montana. I had traveled roughly 2,000 miles of river, and I felt the end was getting near, though nowhere close to being in sight. That was the bright side that I stayed focused on. After leaving Fort Union, I found a partial bison skull in the bank of the river. My ultimate goal of finding a bison skull for a souvenir from my grand adventure may yet come true.

The next morning, Calvin and Dad flipped a coin to see who would ride with me first. Calvin won, so when they showed up at the bridge, they were ready to go. Having someone else so excited to come along on the water gave me new life. It was like having a new set of eyes to see the river with. I had become a little complacent with the sights and sounds of my journey. After twenty-five days on the water, I was having a hard time getting excited about the amount of travel ahead of me. Even though every day brought something new, there was always that tedium of slow travel in between the new sights that began to wear on me.

With Calvin in the boat, the morning had a fresh feel to it. We coordinated with Dad where we would meet him upstream and took off. In no time, we passed a mule deer in the river. Soon we were finding a littering of bison bones in the crumbling banks and stopping to pick up teeth so Calvin could take some home as souvenirs. Geese and goslings scattered at our approach. Ducks, beaver, and myriads of birds delighted us at every bend. There was always something new to be seen, and it seemed that here, in this part of Montana, we had once again found the old Missouri. Maybe this part of the river would be recognizable to someone who had passed this way decades ago. The river wound back and forth upon itself. Cottonwood trees hung out over the sandy edge of the channel and the river took its own sweet time in heading to its rendezvous with the Mississippi. Like me, it seemed that the Missouri was enjoying its time in Montana.

In addition to the wildlife, Montana also had a lot of weather it needed to show us. We encountered just about everything but snow: fog, rain, sun, wind and anything in between. At almost every turn, we were either putting on a piece of clothing or taking it off. For all the weather, though, we had a grand time. We also took longer to get to Wolf Point than we thought. We pulled in around 3:30 that afternoon and met up with Dad. By that time, we were pretty hungry so we went into town and filled up at the local café. Over dinner, we planned out where to meet next. According to the map, I figured we were fairly close

to Fort Peck Dam. To make better time, I proposed to go from Wolf
Point to Fort Peck with just Herschel and then the next day Dad could
ride with me on the lake.

Everyone thought that a good idea, so off I went with Herschel
planning to meet up with the guys in a few hours. The only fault with
the plan was that I had miscalculated the mileage to Fort Peck. What
I thought would only take a few hours took almost six. I didn't make
it to the boat launch below the dam until ten o'clock that night. But,
the trip up river to the dam was a wonderful trip. I delighted at all the
cattle I saw lazing away under the shade of the cottonwoods. Geese still
choked the water and the closer I got to the dam, the more relics I saw
from its construction.

Near the mouth of the Milk River, I passed an enormous skeleton
of a wooden barge run aground. I surmised that this was actually a
dredging barge built during the construction of the dam. In several
places along the banks, I passed the forlorn looking homesteads that
surely were abandoned after the completion of the dam. Old tractors
and vehicles could be seen, their skeletons hidden in the brush. Forlorn
and dilapidated, they crumbled away in the shade of the cottonwoods.
In all, it was a melancholy evening coming up the river, viewing all that
had been left behind in the race for progress.

At the boat ramp, Dad and Calvin were waiting for me with a white
pickup truck. They had arrived and booked a room at the historic old
Fort Peck Hotel and told the story of my coming up the river. After
checking in, they had inquired about a vehicle or trailer to get my boat
around the dam. The guy who ran the hotel graciously offered the use
of his pick up, so I was able to load up my boat the moment I arrived
at the dam. Fort Peck was the only dam on the entire river that I never
had to beg a ride around or wait for a portage. I liked the service.

We ate that night at the Fort Peck Hotel. I had covered 162 miles
that day and thought I deserved to treat myself a little. I indulged in a
hot shower and a few beers with Dad and Calvin. The weather forecast
for the next day didn't look too promising. It called for high winds,
which was exactly what we didn't need for crossing Fort Peck Reservoir.
By bedtime, the wind was already blowing hard. I would not be going
anywhere the next day. Being one who has a tough time refuting peer

pressure, I also caved in and slept on the hotel room floor that night. I cannot say I enjoyed it. After so many nights in the open air with the sound of water close by, I did not sleep well. I was hot most of the night and my roommates snored.

The next morning dawned cool and windy, too windy to even contemplate getting out on the water. So instead, we indulged in a leisurely breakfast at the hotel and planned to spend the day relaxing and exploring the area. The Fort Peck Hotel stands below the dam like a relic from a bygone time. It was built during the glory days of Fort Peck, back when the dam was under construction, and was the hub of activity in Montana. Built in 1936, the hotel must have been one of the most elegant establishments in the area. At any moment, one would expect to see a man in a fedora walking down the narrow hallways. The hotel still held the ambiance of a pre-World War II hotel.

The rooms have not changed much since the building of the hotel. Dark wood trim pervades the building. Each room has a simple metal frame bed and wood floors. Downstairs, the restaurant displays simple elegance. White tablecloths cover small tables that overlook the wide green lawn. The study is the type of room where I imagined men with cigars and suits making deals. Overstuffed leather chairs nestle in the dark, presided over by glassy eyed mounted deer and elk. I thought the entire hotel a wonderful place to sink into and let time waltz by.

But time was one thing I did not want to waste. Midday came and I was ready to be on the move and back on the water. Instead, we drove down to the powerhouse at the dam and looked over the exhibits. Inside were fossils of every size and description, all unearthed during the construction of the dam. Speaking of the construction, there were volumes of photos to look through that documented the building of the first earthen dam on the great Missouri River. It was a project that was enormous in scope, deemed impossible, and yet, done on a budget and time frame that even today could not be matched. At the peak of construction nearly 11,000 people worked on the dam. I must say, as much as I dislike the dams on the Missouri, the Fort Peck dam was a colossal work that showed just how industrious the American nation could be.

Outside of the powerhouse, we toured along the dam itself. Fort Peck Dam is the largest earthen embankment dam in the world. The

Dam itself, excluding the spillway which looks like an enormous bowling alley, is over four miles in length. I am told that years ago on the Fourth of July celebrations in Fort Peck, the town folks would have bowling contests on the spillway. I would love to see such a thing. Imagine a bowling ball careening down several hundred feet of concrete. It must have been quite a sight.

For the most part, the town of Fort Peck seems a lot like the old homestead houses I had seen all along the river since Omaha, abandoned, like the dried, sun bleached bones of a trying time in American history. There are still those who will always be in Fort Peck: dam workers, teachers for the little school, bartenders—the bare necessities. The town will always live in the shadow of its glory days.

That night we had a few beers after dinner and listened intently to the weather forecast. More wind called for later in the day. However, I decided to give it a try early in the morning. My past experience was that the wind did not blow until almost nine o'clock every morning. I thought we should get up before light and be ready to go at the crack of dawn. If we could get past the big open expanses near the dam, I could hide out of the worst of the wind by hugging the bank and skirting the mouths of the channels. It was worth a try.

The next morning was relatively calm. Calm enough to give it a try anyhow, but cold. I bundled up in all my warmest clothes. Dad had decided to go with me and he was a bit shy in the warm clothes department. He brought along a warm blanket from the car and wrapped it around himself to cut the wind. We pushed off a half hour after the first hint of light. The waves slapped against the sides of the boat as we motored from the protection of the marina. Out on the open water, the waves looked to be about a foot and a half high. Rough, but doable. Dad had not been out in rough water before and he balked a little when we started out into the waves. But shortly, he realized the boat could handle it safely. The cold wind whipped across the water and bit at any exposed flesh. Our faces took the brunt of the wind and numbed in the cold. Dad sat up front and huddled in his blanket, most likely wondering how he talked himself into having this much fun. We plugged on and in no time were out of the big water and hugging the north shore, skipping across the mouths of innumerable coves. The waves subsided for the most part, and by late morning, Dad had shed his blanket and began to enjoy the ride.

It seemed as if the only moisture in the world was the water we were floating upon. The land surrounding the reservoir looked like a desert of rock, grass, and stunted trees. Even the rattlesnakes must carry canteens in this country. At noon we stopped to flex our legs and hike around the country. Antelope bounded away from the next ridge as we hiked up to a high spot, scouting the country ahead. Sparse clumps of grass shoved their heads about in the dry soil we hiked upon. Casually walking about, we stumbled upon numerous bits of fossils. I learned later that the dark pearlized little tubes we found were the remains of bacculite aminoids. I found several that day just hiking along taking in the vistas ahead of me. I discovered later these little creatures covered the sea floor 65 to 136 million years ago.

After noon, the clouds broke and sunshine flooded the reservoir. The water calmed and soon we were zipping along over a surface of glass. I think we got awfully lucky to tell the truth. Talking to fishermen in the area, I found that the wind doesn't lie down much this time of the year on Fort Peck. For that little bit of luck I am thankful. The rest of the day, Dad and I talked over the sound of the motor, pointing out sights along the way and in general enjoying all that surrounded us. Come late afternoon we spotted the white minivan. Calvin stood behind it in the shade, waving us in.

Seems Calvin had as much adventure as we did. All he could talk about was how lonely the country was. He had not passed a car in almost fifty miles and had seen few signs of civilization. "Good God, doesn't anybody even live out here?" he asked. Then he looked around at the arid land and thought twice before questioning the lack of humanity.

Calvin had been following the map that I loaned him that morning, looking for an access point to get back in touch with us. I think he was a bit surprised to find the roads shown on the map were gravel. All in all, the long drive he had taken had been quite an eye opener. Calvin was ready to get back to pavement, and soon enough, a gas station. While drinking a beer with Calvin, Dad told him of our adventures, garnishing the story with ample references to the cold wind and high waves. While these two compared notes, I decided it might be a good time to change props on the boat. I had been using the same prop I left Illinois with and it was considerably scarred. The boat ran rough from the vibration of the motor. The constant pull of the motor and vibrating wore me down.

Back on the water, with Dad in the front and Herschel by my feet, the boat literally skimmed across the water. The new prop made everything run smoother, and even better, faster. We looked over the map and decided to be bold and try to get to the Fred Robinson Bridge, effectively the end of the Reservoir, by nightfall. It would mean a total of over 150 miles in one day if we did it. I was ready to be off the big lakes and back to river travel.

By evening we had approached the end of the reservoir. There were reeds growing at the end of the lake, but nothing like I had encountered on Lake Sakakawea. Most importantly, the channel stayed well defined throughout the whole passage from reservoir to river. I was very relieved. Back in the river setting, we began to see more wildlife along the banks. Deer were coming out in the evening cool and beaver could be seen swimming back and forth along the banks. In the short distance from the end of the reservoir to the bridge, we counted 26 beaver. No wonder this area was so important to the early fur trade. I saw more beaver in this one stretch of river than on any other stretch since the beginning of the trip. At dusk we pulled into the campground at the Fred Robinson Bridge. We had successfully navigated all of the Fort Peck Reservoir in one day. Make that one long, one hundred seventy mile day. I was ready to settle down and relax for the night.

CHAPTER 12

*"The hills are high & rugged the countrey as yesterday. I
ascended the highest hill I could see, from the top of
which I saw . . . the meanderings of the Missouri for a
long distance . . . the river was verry crooked and much
more rapid"*

William Clark May 19, 1805

*". . . began to see high cliffs that the area is noted for . . .
high eroded cliffs come down to the waters edge and it is as
quiet as a church in the canyon."*

Chris Bechtold May 17, 1998

ALONG THE WAY ON MAY 16TH, we passed the mouth of the Musselshell
River coming in from the south. Captain Clark wrote in his journals
nearly two hundred years earlier, "Muscle Shell River falls in on Lard.
Side 2270 miles up." I gathered I had come a long way after reading
that in the Journals. Also, Dad and I passed the area where Lewis and
Clark observed their first Bighorn Sheep on May 25th, 1805. Of course,
they shot one to see how it tasted and skinned it out for a specimen. I
never saw any sheep on that day, though I was to see some later on.
Instead, I saw scores of fisherman along the bank near the Fred Robinson
Bridge trying to snag a paddlefish. Once again, it was like a carnival
atmosphere at the boat access points with people scurrying this way and
that around the campground, laughing, joking, and having a good
time; all trying to catch a prehistoric looking fish with a bare hook.
Somehow, the thought of it tickled my funny bone. I slipped down into
the brush along the river and tied up the boat in some thick willows
for the night. To celebrate our longest day on the river, Calvin, Dad
and I hopped into the van and drove into Lewistown, Montana, almost

75 miles away, for dinner and a beer. It being late, we chose to spend the night in Lewistown. The next morning we loaded up with a large breakfast and headed back to the river.

The day was making out to be much cooler than the previous day. Clouds scudded across the sky and a stiff, cool breeze blew from the northwest. When we arrived at the bridge, I immediately rushed down to the water to check on my boat. It bobbed peacefully, just like I had left it. Calvin, who related all of his rural driving adventures to us over beer the night before, had chosen to ride with me this day. It was high time to get out of the van according to him. Looking over a map, we decided to meet up with Dad at Judith Landing at the mouth of the Judith River, so named by William Clark, for Julia Hancock, his sweetheart back in Virginia, whom he later married after completing his famous expedition.

We had scarcely been on the river an hour when I noted to Calvin a shallow bend of river ahead that looked likely to hold bones. We pulled in and took a look around. Sure enough, the bank looked virtually packed with the bones of bison. Scrambling about on the bank, we began pulling jawbones, scapulas, femurs, and other bones out of the viscous mud. We ended up with a coffee can full of bison teeth, but no skulls. A partial one here and there, but nothing worth keeping. It had been a fun hunt, though, about like Easter for a couple of three year olds.

All that day our eyes feasted upon fantastic new landscapes. It proved to be one of the best days of the entire journey. I felt lucky to share it with Calvin. So far, most of my days held some sort of tedium in them. But, this day, I had someone to talk to and share all the grand views and new sights that emerged around every bend. I only wish it was possible that Dad could have enjoyed some of the same sights. I know he would have loved it. This was to be my last day with Calvin and Dad. They planned to turn around that night and start the long drive back to Illinois. I sure appreciated all the good help and good times they brought with them, and even though I enjoyed my solitude, I was going to miss them.

From the Fred Robinson Bridge upstream to Virgelle, Montana, the Missouri River is classified as a Wild and Scenic River. I knew that this area had the the Wild and Scenic Designation, but having never traveled through it, never really knew why. I had traveled very little in eastern Montana and never further down the Missouri than Fort Benton. I was now entering unknown land. Nothing new there. The country I entered upstream from the Fred Robinson Bridge would prove to be much more awe inspiring than any I had encountered further down the river.

My luckiest stroke of planning on the trip was that I arrived at the Wild and Scenic section of river early enough in the year to use a motor. From Memorial Day to Labor Day, the river is closed to upstream motorized use. One can go downstream with a motor, but it must be at river speed and no wake can be visible. Going upstream you can't help but leave a wake. So my first bit of luck was in reaching this area in sufficient time to take advantage of the motorized exclusion.

My second stroke of luck was that there was enough water for me to get through. I hit the mountain spring run off just right. Not too early, when flow rates would still be too low, but not too late, when the river would be raging along with a much stronger current. All the dams up in Great Falls made sure that I wouldn't hit too much spring run off; but I would soon find out, my little motor was to be taxed with the strain of the strong current in Montana.

All of these thoughts are things I worried over late at night or days after they should have affected me. What I had on my mind that glorious day on the river had to do with how lucky I was to be on the river, enjoying what I was doing. Calvin rode up front, positioned strategically to keep the boat on an even keel and give us the most amount of clearance between the bottom of the boat and the river floor. With an eye always on the river, we picked our way upstream. The day before I had changed props on the Reservoir in order to reduce vibrations and increase speed. The new prop was doing a dandy job, but only for a short while. In less than three hours, we encountered a small run of rapids and before I could even think about it, we hit bottom with the prop. My once brand new prop got mangled worse than the one I had taken off the day before.

With a few oaths about paying more attention, we replaced the mangled prop with the one we had taken off twenty-four hours earlier.

I now had a little more incentive to keep my eyes on the river and not hit bottom. I still had only a few hundred miles of river to go, but those miles would be the shallowest and most difficult to navigate. I had to be extra careful at this point, or I would be buying a new prop.

On we continued, through high sandstone cliffs the color of singed buckskin. We had seemingly entered a land foreign to anything thus far encountered. I kept thinking back to the Journals I had read the night before. How the Corps of Discovery had marveled at the land around them. Lewis wrote on May 31st, 1805; "The hills and river Clifts which we passed today exhibit a most romantic appearance . . . it seemed as if those seens of visionary inchantment would never have and end; for here it is too thant nature presents to the view of the traveler vast ranges of walls of tolerable workmanship, so perfect indeed are those walls that I should have thought that nature had attempted here to rival the human art of masonry had I not recollected that she had first began her work." I had nothing to add. I too stood in marvel of a country so wild in appearance, lonely, and somehow untouched by modern encroachments. It was truly lovely.

High cliffs and brushy draws greeted us around every turn. Deer stood along the shore, frozen in place, staring at the loud intruder of their silent domain. That is how I felt with the incessant drone of the motor pushing up through this prairie-hidden paradise. Never before on the trip had I been so acutely aware of the noise my engine was making, but now I felt self-conscious of its modern day scream. Ducks and geese continued to lift in front of the boat like they had since my first day some 28 days before. Only now, I was in a classified Wild and Scenic area, and I somehow felt that the geese shouldn't be flying on my account; rather, if it were possible, I should be lifting off and fleeing so that they could continue on with their day.

In all of this, Calvin sat in the front of the boat pointing hither and yon at every new sight coming forth around the bend. We felt blessed, on this fine day, to see so much. Deer, bighorn sheep, and shortly thereafter, three antelope with young fawns close by. When they ran off, the young fawns looked more like jack rabbits than the graceful runners of the plains they would grow up to be. We soaked up every minute of their escape. For now, we had seen not only the wonder of wild sheep with their young, but now antelope, too. What else would the day bring?

Like pious parishioners, we sat quietly in the boat passing through a cathedral of rock and sagebrush, on every turn a new sight. Geology had taken a new turn for us here. Instead of the dusty, antiquated study of landforms, here it had become a fantastic science of rock and earth. Formations unlike any I ever imagined sprouted from the hills. Large boulders sat upon their pedestals of soil. Hardened flat rocks capped slender sandstone columns like mushrooms. I thought that if those were compared to mushrooms in size, then we now knew what it was like to be bugs. Maybe that's all we were, really, just bugs on a landscape too large for us to fully comprehend or appreciate. Like a bunch of ants, we were continually, incessantly chewing up the world around us. I hoped that we would never reach a point that we cut down these stone mushrooms hidden out here in this sanctuary of the Missouri.

From bend to straight, fast water and slow, we hummed along in bliss up the river. The wind continued to blow and with it came brief, cool showers followed by brilliant shafts of sunlight, alternating our exposure from cold to cool, brief moments of warmth and then back again. Evidence of history never left our sides. Between the towering, tawny cliffs and the sagebrush and cedar filled draws, we would emerge into brief open flats, and at almost every one, we could find the ruins of humanity.

Old homestead cabins bearing the weight of years stood humped up amid piles of debris, their doorways agape like open maws to the elements. With hollowed out windows, they stared complacently at the river. Here was history in a new context. Like the homestead shacks I had passed before, these were the ruins of a life of hardship. But seeing these dilapidated shacks left withering amid this fantastic landscape brought the hardships of those early settlers closer to our reality.

Here, in the arid canyons of the Missouri, I saw the beauty that these settlers must have recognized, but I could also feel the hardships that lay about the place. For the homesteaders that landed here, every day brought a hardship that many of them could not endure for long. Dry hot summers, followed by bitterly cold winters, and a river that could rise up in the spring and take everything, created an isolation almost unfathomable by today's standards. Even now, the folks that live in this part of the world live far removed from fellow humanity. Back then, the distances, while the same as today, took longer to travel.

The burnt ochre and tawny clay that pass reasonably well for a type of stone, turn into a slick gumbo completely impassable after an infrequent shower. Even today, after a rain, one cannot travel in the reaches of the Missouri Breaks. Nature still rules out here. It still makes the inhabitants appreciate Mother Nature and listen to her admonishments. It still determines who stays and who goes upon the face of this unforgiving, yet beautiful land.

Crawling continually upstream, Calvin and I soaked up every sight and sound afforded us. Just when we thought we had to be as far from any other human being as we could possibly be, we rounded a bend to see an old cable ferry along the bank. We pulled in to shore to find out a little about the area and see this old ferry, the first one I had seen on the Missouri since leaving Wood River, Illinois.

The ferry was an old barge with a wood plank deck, capable of holding about two cars, I would guess. It maneuvered across the river on a long cable that stretched from one side to the other. Inside the wheel house of the barge was an antiquated motor, more than likely from a vehicle no longer in production. The motor turned the drum, which in turn wound up the cable and pulled the old ferry back and forth across the river, a very simple and efficient system.

Up from the ferry stood an old trailer house, vintage 1960's or early 70's, obviously the home of the ferryman. We called out to the house but there was no answer, so we hoofed up the hill to knock on the door. No sooner had we given our first knock than the door opened and a small older woman looked out upon us. "I'll be right out, I didn't hear you pull up." She said. I explained to her that we were on the water and didn't need a ride on the ferry. With that she invited us in to sit down for a cup of coffee. We proceeded inside and removed our hats.

Inside, the trailer was warm and cozy with knick-knacks scattered here and there on shelves. The woman introduced us to her husband and the two of them offered us places at the old formica table before settling down themselves. I told them of my trip up the river and we visited about the people they had met on the water, so far removed from anyone else. When the coffee was ready, the old man offered us some peanut butter and bread. I had to decline. He offered once again, then busied himself with a piece of bread to snack on.

From what I gathered from our hosts, I had reached the MacClellan Ferry. There were two more ferrys I would pass further upriver. There used to be one at Judith Landing they told me, but it was replaced by a new bridge. I could tell the old folks hated the thought of losing their jobs to a bridge. They obviously enjoyed the quietude and simplicity of the ferry life. After looking around the country, I had to admit it seemed inviting. They informed me that business was slow this time of year. Roads tended to get slick with the spring showers and there weren't any tourists about yet. But, it would pick up. Pretty soon, there would be folks in canoes going by "pert near every day," and that kept things interesting for the old folks.

They talked and talked and we truly enjoyed their conversation, but it was time we got going. Extricating ourselves from the talk took some doing, but we finally slipped out and went back down to the boat. The old couple waved us on and told us to come back some time for a ride on the ferry. "I'd like that," I hollered back, and we pushed off in the water to buck some more current on our way to Judith Landing.

When we were a ways up the river, Calvin turned to me and asked if I thought all folks down along the river were like that. How so? "Happily eccentric." I thought about it a while and considered maybe we, the ones who always worry about time and what is going on in the rest of the world, are the ones that are so eccentric, and not even of the happy variety.

Back on the water we decided we should keep at it if we were to meet up with Dad before it got too late. The river narrowed down through steep walled canyons. Small rapids, seemingly inconsequential on first observation, slowed our progress. At these little chutes of fast water, I could see the drop in elevation of the Missouri for the first time. Since leaving Wood River I knew, like you know the sun rises every morning, that the river flowed because it lost elevation and the water followed gravity's force down towards the Mississippi, and ultimately the Gulf of Mexico. Previous to this, try as I might, I could never truly discern this fall in the river. Oh, I could look up the river and make myself "see" the gradient, if I tried real hard, but here on this particular stretch of river I did not have to imagine anything at all. The river ahead of me looked as if it were truly flowing down, out of the mountains and towards the sea. From this point on, I would see the river ahead and above me. My trip becoming a climb in the true sense, as I climbed this watery path towards its mountain origins.

The motor strained along through some of the rapids, the small 9.9 horses doing all they could, and we continued to move forward. The scenery persisted to mesmerize us at every bend. Calvin and I sank into a mutual silence, both enjoying the new, strange sights. I think Calvin was also soaking up as much of the remainder of the trip as he could, for when we met up with Dad, both of them planned on heading back home. I believe they both were just beginning to converse with the river. At least I thought so. I know I could hear it talk, like the ferryman in Herman Hess's Sidartha. Looking out over it, it seemed to tell me what to look for, where to turn, and at night along its shores, I could hear it whispering me to sleep. I hoped that both Calvin and Dad could hear the same, could slow down enough to enjoy this murmuring just under our known audible range. I thought they were just about reaching this point.

We knew we were at Judith Landing when we spied ahead of us a solid looking new bridge. Dad was parked down by the side of it at a little boat launch. He couldn't wait for us to get there. When we pulled in, he said we had to go with him to a little town called Winifred for a beer and burger. It was our last night together so I readily agreed. The purpose for his wanting to take us was to show us the Judith River. I have to confess that I never guessed how beautiful the valley was until that night. The drive up to Winifred wound up a steep, little gravel road, curling back and forth upon itself. At the top, we pulled over and Dad led us over to a ledge to look down upon the Judith River. The sun was slanting down in the West underneath a patchwork of scattered clouds. Below us, the valley alternated from a silvery blue, when the clouds obscured the sun, to an iridescent gold as the beams of light danced upon the river. It was a beautiful ending to a beautiful day. After awhile, we piled back in the van, hungry for a bar cooked burger, and drove into Winifred, population: small.

Word got out of my travels as we drank a few beers with the locals, visiting about the river, fishing, BLM, et cetera, and then it was time to go. Dad and Calvin ran me back to the bridge. I hated to see them go. They had been a godsend at my time of need in the silt of Lake Sakakawea, and they definitely had been a lot of fun to have along. But, now it was time for them to head back home, and it was time for me to be alone with the river again. I always enjoy good company, but I have always enjoyed my solitude as well. I hugged Dad farewell and thanked him for all his support, physical and mental. Calvin had been a great help and just fun to travel with. I shook his hand thanking him for his help, too. With that, the two of them loaded up and hit the road. I turned back to the boat and readied my gear for the night. I still thought it looked like it may shower on me that evening. I needed to find a good spot to bed for the night.

Just up from the boat launch was an old rickety house set upon two enormous I-beams. The house was obviously being moved somewhere. Where to, or from where, I had no idea, but the old shell of a house looked like a spot to get out of the weather. I looked inside. The windows were busted out, walls broken in, but to me it was shelter from the storm, if it came. I rolled out my sleeping bag on the floor and settled down for the night. The wind moaned through the open maw of the windows and I could hear the intermittent patter of rain on the roof. I was dry and comfortable which made for a restful night's sleep.

My biggest worry was that a pack rat might run across my bedroll. The Corps of Discovery had encountered a much bigger problem. It was downriver from this site that an enraged bull buffalo stampeded through their camp in the middle of the night, leaving "all in an uproar with our guns in hand." Little chance of that happening to me, I doubted there was even a penned up buffalo within one hundred miles. I don't know how much solace that brought me; I didn't even like the idea of the pack rat running around "camp." Hopefully, like Lewis, I could count on my trusty dog to keep an eye out for anything wrong through the night. I glanced over at Herschel and he was out like a light. Oh well. I settled in on the old wood floor and drifted off to sleep.

I woke up ready to take on the world. Instead, I decided to take on the Missouri. I loaded up after a quick breakfast of coffee and beef jerky and pushed into the current. Scattered clouds still dominated the sky in all directions. I was eager to get moving. I knew that before me lay the strip of river known as the White Cliffs area of the Missouri. I couldn't wait to see this fabled land. I was not to be disappointed.

A few miles above Judith Landing the river narrowed, and I passed from the wide open sage flats where I had spent the night, to the high walled canyons similar to the land I had been in the day before. The boat struggled against the current. It seemed as if the current had gained some strength and the little boat and motor were having a tough time overcoming it. I stopped at one point and rearranged my gear to get the boat to sit a little more efficiently in the water. Even with that adjustment, I was only averaging about five miles per hour. I sure hoped the river did not continue to gain strength.

My mind could not dwell on the speed of the boat for long. The land I passed through captivated my attention. High white sandstone cliffs walled in from both sides of the river. Their shapes like nothing I had ever encountered before. I could not fathom what the early travelers must have thought of this strange land. I at least had a rough idea of what to expect. I had read some books, seen pictures, but none of these prepared me for the fantastic landscape I was seeing.

I know now why some of the formations were named Citadel Rock and Castle Rock. The high towering walls looked like medieval fortresses looming over the river. Add to the imposing sight of these rocks that there may well have been hostile Indians up there and the formations must have seemed quite intimidating to early explorers. I felt lucky to see the river from the angle I did. Upstream, the river had a wholly different look than going down. Every famous river traveler in the past saw the river for the first time while heading against the current. The imposing formations and their intimidating names make a little more sense when seen while bucking the full force of the Missouri.

At one point, near a high natural stone archway called Hole In The Wall for obvious reasons, I looked up to see a forest of turreted sandstone columns. Each one looking for all the world like the onion topped dome of a Russian Orthodox church. For early travelers ascending the great Missouri, this area must have looked all the more like a walled Turkish fortress. How thankful I was that I did not have to worry about hostiles in the region, for I am sure I would have succumbed to nerves and fright long before falling to a well aimed arrow. Maybe that is the very reason the famed Hole In The Wall is omitted from the journals of both Lewis and Clark. Either that, or they failed to turn around to see the stone arch behind them on their way up stream. Actually, it is now thought that there is a good possibility that the stone arch was not as big then as it is today and therefore was undetectable. Or maybe, they had seen so many strange sights, that it did not warrant a clause in their writings.

At any rate, it made a fair impression on me that day. I sat mesmerized in the boat, awaiting each new turn. Herschel, for his part, kept a close eye out for wildlife of any sort, but mostly for beavers. He loved to spot beavers, not so much chase them, as just spot them. It was Herschel who most often spotted geese hiding in the tufts of grass along the bank, or alerted me to movement far off from the river banks. More likely than not, it would be small group of deer, their heads up, ears cupped forward, staring intently at the noise making boat going the opposite direction from all the boats they so often saw.

This day, I spotted my first curlew. I took that to be a sign that we were drawing close to the mountains. From my map I could tell you within a mile or two how close I actually was to the Rockies, but it took a more tangible thing, like the spotting of a curlew or the flight of a mountain bluebird, to register the distance to me. I now was beginning to smell the winds of home. I had not seen the mountains yet, but I knew they were close. All signs indicated that the mountains approached, and I was excited to see them again.

Onward and upward my little motor struggled against the current. The river seemed to get stronger with every mile and the little motor had a tough time overcoming the power of the river with so much weight. The additional weight was due to the fact that since leaving Calvin and Dad, I had once again stocked up on supplies. Of course, that meant a little more beer and a bottle of wine and some groceries that Dad had picked up in Lewistown. My supplies may not have seemed like much, but every pound made a difference in my progress. The main reason for the increase in weight was fuel. I knew there would be no place to fuel up along the next stretch of river until I reached Fort Benton, so I had filled up all my additional fuel tanks. The problem with this manuever was that it increased my weight substanially. Each six gallon tank weighed roughly fifty pounds. Together, the four full tanks added an estimated two hundred pounds to my already heavy boat.

The trade off was six of one and half a dozen of the other. I needed the extra fuel to get up river to Fort Benton, but the added weight slowed the boat down to a mere crawl. By going so slow, I used more fuel and therefore needed the extra containers I carried with me. But it was a risk I was willing to take. For if I tried to lighten my load and make it on one full tank at a faster speed, I ran the risk of running out just short of my destination, and if that happened, it would be a long walk for fuel.

So I continued on at my snail's pace. By evening, I found myself just up stream of the second ferry I was to encounter on the Missouri, the Virgelle ferry. I decided that this was as good a place as any to call it a day. I knew I was about 35 miles from Fort Benton and I had very little fuel left, probably just enough. At least I was hoping so. I made camp in the brush below a handsome grove of cottonwoods. To celebrate my progress, and to also lose a little weight on the boat, I decided to open the bottle of wine that my Dad had given to me the night before. That kept me busy for over a half an hour, for I had no corkscrew and never was a fan of those little Swiss army knives. What kind of Army carries corkscrews to battle with them any how?

With thoughts and ponderings on the logic of the Swiss Army, I set about trying to open my bottle of wine. I had heard from a fellow mule packer that if you tapped the bottom of a bottle of wine against a tree trunk repeatedly, the cork would eventually work its way out of the bottle enough that you could pull it out. Not having anything to lose and a good bottle of wine to gain, I gave it a try.

One does not want to be overly thirsty trying this manuever. It takes time, lots of time. But, I am happy to report, it does work. A half an hour later, the cork protruded from the bottle enough that I was able to grab the cork with my folding pliers and pull it out. I drank the whole bottle that night not so much in celebration of my ascension of the Missouri, but more to celebrate that I opened the damned bottle of wine. Needless to say, I slept well that night.

I awoke early the next morning to a cloudless sky overhead. The morning had the feel of spring all over it. Cool, and damp, but I could feel that it would warm up as the day progressed. I made a small fire and drank coffee, soaking up the sunrise and the morning call of the birds. Then, with Herschel eagerly waiting, we hopped in the boat and cast off.

The boat, sensing my mood, seemed to leap out into the current this morning. Herschel and I were in high spirits this day and the boat galloped up river. With such a small fuel reserve, the weight of the boat was reduced, increasing our speed. Shortly after leaving, we rounded a bend to find three mule deer swimming across the river in front of us. I slowed and killed the motor to watch them make their way to the far shore. One by one, they emerged on the sandy bank and shook off before bounding away up the hills. Herschel kept close watch on them long after they retreated from view.

CHAPTER 13

"The whole party to a man except myself were fully pesuaided that this river was the Missouri, but being fully of opinion that it was neither the main stream, nor that which it would be advisable for us to take, I determined to give it a name in honour of Miss Maria Wood. called it Maria's River."

Meriwether Lewis June 8, 1805

"Passed the mouth of the Marias and climbed up on the hill to take a look around. Probably the same hill Lewis and Clark climbed nearly 200 years ago."

Chris Bechtold May 19, 1998

THE MOUTH OF THE MARIAS RIVER WAS A SIGNIFICANT MILESTONE in the journey of the Corps of Discovery. At this point, the members of the expedition had to determine which river was the true Missouri that would issue them to the famed Shining Mountains. At the time of the expedition, both rivers were roughly the same size; one, the Missouri, ran clear and had a more rock filled bottom. The other, the Marias, ran silty, the same as the coffee with cream colored Missouri they had traveled upon since leaving Illinois and Camp Dubois. The captains split up to reconnoiter the two forks of the river. Lewis ascending the Marias while Clark continued up the Missouri.

After much debating, the Captains decided that the southern fork was indeed the true Missouri river. The men, on the other hand, were convinced that the Marias was in actuality the river that they needed to continue upon. Of course, we all know now that Meriwether Lewis and William Clark were correct in their assessment, and the Corps of Discovery continued upstream on the true Missouri River to reach the

Great Falls, thus confirming that, indeed, the captains had made the right choice.

For me, the decision as to which river was the true Missouri was quite simple. I had expected to see two forks of equal size joining at this point in the river. Instead, I saw a small, muddy river, no larger than some creeks I had passed in the Midwest, issuing slowly into the strong current of the Missouri. The moment was a disappointment to me. I hoped that I could at least have come upon two rivers of equal strength and see this point as a grand joining of forces. But it was not to be. I knew without a doubt, as most any schoolchild would know, that the Missouri River was the southern fork.

Directly above the joining of the two famous rivers is a tall hill overlooking the confluence. No doubt, all the men of the expedition must have climbed it to assess the two rivers and wonder which one was the correct one. I could not avoid the temptation myself and tied the boat up at the bottom of the hill to have a look.

What I saw was a somewhat melancholy sight. The Marias limped slowly through the town of Loma with a look of defeat, giving itself up to the strong, crisp current of the Missouri. Oh, it must have been a sight to see the two rivers in their heyday, each competing fiercely with the other, pouring their strength together to make the wild Missouri. I took in the view from the hilltop. Off to my left I could see the mouth of the Teton river dumping into the Marias, its mouth roughly a mile from the Marias' mouth. I knew I was close to home now. My time on the river was drawing to a close and I hated to see it end. The end of my little adventure was sneaking up on me, for the Teton (which Lewis named the Rose River) was the river that passed along the ranch where I lived in the mountains.

I read the interpretive signs located on the hill and dutifully took in the sights they pointed out. I was surprised to learn of the little town of Ophir that once stood on the far shore of the Missouri, vying with Fort Benton as the drop off point for the steamboat trade that plied the river. Of course, this little town's history is full of deceit and tragedy and it was wiped out by Indians in the late 1860's before it ever truly got started. I glanced around the area trying to fix the images in my mind and see the area through the ages, then slipped back down to the river and headed upstream towards Fort Benton.

As I approached Fort Benton, the water level dropped off enough that I became concerned about the prop hitting bottom. It had gotten mangled enough as it was. When I finally came in sight of the historic little town, I had to choose between two channels, one on each side of a small island below the riverfront. I picked the one closest to town and inched my way toward it. I tried to be careful for I sure didn't want to ground out right in front of the town and make a spectacle of myself. Still, I managed to hit bottom a time or two before I finally pulled into the small dock in town.

Big doings were happening when I arrived. A replica paddlewheel boat was docked below the historic Grand Union Hotel. At the docks where I tied up, an excavator of some sort was being loaded upon a truck. I climbed out of the boat and walked over to the riverfront park where an older woman stood watching. That was quite a show she said. I told her I was a little uninformed, so she filled me in.

The paddle wheeler was to be an excursion boat for river tourists to ride from Fort Benton. The boat made all sorts of press in the little town and its inaugural launching was big doings. That was the day before I arrived. Well, the one thing that had not been planned upon was the low water level this spring. When the paddle wheeler was launched from its truck, it promptly grounded out right in front of the town. The excavator had been used to help get the boat pulled into deeper water and to dredge out a little space to maneuver. This made me feel a little better. At least if I had grounded out on the way into town, it would not have been anything new.

The first thing one sees when walking up from the boat dock in town is a large bronze monument to Lewis and Clark and the Corps of Discovery. The monument is a life size bronze of Meriwether Lewis and William Clark with Sacagawea kneeling beside them. I must admit, it is a most impressive statue. By far, the best monument to the Expedition I had seen anywhere along the river.

From the monument, one can look to the southwest down a long grassy park which overlooks the rivers edge. Lined with tall lush cottonwoods, this little park tells the history of Fort Benton from its early trapper days through its wild and wooly time as the terminal point in the steamboat days. At the far end of the riverfront park is another bronze statue, this one of a dog named Shep. I personally believe Fort Benton to be more famous for the story of Shep than any of its other famed places in history.

The story of Shep is as follows: Years ago, there lived an old man in Fort Benton who had a faithful dog named Shep. The old dog would follow his master anywhere, just like my faithful old dog Herschel, who shows a striking resemblance to the bronze of Shep. At any rate, the old man died and his body was taken to the railroad station to be shipped back east for burial. The man's faithful old companion, Shep, returned to the railroad station every day to inspect each train as it arrived looking for his beloved master. For five and a half years this old dog never gave up his vigil and continued to look for the old man until the day he slipped on the tracks before an arriving train and was killed. For this, the kind people of Fort Benton erected a monument to Shep in front of the Grand Union Hotel.

With my own faithful companion by my side, I wandered the park along the rivers edge reading each historical signboard as I went. The town is much more sedate now. No more gunfights in the streets and wild saloon brawls amongst cowhands and rivermen. Now, the street that once held cowboys, packers, rivermen, indians and rough men of the west, instead caters to tourists looking to see the Missouri before it disappears into the mystical reaches of the White Cliffs. The small shops along the riverfront street sell hardware to the locals, groceries, lunch and souvenirs. The wild west has now been tamed.

At the end of the street, before turning around, I stopped to peek inside the Grand Union Hotel. The hotel was under construction to restore it to its Victorian splendor. Built in 1882, the hotel has been host to many a famous personage traveling from St. Louis to the wild frontiers of Montana. Over the years though, the hotel wore itself out, falling into disrepair until investors bought the old building and, with much effort, restored it to its original splendor and beyond. Today, the Grand Union Hotel offers a visitor a chance to step back in time to a world of opulent splendor and classic style. I am sure that many a traveler looked with relief to the old hotel after stepping off of the steamboats.

A clean bed on solid ground must have been a wonderful delight to the weary travelers.

Unfortunately, I was not to be one of the lucky guests of the hotel. Instead, I decided to head back along the park to visit the museum near what is left of the original fort. When I arrived at the museum, I was the only visitor there. The building houses many artifacts from the riverboat days of the Fort. Old steamboat bells and photos adorn the exhibits. One section that particularly held my attention was an exhibit on the surrender of Chief Joseph of the Nez Perce.

I had heard the story of Chief Joseph many a time, but I never realized that his famous speech where he would "fight no more forever" took place along the Bear Paws Mountains north of Fort Benton. I was much surprised to find that Joseph and his band crossed the Missouri downstream from Fort Benton near the famous Cow Island, and had a skirmish with the cavalry near this point. To my disappointment, I passed the famed Cow Island, stopping point for riverboats in low water years, and never knew it. Just one more instance where I wish I had better prepared myself with maps and historical information.

From the museum, I took a short walk to see what was left of the original Fort Benton. Not much, I am afraid to report. A few ruins of a mud brick foundation are all that has survived. A restoration of part of the fort has been constructed on the site of the old foundations and helps to give a better perspective of what the fort must have originally looked like. Herschel and I wandered about the place and finally decided that it would be best if we got going. I went back to the boat and retrieved two fuel cans which I filled at the gas station downtown. With a supply of gas sufficient to get me up to Great Falls, I headed back to the boat. I concluded that some day I would come back to Fort Benton and soak up some more of the history the little town has to offer.

As we pulled out of the docks and passed the riverfront park, I waved over at who I suspected to be the captain of the replica paddle wheeler. The boat was floating free in the water in front of the Grand Union Hotel, all engines running. I waved a hello and motored by wishing the boat luck. He would need a lot of it with the water level so low. For that matter, I still stand in amazement to think that paddleboats plied the river from St. Louis to Fort Benton.

How they ever managed to get those enormous boats so far is beyond me. It took a great amount of skill and knowledge to maneuver those behemoth boats up the wild and changing channel of the Missouri. There is a an old saying in St. Louis, "The boys go up the Mississippi, but the men go up the Missouri." After having seen the final port on the Missouri, and knowing the river between the two points, I must agree with the old saying. The old river men must have been a tough breed to make it so far.

Thinking back to the men before the riverboat days, one can only say that they no longer make men in the same mold. The strength, both physical and in character, to pull a laden boat up the old Missouri is today unfathomable. When one looks at the voyage of the Corps of Discovery in this light, it makes the Expedition seem near superhuman in its accomplishments. I believe this is why stories of the old trappers and early explorers live on so readily today. They, the early pioneers, accomplished what few, if any of us, could do today and under far more difficult circumstances.

With these thoughts in my mind, I motored away from Fort Benton. Not far above the town, I spied a hole in the high dirt bank overlooking the river. Having time on my side, and always curious, I decided to pull over and take a look inside the little opening. The reason for my stopping was that I thought the little cave, if it could be called that, looked inaccessible and figured it the kind of opening to hold something interesting. Climbing up the steep bank, I found out just how inaccessible the opening truly was. Soon I was forced to dig into the hard clay with my fingers and toes to keep from sliding down towards the water below. I was perhaps fifty feet above the river and a good twenty-five feet from the top of the cliff and level with the opening when I reached across for a hand hold protruding from the clay. Imagine my surprise when I looked closer and realized that I had grasped hold of a bison horn. Not only that, but as I dug franticly with my pliers in the tawny clay, I realized that I had found an entire bison skeleton. Soon I uncovered the jaws and most of the skull. The hump rib protruded ever so slightly. I pulled it from the bank and used it to dig out the rest of the skull.

When I had exposed the entire skull, I gave a great jerk and pulled the head loose from the spine. The weight of the old head, filled with clay, was much more than I anticipated and with the skull held tight to my chest, I slipped from my toe holds and proceeded to slide, bounce, and fall to the bottom of the cliff. But I did not care in the least, for in my arms, I held the only thing I had really been looking for since leaving Illinois twenty nine days before. I had lost my pliers in the fall, but who cared, I had a bison skull and only one more day on the river until I reached Great Falls. I nestled the great skull into the front of the boat and pushed off.

To my dismay, the weight of the skull slowed my progress considerably. Once again I was back to crawling up the river, averaging no more than five miles per hour. But I did not care. I had a treasure better, in my mind, than gold. Something that would always remind me of my journey up the wild Missouri River. The skull was the type of souvenir I could only have dreamt of finding, for it tied the past to the present for me. Reminding me once again of all the changes that had taken place along this river. Changes, some good, some bad, that helped to shape the west and our country into what it is today.

I puttered along content with myself and the coming end of the day. But in my reverie, I failed to notice the increasing power of the current. I was awakened from my day-dream by the bang of the prop upon the bottom of the river. The river had narrowed considerably since leaving Fort Benton and its speed had increased with the narrowness. My little motor struggled to overcome the river, but we kept moving forward and upward. At last, we reached a spot the motor could not overcome. The rapids were not large by any means, but they were strong enough that the motor could not push against them. With no other choice, I climbed out of the boat and grabbed the lead rope. Picking my way through the rocks and swells, I dragged the loaded boat through the cold rushing water.

So this is what it must have felt like, I thought. The men, who had so bravely and tediously labored up the Missouri pulling the keelboats of supplies, had experienced the same thing. Only they had done this day in and day out. I felt humbled after having drug the boat a mere two hundred yards. With Herschel back in the boat, I hopped in and prayed the motor had the gumption to get us up the river to Carter Ferry. It did, and we pulled in to the ferry late in the afternoon. My arrival somewhat perplexed the ferryman. He was dressed in a T-shirt and jeans, with a pistol strapped to his waist.

He asked if I had been fishing and I told him no. I could see his eyebrows go up a little, so I told him my story of how I had come from Illinois. Now his eyebrows really went up. After looking over my gear he believed my story. He also wanted to buy my bison skull which I kindly told him he did not have money enough in the world to buy. He smiled and said he figured he didn't if that was the price.

We visited awhile about my journey and I asked questions about the ferry and how things were going here on the river. The curiosity was killing me, so I finally asked what the pistol was for. "Rattlesnakes," was his reply. That satisfied my curiosity. I then changed the subject to the river upstream. I asked if it were possible to get a boat up to Morony Dam, the bottom dam in a string of five that girdle the Missouri at Great Falls.

He replied that fishermen left the ferry all the time heading up to the dam. Most of them had a jet motor, but they got up to the dam and fished, then came back to the ferry. I asked if he had made the trip himself and he replied "no." I should have taken that little one syllable answer as a red flag. He figured the distance up to the dam just shy of twenty miles. I thought things over and decided to call it a night. The next day I would try to make it to Great Falls. Using the ferryman's phone, I called a friend in Great Falls and got a ride in to town. I spent the night in the Electric City, enjoying a fine meal out and a real bed. The following day I planned to make it to Morony Dam and from there portage around the five dams of Great Falls.

While in Great Falls for the night, I also called the ranch I worked for and let them know my whereabouts. I knew they were anxious for my return. At this time of the year, a lot of work needed to be done preparing for the summer season. The previous fall we started building a blacksmith shed before the ground froze up and winter set in. The shed still needed to be finished and I knew they needed help on the project. In addition, there was a lot of spring fencing to be done and the horses would need to be brought back from winter pasture and shod. I talked to Chuck, the owner, and let him know I was in Great Falls.

He asked if I needed a ride to the ranch, and I replied that I was going to try to make it around Great Falls and I figured if I did, it would only take a few more days for me to make it to Three Forks, the source of the Missouri river. I knew Chuck needed me back, but I desperately wanted to make it to Three Forks. When I hung up with Chuck, I felt the weight of responsibility settling back down on my shoulders for the first time in thirty days.

For the past month, I had only worried about myself and Herschel and where I might find fuel and sleep for the night. I had never felt so free and unfettered in my life. I will bet that none of the early explorers ever suffered from stress and grinding teeth. Yes, I admit they had stress, but it was a wholly different stress than what we "modern" people suffer from today. They did not worry of money, deadlines, missed appointments, bills, and phone calls. They worried about the here and now; food, a bed, keeping your powder dry and staying alive. None trivial items, but all things directly determined by the choices made every day in their lives. No, I will bet none of them ever worried about the far off stresses that "civilized" man has put upon himself.

Now I began to feel a rush to complete my trip and get back to work. Suddenly I started to worry about all the expenses I had incurred to accomplish this trip, and how I needed to fulfill my obligations at work. Well, I figured, it will only be a few more days and I'll be back on the job. I had the next day to think about, and I wanted to get around Great Falls as quickly as I could.

"the current excessively rapid and dificuelt to assend great numbers of dangerous places, and the fatigue which we have to encounter is incretiatable the men in the water from morning until night hauling the cord & boats walking on sharp rocks and round sliperery stones which alternately cut their feet and throw them down."

William Clark June 15, 1805

"I started hitting rapids. Had to pull the boat up the first set. Then the second set came. Had to empty the boat and take the motor off to tow that set . . . Jumped out and tried to tow, but the H₂O was chest deep, and I was afraid I would be swept downstream . . . cut my feet up pretty bad."

Chris Bechtold May 20, 1998

THE NEXT MORNING, I BUMMED A RIDE with a friend back to Carter Ferry. My boat was just as I had left it. I met the ferryman soon after we arrived. He informed me that his wife had called the Great Falls Tribune and one of the TV stations. They wanted me to call them before I left. Truthfully, I was a bit flattered by all this. I promptly called the paper and TV station. I told them my plans to make it to the Morony Dam and gave them a time to plan on my arrival. Wow, I thought, TV.

The ferryman wished me luck and I thanked him for his help, then backed into the river to begin my assault toward Great Falls. I was blissfully unaware of what I was getting myself into. Shortly after leaving Carter Ferry, I began to run into small stretches of rapids. I had unloaded some extra fuel cans and the bison skull with my friend from Great Falls, so the boat was lighter and moved better on the water. The additional loss of weight made a world of difference in how the boat handled the rapids. I was able to ascend a fast spot in the river which was the same size as the one that forced me to drag my boat the day before. The boat slowly crawled through the rapids, but it made it.

The sun shone down on Herschel and I. Creating a good feeling about myself and the day. After all, I had come this far and I knew the river from Great Falls to Three Forks. I could already see myself navigating the upper end of the river in the next few days. My disposition was as sunny as the day. Then I passed what I supposed to be Portage Creek, and realized things didn't look too good. Before me were three stair steps of rapids larger than anything I had encountered before on the Missouri. In fact, they were larger than anything I had ever imagined encountering on the Missouri. I held the boat steady below the rushing waters and looked things over. From what I understood from my map, the dam was less than a mile away and lay hidden just around the corner above the rapids. That looked like an awfully long ways to go from where I was currently sitting.

I studied the rapids from below and plotted a course up through the first set. I knew I had to be careful, one mistake and the prop would be mangled bad enough to end the trip for the day, or worse. Already I could see these rapids were different in the fact that the bottom of the river was comprised of large boulders and solid rock. Nothing was going to give if I made a mistake. Well, I take that back, the boat and myself would end up giving.

I started up my plotted course, easing past the large, submerged rocks, the motor opened up full throttle. Slowly we passed the first obstacles, then, just as slowly, the boat stopped moving. The little motor could not overcome the power of the river. Now I was in a pickle. I knew better than to try and turn the boat in this strong of a current. Instead, I reduced the throttle and carefully backed the boat down through the rapids the way I had come into them. When I reached the bottom, I motored over to shore and pulled the boat onto the gravel bank. Damn, I thought, how in the hell did those other guys get up this thing. The ferryman had said other fishermen made it to Morony, well, if they could make it, so could I.

Herschel had already jumped out of the boat, so the two of us clambered over the steep rock bank overlooking the river, trying to plot a course for the boat. Try as I might, I could not find a better path than the one I had already attempted. That left me no choice. I would have to pull the boat up through the rapids, although that did not look like a safe alternative.

I took off my boots to allow myself a good purchase on the rocky bottom. The cold water stung my feet and soon they felt half numb with cold. With the rope over my shoulder I began the slow, careful ascent of the first set of rapids. The boat actually pulled up through the water much easier than I expected. Most of the boat dragging I had done so far on the trip had been because the water was too shallow and I had to overcome the friction between the boat and the bottom of the river. But here, the boat sat high on the waves, plowing through the rapid waters. The difficulty lay in being able to maneuver myself through the rapids.

Sharp rocks on the bottom of the river cut my feet as I inched forward. The cold water bit into my legs as I struggled against the current. The water level increased. It became more and more difficult to keep my balance and continue to pull the boat. Soon, the boat began to feel heavier and heavier in the strong current. By this time, the water was up to the bottom of my ribs and my feet ached from the cold and sharp rocks. I finally struggled to the edge of the water and hauled the boat on the shore. I had made it through the first set, two more to go. If only the water level was deeper near the shore, I could have pulled the boat up without having to get so far out in the water. But rocks littered the water close to the bank, making it impossible for me to drag the boat through that course.

I rested on the shore a short while and let my feet thaw out in the sunshine before scouting out my next attempt through the second set of rapids. The second set looked even faster and larger than the first. I plotted a course along the bank that looked plausible, then walked back to the boat to give it a try. No sooner had I begun than I realized I didn't have the strength to pull the loaded boat against the overwhelming surge of the current. I quickly slipped over to the bank and pulled the boat up on some rocks to hold it. I would have to empty the boat and try it without so much weight.

After unloading all my gear, I pulled the motor off the boat and carried it to shore. Then back into the current I went with the lead rope held firmly in my hand. The second set of rapids proved to be much stronger than the first, but the empty boat towed easier. I clawed my way up against the surging waters and with luck and much effort, I made it through. My feet by this time were bleeding, leaving little red wisps in the slow moving water along shore. I climbed out of the river and hiked down the bank to begin ferrying my gear up to the boat. Deciding that I had better try to get through the next and final set of rapids while my feet were still in some sort of condition to do so, I carried only the motor to the boat before entering the water to try the third set. When I got through the final set, I knew I would need the motor to move about in the current and find a spot to portage my other gear around to.

Each set of rapids seemed to get a little stronger than the last. The third set surged around a steep-sided rock bank. I knew if I could get around that bend I would have it made. I could then get close to the water from the shore and pull the boat up the final stretch to the dam. My feet ached more and more with each step, so I started back down into the water once again, the cold numbing the pain. With the empty boat behind me, I again started to inch my way against the over-powering Missouri. To say I struggled against uneven odds would be understatement. The water got deeper and deeper so that I struggled just to keep from being swept downstream. The boat bobbed along happily behind me, while I strained to keep from losing my precarious footing on the river bottom. With the dam in sight, I reached the point that I could go no further. The current threatened to sweep me downstream and I had but a faint toehold on the rocks. If I slipped loose, I was going to be carried down into the rapids with nothing but my life jacket on and a loose boat somewhere ahead or behind me.

A large flume of water poured between me and the bank, large enough that I knew I could not make it across. Herschel stood at the waters edge nervously watching me. I could tell he wanted to come out to me, but he knew better than to jump into the rushing water. The large rock I held on to parted the water in strong, rushing flumes on either side of me. If only I could find a way to get around that rock and get a solid hold, I thought, I might just be able to make it. But it looked hopeless, and there in sight right ahead of me was the dam. Damn, or should I say Dam, I didn't think I was going to make it there. I had to turn around, and oh, how I hated to do that being so close to my destination. Especially knowing that there were people waiting for me up there, expecting me to show.

I fashioned a crude loop out of the lead rope of the boat and flipped it over the rock in front of me. It caught on the sharp tip of the boulder enough to hold the boat. Quickly, I grabbed the bow of the boat and hoisted myself up into it. The loop slipped loose as I did this and in one fluid motion we were off, descending the rapids with the prop up and only a single oar to guide myself with.

I got my footing in the middle of the boat as it spun around in the current. Using the oar as a jousting pole I fended off the rocks as the boat bounced and jumped down through the rapids. I was afraid that at any moment the boat would slam into one of the large boulders sticking out of the water and capsize. But the little boat held tough, it bounced and careened through the froth, never once threatening to flip over. I, for the most part, stayed braced in the center of the boat and did my best to stab at boulders speeding by. After descending the second set of rapids, there was enough of a lull for me to get to the motor, drop it into the water and with one quick pull, start it. Luckily, I got this done in time to prevent having to careen down the final set of rapids. I turned the boat towards shore and headed, quite conveniently, to my gear, which lay piled there.

As I dragged the boat up through the rocks on shore, Herschel ran out into the water to greet me. I think he had been more nervous than had I. Things happened so quickly that I never had much time to worry. On shore, I sat down to catch my breath and look over my cut and bleeding feet. I had been in sight of Morony Dam, but it might as well have been on the other side of the continent. No way was I going to try to ascend the third set of rapids again. If the fishermen were going from Carter Ferry to Morony Dam, they were better men than me, or they had awfully damned powerful motors. Enough was enough. I decided to cut my losses before I got drowned up here all alone. I hated to think I had made it all the way to Great Falls, Montana from Illinois only to be killed in the last quarter mile. No, I had pushed my luck far enough. I decided to go back to Carter Ferry and get a ride.

Before heading back to the ferry, I changed into dry clothes and carefully cleaned the cuts on my feet. Climbing to the top of the hill along the river, I pulled out the cell phone Mom had given me and dialed up the number of the reporter from the newspaper. I told him where I was and that I wasn't going to make it to Morony Dam. I was headed back to Carter Ferry. Then I sat down amongst the dried grass and prickly pear and looked down at the river.

I had been so close. Just yards really, from making it past the rapids and motoring up to the dam amid the TV crew and photographer from the paper. It could have been a grand entry into Great Falls, one that all my friends could have seen. I felt like that was my one shot to make my crazy trip legitimate. After all, this was just a crazy trip, some off the wall idea of mine that I had unbelievably followed through on. I just wanted the rest of the world to know about it. To know I had done it, and I hoped that maybe this could have led into something else. I didn't really know what. But I hoped something greater than what I had been doing. Something where I could be out on the river, my own boss, showing others what all I had seen. But I had not made it. I fell just a quarter mile short.

I sat up on that hill a good half hour or so, just looking down at the water and thinking. I didn't want this journey to end. My freedom that I had enjoyed for thirty days was coming to an unwanted halt. I knew it was bound to end, but I didn't want it to happen like this. Now I looked back on the previous weeks and hoped I had not squandered them. I regretted already not having stopped more, having walked the river's edge more, having loafed more on my odyssey. Now, it was time to get back to work. I had put it off too long and I needed to make some money and get my feet back under me financially. I had a boat and motor that had taken a big chunk out of my checking account and I needed to pad my wallet a little.

As much as I hated to do it, I needed to call it quits here in Great Falls and go back to work. If I bypassed Great Falls and continued on to Three Forks it wouldn't look too good for my job. There was a building that they needed to finish at the ranch and a lot of chores to get done before the summer season started. Besides, I had told Chuck I was only coming to Great Falls. Well, I kept my word. Now was no time to break it. Damn. Dam it all.

Back at the boat, Herschel had already adopted my meloncholy mood. I loaded up all the gear and together we hopped in the boat and backed out into the current. I chose a course through the rapids and raised the prop to keep from tearing it up as we coursed down through the rocks. Below the fast water of the rapids, I started the motor for our retreat to Carter Ferry. For the first time in thirty days, I was heading downstream. How easy it was. In no time, we rounded the final corner and came upon the Ferry ahead of us.

The ferryman came out to meet me as I pulled in alongside the ferry. "No Luck, huh?"

I told him about my morning. "Well, I never been up there myself" he said, "but they say the Dead Man Rapids are rough ones."

So that was it. They were called Dead Man Rapids. I was later to find out that the so called fisherman that go to the dam never ascend the rapids at all, just fish below them. In fact, no one ever tries to go up the rapids. Now they tell me. Well, a lot of good it does now, and besides, I don't know if any of that information would have changed anything. I probably would still have had to find out for myself. Some way to end things, I thought.

Now I had to find a ride to Great Falls. All of my friends were working and I hated to call anyone at the ranch to come out on such short notice. While I was trying to come up with a name of someone to call, a car pulled up at the Ferry. It was the newspaper reporter. He had been waiting for me at Morony Dam and now had driven all the way out here to talk to me. I told him about my luck trying the rapids and answered a myriad of questions about my trip up the river. After taking a picture of Herschel and me, he said he had better get back to Great Falls. He offered me a needed lift back to town.

I actually had no destination in mind while I rode to town. The reporter mentioned to me that the director of the Lewis and Clark Interpretive Center would like to talk to me. With no other plans, I asked if I could be dropped off at the center. After thanking the reporter for the ride, I went inside and introduced myself. There followed a brief flurry of introductions and many questions about my journey. I spent a few hours at the center visiting with folks and at five o'clock called up my friend for a ride.

The next morning, I was surprised to find a photo of Herschel and me on the front page of the Great Falls Tribune. The biggest change in my daily routine was not being able to get in the boat and take off up the river. I felt like a fish out of water, pardon the obvious reference. Suddenly, the realization that my trip was over hit me like a gale force wind. I was done, and I had not even made it to Three Forks. How could I be done, and not have made it to the end of the river. I felt like a quitter. But it was too late to keep going now. I had already called Chuck. He and his wife, Sharon, were on their way to fetch me. This was it, the end, and an anticlimatic one at that.

Chuck and Sharon picked me up in Great Falls and we rode out to Carter Ferry to pick up my boat. After piling it all in the back of Chuck's truck, we set off back to the ranch, my journey completed, for now. I came off the river in Great Falls on the 20th of May, exactly thirty days from the day I left Wood River, Illinois.

After arriving in Choteau, Chuck took me directly to the elementary school where I gave an impromptu presentation to the fourth grade class, who were studying Lewis and Clark at this time. From there, we made a brief stop at the local paper and I told a short version of my trip to the editor of the Choteau Acantha. To me, the trip seemed to be rolling up much too fast. My gear had barely enough time to dry from the river. Now, I was back at the ranch and it was all over. I could not adjust that quickly, and I could not forgive myself for not having finished the trip to the end of the river.

Life settled down at the ranch and soon, it was as if my trip on the Missouri was nothing more than a remembered dream. I found that what had been hailed as a considerable feat in the Midwest was acknowledged as no more than an extended trip here in Montana. Soon enough, I began to consider the expedition the same way myself. But, I had work to do, and that kept my mind off of such things.

Yet, deep in the back of my mind, I had not closed the book on my personal journey. I said that I was going to follow the Corps of Discovery all the way to the ocean, and I planned to do so. I just had to get the time to follow through on my word. The first chance I got, I was going to make it to Three Forks. Come hell or high water.

CHAPTER 15

"I begin to be extremely impatient to be off as the season is now waisting a pace nearly three months have now elapsed since we left Fort Mandan and not yet reached the Rocky Mountains"

Meriwether Lewis June 30, 1805

"Made plans to meet . . . in the morning and head on back up the river . . . Got off to a slow start then headed upstream."

Chris Bechtold June 15, 1998

NOW IT WAS THE 15TH OF JUNE and I had two days off from work; two days, and a lot of river to cover. A friend of mine, Brian, had shown serious interest in my trip since the day I had arrived back at the ranch. When we both got a day off, he jumped at the chance to ride along with me while we tried to cover the section of river from Great Falls to Wolf Creek. I looked forward to the company on the river, and also needed the use of his pickup to get the boat and gear from Choteau to the river.

We left the night of the fourteenth and drove into Great Falls to leave the boat at a Marina near White Bear Island, so named by the Expedition for the amount of grizzly bears found there. This freed up the pickup so we could run around town and not worry about losing something or getting a ticket for having a fourteen foot boat hanging out the back of an eight foot bed. The next morning dawned clear and sunny, perfect for boating on the river. Brian and I loaded our camping gear into the boat plus Herschel and Brian's dog Katie. This being Montana, everyone brings their own dog. With the two of us, our dogs, gear and fuel, the boat sat low in the water.

Low and slow is how we traveled, too. I think Brian must have thought me crazy to have traveled as far as I had at such a snail's pace, but I assured him that with only myself and Herschel, we moved much faster. He looked me over, not sure if I was telling the truth or just trying to convince him I was not crazy. All that day we motored slowly up the river. Taking in the sights of cabins along the shore and cattle sauntering along the banks. Brian had grown up in Great Falls, but never had seen the Missouri river like this.

That morning setting out, we traveled downstream so as not to miss any of the river. We went past the mouth of the Sun River (known to Lewis and Clark as the Medicine River) and continued towards the city park of Great Falls before turning and starting upstream. In this way, I tried not to miss any more of the Missouri than I absolutely had to.

As the day wore on, clouds began to build in the west. With the clouds came an ever increasing wind, and before we knew it, along came storm clouds. We had prepared for every eventuality, but still we did not look forward to a chilly June thunderstorm, but that is just what we got. The wind began to whip at us and soon sheets of rain and small beads of hail peppered our skin. The dogs looked up at us miserably, no doubt reflecting our own countenances. Before as I traveled, I would pull over to make a fire, or wait out the storm, but traveling with a companion on our limited days off precluded any chance of doing that. So we doggedly continued in the rain.

When the rain looked to settle in for the night, we decided to forego our camping plans. Instead, we drove on to the small town of Cascade, Montana and tied up for the night. Soaked to the bone, in a pouring rain, we trudged down the lonely streets to the Red Angus Café to warm up with a burger and a cup of coffee. With that done, we took advantage of our ill fortune and spent our evening in Cascade style. With two wet dogs on our heels, we sauntered over to the Driftwood Bar and enjoyed our Saturday night in the little town. At some point in the evening we remembered we had no vehicle to get us back to Great Falls, so we called a friend to take us back to the big city.

A short night, and a long, slow moving morning later, Brian picked me up in his truck and we headed back to Cascade. The weather looked much more promising this day, even though our outlooks didn't. Parking in Cascade, we headed down to the boat and loaded back up, dogs and all. I had to bring the boat up to full speed to pull the plug and drain all the rain water out of the bottom of the boat. That accomplished, we took in the scenery, each man left with his own thoughts and his own dog.

From Cascade to Wolf Creek, Montana, the Missouri River is classified a blue ribbon trout stream. People come from all over the world to fly fish this segment of the river. Not only is the fishing great, but so is the scenery. High granite cliffs force the river back and forth, curving this way and that over a gravelly bed. The water at this point is clear enough to spot fish several feet under the surface. Threading its way through the canyon, the river crosses time and again under Interstate 15. In this way, the river of the West comes in contact with the concrete river of highway, and beside that the steel ribbon of a railroad. The three make an awkward contrast through the narrow canyon, each having their time in history as the predominant means of travel for those seeking the West.

But Brian and I were not interested so much in what took place on the interstate. Instead, we kept our eyes glued to the drama taking place around every bend of the river. At each curve we encountered fishermen trying their best to hook the famed trout of the Missouri, each adorned like the centerfold of an Orvis catalog. The entire journey up the river had been like an evolution of fishermen. Near St. Louis on the lower Missouri, I had passed commercial fishermen plying trotlines for catfish and buffalo. Then as I traveled further upstream, I began to encounter bank fishermen also fishing for catfish and perch. The further west I got, the more fishermen I ran into. By the time I got to the Dakota's the water teemed with walleye fishermen. At the mouth of the Yellowstone, I hit a glitch in the evolutionary ladder with the paddlefishermen; but then the progression continued with more walleye fishermen until I finally reached the upper Missouri and the purist fly fishermen. Of course, they will argue that they are the top of the evolutionary chain, one step down from God himself with a rod and line, but I am not so sure about that.

Most of the fly fishermen we passed that day did look good, but we failed to see too many of them reeling in fish. I firmly believe fly fishing to be a chance to dress up in flashy duds and stand in cold water. Needless to say, I wasn't too impressed. From the looks we were getting from the fishermen, I don't think they were too impressed with us either. Nothing bothers fishermen worse than having their peace and quiet disturbed. Nothing is more disturbing than two cowboys with two dogs motoring by with no interest in fly fishing whatsoever.

Our day continued like this until midafternoon when we finally reached Holter Dam in Wolf Creek. Now I was truly on familiar territory. The ranch that borders the dam is one I had worked on for two years. For those two years, I looked off my front porch at Holter Dam and Reservoir. When we pulled up to the boat launch, I had Brian tie up the boat before we started hoofing it to the main ranch house. I still had friends who worked at the ranch and I was looking forward to visiting with them. I knew that they never expected me to drop by for a visit like this and I couldn't wait to see the looks on their faces.

For two years, I looked out over the blue waters of Holter Lake Reservoir. Time and again, I wondered what the river must be like downstream, where the waters went and how they changed on the long trip to the ocean. Well, now I knew. I knew only too well how the river changed from one curve to the next and just how long, or short, the trip could be. My dream of floating the Missouri had become reality.

My friends, Ken and Anne, were home at the ranch and I surprised them. They offered us dinner and a beer, which we gladly took them up on, and we offered them stories about our two day adventure from Great Falls. Before it got dark, I talked Ken into giving us a ride down to Cascade to pick up Brian's truck. Once again, I had to say goodbye to the river. Both Brian and I had to be back to work the next day and I was not sure when I would get the chance to complete my vow to reach Three Forks.

Brian, for the most part, had a ball on the river. He said he could have done without the rain and cold, but that just makes one appreciate the river all the more, as I told him. The next week both of us had stories to relate at work. I enjoyed having someone around who actually knew what it was like on the water. At least now I was not the only soul to know the river. From here on, Brian would have a little something to share with folks when they asked about the journey.

Unfortunately, the rest of the summer got busy, and I was unable to slip away again for the two days I thought I would need to finish up. Summer turned to fall, when I found myself back in the mountains guiding once again. I was afraid, at this point, that I would not get a chance to get back on the water until the next spring. I desperately wanted to finish up. I felt like I had cheated myself until I accomplished what I had set out to do.

Soon it was mid-October and I was still in the mountains. Winter reached out and warned of what was to come, and I could not get a chance to slip away. With the cold northern winds blowing, I finally got the break I was looking for. I grabbed a day off and loaded the boat onto my pick-up.

Back in Wolf Creek, the weather looked anything but promising for boating. Holter Lake heaved and sighed on the rocky shore, its water the color of dark slate. A cold wind blew down from the north chilling every bone in my body. I wrapped up in a wool coat and strapped on my life vest underneath, then zipped Herschel up in his life vest and with that we were off.

Since I was solo, my plan was to motor up to Hauser Dam and then back to my truck, at least this way I could get one more reservoir closer to Three Forks. I hated the fact that I only had one day to do this. But one day was better than none. By the time I had gathered all my gear from storage and driven to Wolf Creek, it was one o'clock. Undaunted with the late start and moving slowly from my taste of freedom the night before, I pushed off into Holter Lake. I had brought along very little gear in order to make the fastest time possible on the water. With me I had only the bare essentials: gas, camera, matches, a thermos of coffee and food. The boat seemed to skip across the water with such little weight. I use the word skip loosely, one might better explain the rhythmic pounding on the waves better by saying bounced, or hammered. The "Teddy Roosevelt" was living up to its name that day. My back and backside were feeling every little wave we pounded against. So was my head. But I had no fear of the waves. I had encountered much worse before and I knew what the boat could safely handle. My only concern today was time.

It is a shame to have to condense such a wonderful experience to such a short time frame, but by this time of the year, I was racing not only old man winter, but my ability to get away from work. I could only justify the hasty passage of the upper river by telling myself that I had lived around here and seen much of the country before, though never from the river perspective.

I wove my way around the famed oxbows of Holter Lake, passing a small band of Bighorn Sheep. The group was comprised solely of rams who seemed not the least bit interested in my noisy boat or pointing dog. Like Captain Lewis, I was amazed at how the bighorns moved about on the "immencely high and nearly perpendicular clift." I slowed enough to take a few pictures before racing on in my pursuit of the river's source. Later that day I was to pass numerous deer, a few eagles and a small herd of about fifty elk, the wild bounty of the Missouri seen upon every shore.

Just a few miles above the oxbows, I entered what Meriwether Lewis named the Gates of the Rocky Mountains, a name that stuck to this very day. As inspiring as the gates are today with their high limestone cliffs pressing in on the waters, I could only imagine how imposing the stone walls must have been one hundred years ago when the river ran unfettered through here. Nowadays, the water level is much higher than in the days of Lewis and Clark; therefore, they looked at higher walls than the ones we see today.

The sound of the little outboard motor seemed to blaspheme the cathedral-like silence of the canyon. Three miles later, I broke from the walled gorge into a wide open expanse of reservoir known as Upper Holter Lake, aptly named. With engine going full throttle, I sped on, winding with the river through the low mountains to reach Hauser Dam. I believe I surprised the few fishermen out that day when I attacked the small rapids below the dam. I passed by with a friendly wave, only to reach the dam, turn around and retrace my path with another wave in the fishermen's direction. They must have thought me a crazed duck hunter.

So that was that. I had one more obstacle to overcome, and was a few more miles closer to Three Forks. But I was not satisfied with the accomplishment. It all seemed too rushed, hurried. I never felt like I had a chance to connect with the river again. Instead, I felt like a pleasure boater out on a Sunday ride, totally unconnected with the deeper meaning of my trip. Disgusted with myself, and the circumstances that forced me to hurry this way, I loaded up the boat and drove north to Choteau. I was feeling like the fates were planning against me and I would never make it to the river's source.

No sooner than I had arrived at the ranch when it was time to go back into the mountains. Once again, I could feel the pinch of winter moving in on me. I wondered if I was going to get one more chance to finish up before winter's cold grip throttled the river and iced me out. I vowed that if I got any more time before things froze up, I was going to make it all the way to the beginning of the river, weather be damned.

The Gates of the Rocky Mountains

CHAPTER 16

*"we proceeded on a fiew miles to the three forks of the
Missouri."*

William Clark July 25, 1805

*"It was exhilarating to be back on the river . . . I did it. I
floated the entire River."*

Chris Bechtold November 7, 1998

MY CHANCE FINALLY CAME ON THE SEVENTH OF NOVEMBER. I had the
weekend off and I planned to make good use of it. I loaded the truck
the night before and stashed all my gear in the cab and under the boat.
Once again I was going solo, so I had to make preparations to back
track to the truck at each dam. The weather was cold and overcast. I
never asked for help, figuring it foolish myself to be boating up the river
in such weather. Why would anyone be interested in ferrying around
a madman in a jon boat at this time of year?

The next morning, I left Choteau before daylight headed for Hauser
Dam. I had a full day planned if I was going to make it to Three Forks.
I arrived at Hauser Dam a little after first light. In a rush, I backed the
boat up to the boat launch at Hauser and unloaded it from the truck.
Once again I had packed coffee, food, and only the bare essentials. Time
was of the essence. I needed to be able to load and unload the boat
quickly, not to mention drive it quickly on the water. In a short time
I had everything prepared to go. Wearing insulated overalls and a heavy
winter coat, I looked more suited for driving a snowmobile than boating. While zipping up my life vest under the heavy layers of clothing,
I chuckled at the thought of what I was doing. If I went overboard in
the frigid water with these heavy clothes, I was going to sink like a rock.
Well, that was incentive not to go overboard. When I finally finished

bundling up, I doubled checked the boat for my camera. I planned on using it when I reached the river's source. Hopping into the boat, I again roared up the lake with Herschel sitting up front like a hood ornament on a late fifties Mercury.

At Hauser Reservoir, the mountains pressed in a little closer than at Holter. Tree covered hills slipped down to the water's edge and shadows loomed over the water making for a chilly ride to Canyon Ferry Dam and back. Hauser was to be the smallest of the reservoirs I traveled upon and it took me little time at all to cover its surface.

Once again, I unloaded the boat and wrestled it back onto the truck, cursing my failure to invest in a boat trailer. I never needed one until this day, always thinking them a frivolous expenditure. At this point, I was beginning to think I would pay a pretty penny just to borrow one. Loaded up, I hit the road again. This time I drove out through Helena on the interstate, then south towards Townsend, Montana. I made up my mind that I was going to make it all the way to Three Forks, come hell or low water. I had little time and my old truck had traveled far enough. I did not want to get almost to Three Forks then have to drive all the way back the next day just to finish a few miles. I was too tight to spring for a hotel room and it was too cold to camp out. I had just spent the last two and a half months camping and guiding in the mountains. I didn't feel like sleeping out in the cold again so soon.

With these thoughts in the back of my mind, I hurried to unload the boat at a launch area called the Silos, midway the length of Canyon Ferry Reservoir. Having unloaded, I zipped down to the dam and looped in front of it. Then with the wind at my back, I raced the length of the reservoir until I reached the entry point of the river. Here, the river had poured not silt, but gravel into a web of shallow channels. I dodged from one to the other trying to find a passage, but to no avail. I gave up at this point and sped back to the truck to repeat the unloading and loading process.

By this time, it was noon at a time of the year when the days are getting shorter. I knew I wasn't going to make it by nightfall, but damned if I was going to quit now. I had set my hard head to go to Three Forks and I was sure as hell going to make it. This time I jumped in the truck and headed back to the highway looking for an access point to the river.

I had a lot of miles to go yet that day. All of the river from here on I knew nothing about except those portions I could see from the highway. Once again, the river held a few surprises.

I passed through Townsend looking for a place to put my boat back in the water. I could have put it back in the water right below town, but I hated to fight the low water and I admit I was rushing in my quest to finish. Instead, I found a fishing access at Toston. In the process of looking for a good access point, I ended up driving about fifteen miles south of Townsend. That meant I had a substantial portion of river to backtrack upon.

Hurriedly, I unloaded and readied the boat in the water. At this place on the river the water looked shallow and the bottom much too rocky for my liking. I was going to have to be careful or I would mangle the prop beyond repair. Pushing off I headed downstream. This proved a little disconcerting, for I was used to always heading into the current and judging the water level from below. I learned quick enough where to point the boat. Soon, I learned what was too shallow for the boat to pass through. I bounced and skidded through the shallow portions, knowing only too well that I was going to have a tough time making it back upstream.

I had gone roughly six or seven miles when I decided I had better quit pressing my luck. The water level looked much too low over some of the riffles ahead of me and I did not have my hip boots with me. If I ended up in the water I would freeze my feet. I was cold enough already. Choosing a good spot, I turned the boat around and headed back into the current. Like I had anticipated, my progress slowed considerably. Thankfully, I had little weight in the boat. This fact alone made it possible for me to climb back through the riffles I had skimmed over previously. My poor little prop took a beating on the return to Toston.

Back at the truck, I decided to continue on upstream as far as feasible. According to my maps, I had only one more dam to portage around. The Toston Dam, which is a small irrigation/ electrical dam about 5 miles above the truck. I headed for the dam hoping to get an idea of what to expect. These miles passed fairly quickly and being in a hurry I turned around before I actually saw the dam across the river. I knew I was close to the dam from the narrow gap in the canyon ahead of me. Turning the boat, I zipped back downstream to the truck. Again, I took off the motor and unloaded the boat. I wrestled its two hundred fifty awkward pounds onto the flatbed and secured it. Then Herschel and I drove over to Toston Dam. The last damned dam on the Missouri River.

After having seen the huge dams at Yankton, Pierre, and Fort Peck, the small electric and irrigation diversion at Toston seemed like a child's dabbling with the river. But small as it was, the dam still had the power to hold back the Missouri, and that was power enough to respect. By this time, evening was fast approaching. I didn't know if I could make it to the headwaters by dark or not. But, damned if I was going to quit now. I unloaded and got the boat in the water.

The temperature hovered around thirty-two degrees. Here in the shade of the canyon, I could feel the cold seeping over everything. In a very short time, the temperature would fall below freezing. It was now or never. Herschel hopped into the boat with me, sensing the excitement in the air. The exhilaration of seeing the end in sight had my heart racing. This was going to be the moment I had dreamt about. I just had an estimated twenty or so miles to go. Bundled up against the cold, we raced off up the river.

This final stretch of river proved to have a beauty all its own. At least I thought so. It could have been the excitement of the moment. The river width fluctuated from wide and shallow, where the boat would sputter across the rocky bottom, to narrow and deep between high rock walls. These narrow points were at most 150 or so yards wide. I laughed out loud scooting through the narrow walled canyon, thinking of how the great Missouri had shrunk in size, and how Herschel and I had seen it happen.

Along the east shore of the river, a railroad track traced the outline of the river, but I never saw a train. I was alone on the river, darkness closing in, and the end of my long journey on the Missouri. When I emerged from the high tawny colored walls of the canyon, a broad flat greeted me. From here I could see ahead the open valley where the three forks—the Jefferson, Madison, and the Gallatin—combined to form the Great Missouri. Off to the east, across the flat loomed the Horseshoe Hills, visible only as a purple-gray outline in the looming dusk.

I strained to see the river ahead of me. The prop continued to hit bottom, time and again, and I knew I was chewing up the blades terribly, but I didn't care. This was the final stretch and I wasn't planning on using the boat in the winter. Off to my right I passed a cement plant, lights blaring into the night. Shortly after passing the plant, I saw a small sign at the rivers edge. I pulled in to read it and get my bearings.

The sign said I had reached the Headwaters of the Missouri River. I had done it. I had traveled the entire river, some 2,300 miles from its mile wide mouth to its humble beginnings here at this sign. I could have hollered out loud, there being no one to hear me. I was alone in the dark. Herschel sat in the boat and looked back at me. We were the only ones to know what we had accomplished. I wasn't ready for it to end this way. Besides, Lewis and Clark had followed the Jefferson River up past Dillon, Montana to straddle the tiny beginnings of the Missouri River at the continental divide. I was not going to stop until I, too, had made it to the Jefferson River.

With darkness surrounding us, I navigated the river by the reflection of the last light in the western sky. The mouth of the Jefferson was not much further and shortly I came upon it. The prop ground in the rocks, the boat banged noisily on the rocky bottom, and I pointed its nose into the waters of the Jefferson. Letting the current push us back, I swung around and ran the bow aground on a gravel bar. This was it. This was the end of the line for Herschel and me.

Standing on the rocky, little, gravel island, I listened to the waters gurgling around us. It was full on dark by this point, the temperature below freezing, and not a sole in the world knew where I was or what I had just accomplished. It was just Herschel and I, standing where we knew the journey ended for us. I wanted to yell, jump up and down, and at the same time cry. All alone I tried to soak up the moment. A moment I had never imagined would end in this way. I always imagined it to be something a little more noteworthy, a little more climactic.

I brought along my camera to document this great moment in my life, but it seemed so trivial at this point. But I wanted this moment documented on film, proof for my children, should I ever have any, that I had done this. Putting the camera on a small rock, I stood back with Herschel at my side and took a few photos with the self-timer.

Looking back at the pictures now, I find them quite humorous. It was so dark that Herschel's eyes glow in the sharp glare of the flash, and I look like I had just come in from calving rather than someone who had just finished traveling the entire Missouri. But, we can only make do with what we have.

My final challenge, like an extra credit question on a high school exam, was to navigate the river back to the truck in the dark. What had proved to be so challenging coming up river from the dam during the day, now was much harder to do going downstream in the dark. I could not afford to make any mistakes. The temperature was below freezing and no one knew where I was or what I was doing. If I messed this up, I was going to get in trouble.

With only starlight to see by, I put the boat back in the water and strained my eyes watching the water ahead of me. Having just come up this way, I used remembered landmarks to keep me abreast of my location on the water. In this way, I had a rough idea of which side of the river to lean to, and what to expect ahead. Still, there was little solace in knowing that one wrong turn on a big rock could ruin everything. Plus, if I hung up in the shallows, or anywhere for that matter, I didn't have waders to slip out into the water with. If that happened I was going to get wet and very cold.

On top of all these other worries, I figured I had hardly enough gas to get me back to the truck. I sure didn't want to run out now. I needed the motor not so much for power at this point, but to steer with. Without it, I could end up being carried into rocks and debris that would make a mess of my evening. Also, I had to think of the dam ahead. I surely didn't want to drift into that damned thing.

All these thoughts soon combined to erase the elation I had earlier felt and set my nerves on edge. With tight jaws and grinding teeth, I strained my eyes on the inky water ahead of me. To conserve fuel, I would kill the motor and let the current take me through the spots I knew to be safe. These times were like icing on top of the cake. I could relax at these junctures, listening to the water lap at the boat, gazing up at the stars, and be happy. Then, I would hear the water change tone ahead, and starting the motor, I would tense up for my next challenge.

I finally rounded the corner to see the lights of Toston Dam as I slumped my shoulders in relief. I was cold, tired, and full of a sense of accomplishment I had never felt before. For the last time, I unloaded the gear from the boat and wearily loaded the empty boat onto my truck. Herschel hopped in by my side and we drove off towards Choteau. That was it. I had the monkey off my back, and the Missouri River behind me.

CHAPTER 17

*"have sufficiently informed himself with rispect to the state
of the river &c. as to determine us whether to prosicute our
journey from thence by land or water. in the former case
we should want all the horses which we could perchase and
in the latter only to hire the Indians to transport our
baggage to the place at which we made the canoes."*

Meriwether Lewis August 17, 1805

*"I'm getting excited . . . Will put in at Canoe Camp where
L&C put in with dugouts after branding horses."*

Chris Bechtold December 11, 1999

NOVEMBER SEVENTH, 1998 was the day I finished my journey up the
Missouri River. For a while, that was enough of an accomplishment. As
far as I knew, I was only the third person to ever ascend the entire river
by boat in the last one hundred years. For sure, I did it on the smallest
budget, and for the most part, solo. Yes, I had much support and help
from my family, but for the most part I made the trip alone. I was
proud of this accomplishment.

The next spring found me working back at the ranch. I kept busy
wrangling and packing, taking care of the horses, and any other thing
that needed doing. Like always, time away from the ranch was hard to
come by during the busy summer season. Invariably, folks would ask if
I ever planned on finishing my journey retracing the path of the Corps
of Discovery to the Pacific.

I always responded, yes, I planned to finish up some day when I got
the time. Well, the time never came. I stayed busy all that summer and
well into fall. It was a friend's phone call that finally spurred me on to

action and finishing what I had set out to do. She joked that I had only really finished half of what I set out to do. Hearing someone else say this hit me hard. The truth, especially from someone else, can hurt. I realized that she was right. I truly had only accomplished half of what I started. In fact, the more I looked at it, the more I realized I was being a quitter. No one stops halfway. I vowed that late fall day that I was going to finish this trip before the year 2000 no matter what.

Just because I made a promise to myself to finish the job, didn't mean I was going to find the time to do it. I first had to fulfill my obligations at the ranch. That meant finishing up the fall season, pulling shoes off of the horses and winterizing the cabins. Only when these jobs were done and the ranch buttoned up for the winter, did I feel I could slip away for some time of my own.

I knew next to nothing about the country I planned to travel through. Back to the Journals I turned to learn a thing or two of what to expect. Not that the Journals could be termed a travel guide for the rivers today. I knew enough to know that most all of the Columbia River was dammed and the Snake had a few dams of its own in the stretch I planned to travel on. First off, I had to find a starting point.

The Journals provided this information. I decided to put into the water at the same place the Corps of Discovery did. I figured that I would never get a chance to follow the Trail of Lewis and Clark all the way overland, so I might as well do my best to follow the water portion of the trail. I already had accomplished half of that.

According to the Journals, the Corps of Discovery built dugout canoes near what is today Orofino, Idaho. I decided to put into the river there on my way to the Pacific Ocean. Unlike my trip up the Missouri, or maybe like it in a way, I failed to prepare adequately. I also failed to research the river as much as I should have. I just assumed that nothing could be as challenging as the Missouri River. Besides, I was going downstream, what could be easier than that? Those were not the best guidelines to use to prepare a trip.

I decided to leave from Orofino by way of the Clearwater River. According to the maps I had acquired, it looked like a short trip down the Clearwater until it joined with the Snake River at Lewiston, Idaho. At Lewiston, I would encounter my first dam. I researched this problem a little more extensively. First, I called the Army Corps of Engineers and checked to see what the regulations were for locking through the dams. Unlike the Missouri, all the dams on the Columbia have locks, which allow boats to float right through, or at least that was the simple impression I held.

Gee, everything seemed to plan out so well, I couldn't imagine that I would have any trouble at all. From my perspective, it would be a fairly simple trip. I would drive to Orofino, put in on the Clearwater River, follow it down to the Snake River, lock through the dams on the Snake, join up on the Columbia and again lock through any dams and before you know it, I would be at the Pacific Ocean. A total distance of roughly 850 miles or so, not too much of a problem, and all downstream; easy, I told myself.

At the Pacific, I would try to call someone for a ride back to my truck, or maybe just hitch hike a ride to Orofino. Who knows, I thought, it wouldn't be that hard to just boat back up to the truck, either. With this simple plan, I began to get things ready for my trip. I already had all the equipment. All I really needed to do was gas up my fuel containers, buy a little food and hit the road.

I started to make plans to for my big journey. Like always, there wasn't a lot of time for me to get away. At last, with the ranch shut down for the winter, I planned to slip away and begin the second part of my grand adventure on December 11th. This would give me plenty of time, by my calculations, to finish the trip and still be home by Christmas.

December isn't the best time to plan a long camping expedition, but it was the only time I was going to get. For that matter, the Journals show that Lewis and Clark traveled to the coast at about the same time of year. That would make things even more interesting. I could compare all that I saw with what Lewis and Clark saw in the same season.

Understandably, my folks thought I was out of my mind when I related my plans to them. I believe they thought me crazier than Chuck and Sharon did at the ranch. Everyone I worked with just looked at it like another river trip. Being folks who work in the mountains, they didn't think much of long trips and thought it was bound to be warmer over on the Columbia. I didn't think it that big of a deal either. I just wanted to finish the trip as soon as I could. I had one thing on my mind at this point and that was reaching the Pacific Ocean with the same little boat I left Wood River, Illinois in.

What I had not anticipated in my preparations was that my Dad and Calvin would want to come along. I really couldn't imagine that anyone would want to go with me at this time of the year. So, I was quite surprised when Dad called on December 5th and asked if he could come along. How do you say no to that? I said sure, come on out. Dad hung up and told Calvin of the plan. In no time, the two of them had bought plane tickets to Spokane, Washington. My plans for one quickly amended to plans for three.

I made arrangements to pick them up on my way to Orofino on the 11th. Suddenly, with all of my plans in place, I realized I had more to do than I thought. I was going to need new tires on the truck for one thing. The old slick things on my truck would never make it over a snowy pass. I was also going to need to prepare my gear a little more seriously. For one thing, I needed to make sure my motor would still start.

Two days before I was to leave, I decided I had better check out the boat and make sure it was still "sea worthy." I had been storing it upside down on the ground by my cabin. In the year since I had last used it, rabbits had moved in underneath it and I am sure several families of mice resided in the nooks and crannies of the gunnels. More importantly, I needed to check out the motor.

After my last day on the Missouri, I had simply drained the gasoline out of the motor and put it up in the loft of the cabin. No recommended maintenance or servicing, I just shoved it into a corner of the loft. Now I began to worry about the readiness of my little workhorse. My biggest fear was that some O-rings may have dry rotted or the injectors might have gotten dirty. I needed to test everything before I got to the river in Orofino. A little preparedness wouldn't hurt.

My problem now was finding the time to test the boat, and also finding a body of water close by that wasn't frozen over. There is a reservoir, roughly 16 miles from the cabin that I thought about going to, but hardly any water was left in it, and what was there was frozen. I could have tried the Teton River across from the cabin, but it had hardly enough water to float the boat. Then I thought of a place.

At the turn off to the upper ranch, beavers had been busy all fall building a dam in the slack water of the Teton River. There was just enough current flowing across the beaver pond to keep the water open, and I guessed the water level about four feet, enough to float the boat and test the motor. Off I went up the mountain road to field-test my set up in a beaver pond. I know it sounds silly, but that is exactly how I prepared for the waters of the grand Columbia River.

Backing up to the edge of the beaver pond, I pulled the boat off the truck and slid it across the snow into the water. Next I attached the motor and hooked up the fuel tank and with only one pull, the motor sprung to life. I couldn't believe it. My darned old truck wouldn't even start that fast. I flopped down on the seat and backed into the pond.

The pond itself was only about fifty feet across and maybe seventy-five feet long, but it was enough to test things out. I opened up the throttle and did some tight turns on the water. I must have looked a little funny with a fourteen foot boat out on a small beaver pond in the snow-covered mountains. Wouldn't you know it, one lone vehicle passed by while I was sitting out there in the boat. What could I do, but wave? I am sure they thought me certifiably nuts.

With the motor checked out, I was now ready to go. I had only to drain the water from my cabin and winterize it before I left. The cabin heat was primarily an old coal burning pot-bellied stove, so I needed to make sure things were buttoned down or I would come home to busted water pipes. It being close to Christmas time, I decided to have a little fun before I left and attended a Christmas party in town the night before. I am certain that is not a good pre-trip policy. I felt terrible the next morning as I loaded up all my gear in the truck. The weather was overcast and blowing with snow forecast, and I had a well-deserved headache, typical cowboy style.

On top of my own miserable physical state, the roads went from bad to worse. Thankfully, I had put some good tires on the truck the previous week. Not new tires, but they had a lot more tread than the ones I had. They did the trick, too. The weather alternated from snow on the passes to sleet and snow everywhere else. Three hundred miles later, the sleet and snow turned to just plain rain. I drove straight through Spokane, Washington to the airport outside of town. With perfect timing, I strolled up to the arrival gate just as Calvin and Dad stepped off the plane. It was sure good to see their friendly faces again.

Not wasting time, I took them out to the truck where we rearranged all the gear in order to fit their duffle in the truck bed with the boat. Then we all piled into the front. We must have looked like the Beverly Hillbillies with Herschel, Calvin, Dad, and myself all piled into the front of my old pickup. On the back of the truck, my boat was strapped upside down, hanging off the back of the flatbed a good six feet. Bags of duffel littered the open spots along the sides of the boat with bungee cords and straps criss-crossed back and forth across them. What a sight we were. With a hot cup of coffee to keep us all awake, we left Spokane headed for Orofino, Idaho.

CHAPTER 18

"all the Canoes put into the water and loaded, fixed our
Canoes as well as possible and Set out . . . proceeded on
passed 10 rapids which wer dangerous."

William Clark October 7, 1805

"Raining this morning . . . The upper river was shallow,
but do-able . . . Grounded out a few times and once had
to get out and pull . . . quick water"

Chris Bechtold December 12, 1999

WE ARRIVED AT OUR DESTINATION AMID A STEADY RAIN. Dampness pervaded everything. Orofino is nestled tight between the mountains in a narrow valley through which the Clearwater River runs. Compared to the sparse, rugged plains of north central Montana, this region seemed lush as a jungle. Directly across Highway 12 from downtown Orofino looms the massive concrete wall of Dworshak Dam. Just below this dam, a small park sits quaintly along the river's edge. The park is a memorial to The Corps of Discovery, aptly named Canoe Camp Park.

Here is where the men of the expedition carved their dugouts from the trunks of Ponderosa Pines. The boats took the men roughly two weeks to build, a tedious prospect of burning out the center of the large logs and then chopping out the burnt remains. Luckily for me, my boat was ready to go.

While I was prepared from my moment of arrival to take to the water, at this location the men of the expedition had much to do. For one thing, it was here that the Corps of Discovery emerged emaciated from their trying journey through the Bitterroot Mountains. After coming from the mountains, the men were greeted by the hospitable Nez Perce

179

Indians. Camping at this spot, they recuperated from the arduous trek through the mountains by dining on dried salmon and camass root. Some of the men, Lewis included, did little actual recuperating. The switch from a lean meat diet to the fatty salmon and starchy roots wreaked havoc on their bowels.

I, for one, looked forward to a meal of salmon. I could not wait until I got closer to the coast where I planned to dine on a fine meal of fresh salmon. That was one meal I got little of in Montana. Like me while back in Choteau, Lewis and Clark had to take care of the horses before they could begin their journey by river. All in all, I had it much easier in every aspect than did the men of the expedition. Yet, looking closely, I did see some similarities.

I was to find out soon enough that the most striking similarity between my own journey and the Corps of Discovery's was the weather. Rain and wind were my constant companions on this leg of my journey. I felt as if moss had grown on my back by the time I made it to the ocean.

At this spot, where Lewis and Clark readied themselves and the men for the transition from land to water travel, I stood and looked over the Clearwater River. It looked smaller than I had expected. It definitely had more current than I expected. From on shore I could see fast moving water rushing around some pretty good-sized rocks.

That night, Dad, Calvin, and I got a room in a small hotel in Orofino. The weather was cold and rainy, bordering on turning to snow. I slept like a log after the drive, and unlike my trip up the Missouri, I had no apprehensions whatever. The next morning we woke early and loaded up on a heavy breakfast at the local diner. At first light, we took the boat to the access point on the river. I had on my rain gear, waders, and life vest. All of us scurried back and forth from the truck to the boat, loading gear and equipment.

As I stood in the boat arranging my gear and readying the motor, I looked up to see a couple about my age drift by while fishing. I never gave it a thought. A moment later I heard a voice ask, "Chris?" I looked up to see John, a friend from my college days, fishing with his wife. I had not seen him in seven years. He asked me what I was up to and if I planned to fish. When I told him my plans, his eyebrows raised in amazement. I went on to answer his questions as best as I was able. I could tell from his questions that he obviously knew the river much better than I did.

I reversed the questioning process and asked him to fill me in on what to expect. We visited for a bit before I told him it was time I got going. John wished me luck and with that, I looked up at Dad and Calvin on shore. As I backed the boat into the current, I told them I would meet them in Lewiston, Idaho. The current was strong enough to carry me quickly away from the ramp. I turned the boat into the sweep of the current and for the first time in over a year, I was running down river, the current at my back. I instantly enjoyed the feel of traveling downstream. I knew this would be a quicker trip than my Missouri voyage and set about looking over the country around me. A short way ahead I approached my first set of rapids. Picking a route through, I revved up the motor, gathering enough speed to steer my way through the rushing waters. I misjudged at one point and banged the prop on a large rock, but did no damage.

I relaxed after completing the first set of rapids, my confidence back. From there on, I would encounter several fast spots on the river. At one such point, my old friend John passed me to show me the safest way through. Other than that, I was on my own. Further downstream, I passed a fast moving jet boat roaring up against the current. I waved a hello, not a bit envious of the boat going upstream. I had my fill of upstream travel already. Soon, I was approaching Lewiston, Idaho.

The town lies at the junction of the Clearwater and Snake Rivers. Surprisingly, it took little time at all to reach Lewiston. I spied Dad and Calvin standing on the shore waving me over. I pulled in and took them up on their lunch offer. We ate at a small truck stop across the river from the Potlatch lumber mill. After the sandwich, I told the guys I was anxious to get back on the water. Things were going quite well and I knew that I would not encounter any more shallow water from here on out. I decided to install a new spare prop I carried in case of emergencies.

After changing props, we all decided Calvin would be the first to ride with me. He eagerly hopped in. I say eagerly, because the rain had stopped. I never once had them volunteer to ride when it was raining and now both he and Dad were ready to get on the river. Leaving

Lewiston, the water slowed noticeably at the confluence of the Snake and Clearwater. I was on big water now. Off to the north, a barge sat tied to the shore.

The barges of the Columbia River system are markedly different than those I saw on the Missouri. Instead of being wide and squat, sitting low in the water, these on the west side of the divide had high sides and were shorter in length. I never got a chance to talk to a riverboat captain on the west side to ask why this was so. Maybe it made them easier to maneuver on the smaller rivers. I don't know.

At any rate, the water lay ahead of us like a large sheet of glass. The boat skimmed across the river's surface leaving a wake that drifted a quarter mile behind. I was happy with my progress. Here it was, first day out and I was already on the Snake River and making good time. Ahead of me I could see the concrete ribbon that was Lower Granite Dam stretched across the river.

I called the Army Corps of Engineers in preparation to my trip and received the protocol for locking through the dams. At this time of the year, there was no set schedule of lock activity. If I were the only boat around, the locks would be obliged to let me through. If there was a barge in the near vicinity, the lockmaster would wait and lock me through with the larger craft. But law mandated that I had a right to lock through no matter the size of my craft. Still, I was nervous about my first passage through the locks.

When we approached the dams, I followed the buoys that marked the correct approach to the lock entrance. There, I found a long rope dangling along the concrete bastion at the mouth of the lock. According to the information I received in the mail, I was to pull the rope to signal the lockmaster of my intentions to lock through. This could also be done via marine radio, but I had no radio, nor did I want one.

With Calvin in the front of the boat, I inched up alongside the concrete wall; Calvin reached over the bow and yanked the rope, setting off a alarm that alerts the lockmaster. I didn't like this rope-pulling bit at all. For one thing, the wind picked up a little just as we arrived at the dam. This created some small waves that kept my little boat bobbing like a small fishing bobber alongside the high wall. I continually worked the motor to keep from being washed against the concrete wall.

Not knowing what to expect, we waited for upwards of twenty minutes while the lock filled. Next, we saw the steel gate that covers the entrance of the lock slowly descend into the roiling waters. A red light stayed lit along the entranceway. When the gate had been submerged for a minute or two, the light turned green. I took this to mean go and we motored slowly into the lock chamber.

It was like being in an enormous concrete swimming pool. The lockmaster came on over the intercom speaker and directed us to the mooring bit where we were to tie off. Then a loud rumbling commenced and the gate that had submerged before us appeared out of the water behind us to seal off the river from the lock chamber. As soon as this happened another rumbling noise commenced and in a moment, I noticed from the watermarks on the wall that we were descending.

As the water level dropped inside the lock chamber, the buoy we were tied to rolled slowly down its track inside the massive chamber walls. I admit I was pretty nervous about this time. All the roaring and rushing sounds echoed back and forth inside the immense chamber drowning out the sounds of all else. There we sat in a little fourteen foot aluminum boat tied to a steel buoy the same size. What if the buoy caught on something in the track? I was afraid our lead rope would hang us over the descending water level. All sorts of worrisome thoughts filled my head. Maybe I had drunk too much coffee, but I could not sit still in the boat. I fidgeted around in my seat trying to take in everything and worrying that something was bound to go wrong.

Behind me, a "small" leak poured down from the entrance gate, the same gate that held the river back above us. By this time, we had descended about fifty feet in the chamber. I asked Calvin if he saw the leak. He said he did. I told him that if the water from a leak like that hit the boat floor from that height, if would knock the bottom right out of the boat. He laughed and told me to relax. Yeah, right. I don't tend to get worried much when I am outdoors and on my own, but in this manmade swimming pool with only a steel gate holding back the Snake River, I was admittedly worried.

At last, the water level stopped descending. We had dropped a total of one hundred and five feet. Up above us, at the level we had started at, I could see the outline of a man leaning over the steel railing. It was my Dad; he waved at us and shouted something we could not make out. The acoustics were terrible at the bottom of the chamber. A deep rumbling started once again. At the far end of the lock, two enormous steel doors slowly parted. Through them, I could detect a sliver of light. A minute later and the doors were wide open. I heard a bell go off and with that we were cleared to leave. I couldn't get out of that lock fast enough.

We rushed out the bottom of the lock and once clear of the gates, I slowed and turned the boat to look back at the dam from below. It appeared monstrous. An immense concrete structure capable of holding the entire Snake River loomed above us. It sent a shiver down my spine. There was a lot of power being held back, one hundred five feet of the Snake River, to be exact. I didn't hang around long to contemplate things. Revving the motor, I sped us downriver as quickly as the little boat would take us.

Further downstream, we approached a highway bridge over the river. The water had a little chop to it, but not enough to slow us down, just enough to make things a little bumpy. We pulled at the bridge where we saw Dad standing along shore. He asked how things were going and where we wanted to meet him next. I looked over the map Dad brought along and decided things were going so well, we might as well try to make it to Little Goose Dam for the night. It was a short distance ahead, maybe ten miles and I guessed with the progress we were making, we could be there by nightfall.

Calvin asked if Dad wanted to take a turn riding, but Dad replied that he would ride the next day. With that decided, Calvin and I said "So long," and backed into the river. We would meet Dad at the boat launch above Little Goose Dam before dark. Little did we know what was in store for us.

CHAPTER 19

"one canoe in which Sergt. Gass was Stearing and was nearle
turning over, she Sprung a leak or Split open on one side
and Bottom filled with water & Sunk on the rapid the men,
Several of which Could not Swin hung on to the Canoe,"

William Clark October 8, 1805

"We were hitting five and six foot waves in the rain in the dark.
It was damned serious and we could easily have capsized."

Chris Bechtold December 12, 1998

NOT LONG AFTER PULLING AWAY FROM THE BRIDGE, a light rain developed. Shortly thereafter, we looked ahead of us to see a wall of rain coming down the river channel. This front had with it strong winds, which turned the moderate chop of the waves into serious swells with white caps. Still, it was light out and we decided to keep heading into the wind. Dad expected us to meet him at Little Goose Dam and we had no way of getting in touch with him. We had to get there or Dad would be worried something was wrong.

I actually hoped Dad would see how bad things were getting and meet us at a point where the river approached the road. Unfortunately, the river has no road access to it until it reaches Little Goose Dam. Dad knew this, because he had the map. We did not. Still, we held out hope that we might see Dad standing along the shore ahead.

Our situation continued from bad to worse. The rain increased and with it, the wind. Waves by this point were getting high enough to toss the front end of the boat out of the water. I asked Calvin to kneel in the front of the boat to keep the front end down. We were getting soaked from the driving rain and visibility was deteriorating rapidly. I could see the shore, but not too well, it being difficult to look into the driving rain. All of the obstacles facing us now only combined to slow us down. Our progress in the high wind and waves slowed to a crawl.

A new dilemma now faced us. With our pace so slow, and all the detrimental weather blowing into us, it began to get dark. We were in no position to do anything to improve our condition. We had no idea of our distance from Little Goose Dam. We continually hoped that it was right around the next bend, but it never seemed to be there.

This is where I began to wish that I were traveling alone. For if I were alone, I would not have been in the situation I was finding myself. I would have pulled into a sheltered spot on shore and made a hasty camp to wait out the weather. Since I had Calvin with me and I said we would make it to Little Goose Dam, we had no choice but to get there.

Now, it had turned dark on us, and we really did have no choice but to get there. I could not make out the shore too well, but I knew there was not much of a chance of getting to it safely. The banks of the river in this country were rough, steep, and rocky. The water crashed upon the banks hard enough that if we did head to shore, we would have been smashed upon the rocks.

I continued to steer the boat even though I could not see much beyond the bow. Calvin was still kneeling in the front hanging with both hands onto the gunnels. The waves were high enough at this point that I could see the white caps above Calvin's head. I kept the boat pointed directly into them and hoped that we were hitting them straight on. If I got too much of an angle upon hitting each crest, I was afraid we would be swamped. I was mighty worried at this point, as was Calvin.

With each wave, a bucket full of water would splash down upon me. The back end of the boat was filling with water, which only caused the front end to raise higher, making each wave hit all the harder. I couldn't have turned the boat to head for shore even if there was a sandy beach to go to. I admit that I was thinking we were going to end up swimming before the night was through. I thought of all the things I would need to do if the boat flipped over and we ended up in the river. I hoped Calvin was preparing himself in case things got any worse.

When I had just about given up hope of the boat's being able to withstand any more, I saw a faint light ahead of us. It had to be the light of Little Goose Dam. Just as soon as I saw it, the light disappeared, when I turned the tiller of the motor it appeared again. That could only mean that there was a point of land ahead of us. I began to have some hope. As I slightly turned the boat to the south between each wave, I inched toward the bank and the light disappeared ahead of us. I kept this maneuver up until I could see the white foam of the waves hitting the rocky shore off to our left. Soon the severity of the waves let up enough that Calvin and I could shout back and forth to prepare for the next onslaught.

Steeling ourselves, we rounded the point into what we thought would be the ferocious waves, but they proved to be less severe than we had encountered before. I kept us as close to the shore as I dared and when we had gotten completely around the point, I could see a set of head-lights shining through the rainy darkness ahead.

I turned the boat into the waves and headed straight for the lights. We were in a small cove and soon enough we could see the boat dock in the glare of the truck's headlights. I pulled in alongside the dock and Dad rushed out to grab the lead rope. He tied us off to the dock. As we climbed out of the boat, he gave each of us a big hug. He had thought we were done for.

I think the stress of the situation had been worse for Dad than for Calvin and me. At least we had something to keep us occupied. Poor old Dad could only sit there in the truck and worry. He had no way of knowing if we were still surviving out in the inky darkness or not.

At one point, he said he had made up his mind to call for help and notify the search and rescue that we were out on the water. But he did not know if we were still out there or not. He thought we may have gotten to shore and could have been walking back to the dam. Instead, he sat in the truck, at wit's end, listening to the wind and rain buffet the side of the vehicle, and worried. According to Dad, he never heard such a sweet sound as that of the pounding of the boat upon the waves. He knew then we were all right.

Luckily for Herschel, he had traded places with Calvin back at Lewiston and ridden shotgun with Dad. He ran back and forth upon the boat dock, glad to see me. On the ride into town, he stayed pressed up against my side the whole way. Of course, there was no other place for him to sit. We were all packed into the front of the truck like sardines. We were wet and thankful to be safe for the night.

For dinner that night, we drove to the nearest town and were the last ones in the door before the café closed. Our dining place was a small café in Starbuck, Washington. I had a cheeseburger and savored every morsel with a hot steaming cup of coffee. The wind continued to blow outside and the rain showed no signs of letting up. Sitting in the café, I did my best to stick to my guns and camp out for the night. Lewis and Clark had roughed it through here, and so could I. I planned to camp out on principle.

All the way up the Missouri I had slept out, and I didn't want to change things now. If I had been traveling alone, like I planned, I would not have even had the option of staying in a warm motel room. I insisted that Calvin and Dad take me back to the boat. They relented, voicing the opinion that I was plumb crazy. After our hot meal we went back to the boat.

When they dropped me off, the wind was still blowing, sending rain down in slanting sheets. I waved them off, with Herschel by my side, as the truck pulled slowly away. I knew those two would drive a hundred miles if they had to, just to find a motel room since my Dad's idea of roughing it is sleeping in a twin bed.

I had a lot yet to do. The only light I could see was the faint glow coming from the lights of Little Goose Dam. It was not enough light for me to see very well. I fumbled around enough to get my sleeping bag out, and a rubberized tarp, the same I had used when ascending the Missouri. There were hardly any trees around this little boat launch, and certainly none that would work for me to set up a lean-to. I wandered around peering at every little spot of shelter and finally hunkered up along the lee side of a small tree.

Hurriedly getting into my sleeping bag, I put all my wet clothes up against the base of the tree, hoping that the blowing wind might dry them out a little bit. Then I grabbed hold of a corner of the tarp and rolled myself up inside of it like a hotdog in a piece of bread. Suffocating in the stale air of my sleeping bag and rubber tarp, I tried to fall asleep.

I didn't have much luck. The wind continued to whip across the little flat and soon the tarp began to flutter in the wind, waking me.

The rain pelted the hard rubber surface of the tarp, creating a racket that was anything but peaceful. Meanwhile, Herschel lay curled up dejectedly at the base of the little tree, wet and sad faced. I laid in my bag that way for upwards of an hour, until I couldn't take it anymore.

I had seen an outhouse in the lights of the truck as we pulled in. Jumping up in the wind and rain, with my sleeping bag and tarp in tow, I ran for the outhouse. To my surprise, it had a little overhang entryway to it. I tossed my bag in along the door, then ran back to the tree and grabbed my wet clothes. I crawled back into the opening and spread my sleeping bag out once again. It was just a little too long to fit. The foot of the bag stuck out into the wind and rain. No problem, I pushed the door open and found just enough headroom to make a usable, if not pleasant, shelter.

Herschel curled up against me and the two of us slept reasonably well. I spread my wet clothes out upon the tarp that covered me up. So ended my first day on the river west of the divide. When I awoke in the morning, my clothes were dry enough to wear again, not that I had much choice.

The wind howled enough that morning that my little cook stove would not stay lit in the strong gusts. I hunkered down around the little stove with the tarp wrapped over my shoulder to shelter the stove so I could boil my morning coffee. About the time I finished drinking my coffee and eating my bagel, I heard the truck approaching.

Dad and Calvin arrived bright eyed and bushy tailed. The truck held the remnants of a box of donuts. My companions assured me they had gotten good nights sleep, though not at the best accommodations. The motel they found the night before sounded like something out of a bad movie, but the beds were soft enough for the two of them and the heater worked enough to keep the frost off. They reported that the wind chill that morning was at zero degrees. I could well believe that.

The wind had not let up since I first awoke, and if anything, it had increased. The lake roiled in front of us, a sea of whitecaps and spray. I had no intention of even contemplating a launch. Dad said he was still recuperating from last night's worry and sure didn't want to see me go back out on water like that. With that settled, we decided to portage around the dam with the truck. Locking through the dams really didn't appeal to me anymore. I felt like a tin can in the ocean at the last lock and I could just as well pass on going through any more locks.

We loaded up the boat onto the back of the truck and motored around the dam. It was nine o'clock by the time we unloaded at the boat launch below Little Goose Dam. I noticed no one volunteered to ride with me this morning. Calvin showed no interest in getting back into the boat at all, in fact, he said he wasn't feeling too good this morning and thought he should ride in the truck. Dad looked out over the choppy water below the dam and said he sure as hell didn't want to get out on the water. He had enough new gray hairs from worrying about me the night before. He didn't want to add to them by worrying about us both.

With those two votes of confidence, I loaded up in the boat with Herschel. At least my dog had no qualms about riding with me. One thing about a dog, they are loyal to a fault. The water below the dam was not near as treacherous looking as above the dam, so I decided I had best get going while the going was good. I told Calvin and Dad I would meet them at the next dam, about thirty miles downstream.

Out on the water, the waves were not near as bad as they had looked from shore. I negotiated the chop with ease, although the ride was not very smooth. Herschel, I believe, had missed not being in the boat the day before and manned his post at the bow with a grin on his furry face. I took the opportunity to look over the countryside a little and try to relax in my solitude.

The land in this part of southeastern Washington is a continual rise and fall of steep sided hills. Each hill rose sharply from a small, usually dry draw then crested in a smooth roll and dropped quickly back to the next draw. Everywhere the land looked dry and brown. Even with all the rain I had just been subjected to, the land still looked desiccated. The primary vegetation looked to be grassy hillsides and where it was feasible to get a tractor, wheat covered the slopes.

I had entered the desert regions that made up the country from the foothills of the Cascade Mountains to the foothills of the Rockies. From what I read in the Journals of Lewis and Clark, even they had a tough time finding enough firewood to build a decent cook fire. Most of the wood they did find was driftwood taken from the banks of the river. I believed it. From the view I had of the land, there looked to be little chance of seeing a tree. Everywhere were steep grass covered hills. The shoreline of the river consisted of large reddish rocks that climbed rapidly from the waters surface; as soon as the rocks leveled out, grass would take hold. Back farther on the hilltops, wheat grew.

The other thing that surprised me about the area was the lack of people along the river. Even with all the dams scattered along the river's course, I saw hardly a soul on the water. Maybe for good reason, considering all the rough water I had encountered so far. That second day, I never passed another vessel upon the water. For that matter, I saw very few areas that had access points to the river. The steep, hard land seemed to hide the river, not letting the world know the bounty of water hidden in its deep valley. In the river bottom I felt quite alone. Not even the sight of a road broke the monotony of grass and sky.

After about sixteen miles, I saw a highway bridge ahead and the truck parked alongside it. I motored over to check in. The guys were having a good morning looking over the country. All was well with them, so I told them I would keep going and meet them at Lower Monumental Dam, my next impediment on the Snake River.

In what seemed to be no time at all, I came in sight of the dam. In fact, I made such good time that I had beaten the guys to the dam. I pulled in alongside the boat dock and waited for their arrival. My distaste for locking through was still in my mind as I waited, so I began to unload all the gear from the boat and prepare it for a portage on the truck. When the guys came into sight, I could see them laughing at my preparations. They thought my fear of the locks quite funny. I didn't care what they thought. I didn't want to go through that procedure again if I could help it.

We loaded up the boat then took a break to eat. It seemed I had come a long way for it to be only noon. After our quick lunch, we drove down to the boat launch below the dam. From the looks of things, the waves had gotten worse below the dam. I studied the water for quite some time before deciding it would be too risky to go out.

As much as I hated to, it made no sense to wait away the day hoping for the wind to die down. If I had been traveling alone, I would have had no choice but to wait, but Dad and Calvin were on a schedule. I had to make it to the ocean by the twentieth of December in order to get Dad and Calvin back to the airport in Spokane by the twenty- first. Today was the thirteenth. This was the disadvantage of having someone along on the trip. Of course, the advantage was the comfort of seeing a friendly face every day. These were the pros and cons. Still, I hated to skip a section of the river. I felt it lessened what I was doing. Even though I was not doing this for any one but myself, I hated to lower the accomplishment in my own eyes. I still had a lot of time, but I didn't know yet what was in store and couldn't afford to wait around this early in the trip. Submitting to the conditions, I got back in the truck and we drove off looking for another access point to the river.

I determined from the map that we could get the boat back in the water near a little town called Snake River, a fitting name for a town around these parts. When we got within sight of the river, my heart sank. The waves had gotten even higher since we left Lower Monumental Dam. The wind blew hard and straight from the southwest. Unfortunately, the river turned at this place and headed southwest, straight into the teeth of the wind. There was no use in even thinking about getting on the water. Dad turned the truck around and we drove the twenty miles to Ice Harbor Dam. I felt completely disgusted with the situation and having to cheat the distance between the two dams. But at the same time, I felt I had no choice if I was going to make it to the Pacific.

CHAPTER 20

"proceeded on Seven miles to the junction of this river and the Columbia which joins from the N.W. In every direction from the junction of those rivers the countrey is one continued plain low and rises from the water gradually, except a range of high Countrey on the opposit Side about 2 miles distant from the Columbia."

William Clark October 16, 1805

"I passed from the mouth of the Snake onto the Columbia River . . . no trees yet to speak of."

Chris Bechtold December 14, 1999

AT ICE HARBOR DAM, MY LUCK CHANGED. The wind subsided enough that I felt I could make the eight or so miles to Pasco, Washington. Dad and Calvin looked at the map and told me they would meet me at the bridge going into Pasco. There looked to be a small park there with a boat access. I told them I would race them there and took off. They beat me, and I am sure their ride was much smoother than mine.

I called it a day at Pasco. With the boat tied up securely at the docks, we all piled back into the truck and went into town to get dinner. Calvin didn't look too good and said he felt he was coming down with something. As soon as dinner was over the guys found a motel at the edge of town. I took a hot shower to refresh myself and warm up before heading back to the river.

All of my early impressions about this trip were that it would be a quick and easy downstream trip to the ocean. I never even thought about the wind I might come up against. On the Missouri I ran into some bad wind, but nothing like I was seeing here. Worse yet, the wind showed no signs of letting up. Living in Choteau, Montana, I was used

193

to wind, but I never was out on the water in a boat with the wind blowing like it did here. I began to get a little worried about the next few days. The river had my attention; I just hoped that was all it was going to get.

I slept that night under a tree in the small park at Pasco. Just my luck, it rained throughout the night and I was forced to roll up in my tarp again. The trees were much bigger at this park than at the previous night's camp, however, so I stayed relatively dry. My nemesis this night was traffic. The sound of trucks roaring across the bridge beside the park made it hard to sleep deeply.

I lit my stove the next morning to warm up for the day. After packing all the gear in the boat, I saw Dad and Calvin approaching. Just as I was hoping, they brought hot coffee. I have a serious addiction to coffee and doubt I could even think about the trip, much less accomplish it without coffee.

The morning sky loomed low and overcast. Looking over the water, I could only detect the slight rise and fall of a few swells. I hated to waste time and told the guys I better get going. By the time I finished my coffee and donuts, the waves were beginning to form in a light breeze. It was eight o'clock. Against my better judgment, I decided to go.

From the Pasco bridge to the mouth of the Snake, where it joins the Columbia River, is at most one mile. The waves proved to be of little concern in this short passage, but the moment I rounded the point into the Columbia River, things got ugly. The wind again blew from the south. At the junction of the two rivers, the wind had a long run up the Columbia to gain speed and build waves. Having turned on to the Columbia I was committed. The waves started to batter the boat and soon the front was leaping and pounding from wave top to wave top.

I tried to swing towards the eastern shore, but, to my surprise, the water depth diminished quickly. A soft sand bottom reached from the banks out about one hundred yards, making it impossible for me to get the boat to shore and out of the waves. To add to the problem, the shallow water made the waves even choppier, carrying the boat into the sandy bottom between swells. At one point, the prop hit bottom hard enough to kill the motor, leaving me sideways to the high waves.

Water washed over the sides of the boat. I was afraid I would be swamped. I could have gotten out of the boat, but I was unsure how solid the bottom was and if the water level was consistent all the way to shore. I needed to stick with the boat. I got the motor going and by gunning the engine on the upswells got out to deeper water again. I scanned the bank looking for any way at all to get off the water, but to no avail. I would have to keep going until I saw a place to escape.

Meanwhile, it had started to rain again. Not that I noticed immediately since the spray from the waves soaked me thoroughly once again. With reference to rain and for comparison, Choteau, Montana gets very little precipitation, roughly eleven inches a year, and that comes mostly in the form of snow. I prepared for rain about as much as I had prepared for the rest of the trip, namely little. I wore an old Gore-Tex coat I received four years previous and my trusty old hip boots over wool pants. On my hands, I wore wool gloves and for headwear, a wool hat. I soaked up water like a sponge. I stayed warm, though. There is nothing like wool to retain warmth while being wet, but I took on a lot of weight with all the moisture. That old Gore-Tex coat had seen better days, too. It was leaking water like a paper shirt.

Being wet was not my biggest concern at that moment. Actually, my biggest concern was trying not to get completely wet by ending up swamped in the river. The waves just seemed to get larger and larger. The whitecaps were dishing out a beating to my little boat. I could see no end in sight to the rough water. Keeping a tight hold to the motor with one hand and my little bench seat with the other, I kept pounding onward, hoping that somewhere ahead I would find a way out of this terrible predicament I found myself in.

Just off to my left, I could see traffic passing on the highway along the river. I wondered if any of those people knew my situation. I doubted it. I actually doubted that any of them noticed me at all. I wasn't going to let them hear about me on the evening news either. Ahead of me I could see the river taking a turn to the west. At this bend was where the Walla Walla River dumped into the Columbia. Stealing a glance between the waves, I saw the truck parked along the water with its headlights flashing. I scanned the water between the truck and the boat and tried to pick a path that would get me to shore with out hanging up on the sandy bottom of the river.

Using the channel of the Walla Walla, I was able to get in close to shore and hop out. I towed the boat the remaining distance to the truck. With Calvin and Dad's help, we carried the boat up the bank and got it onto the back of the truck. Once again, I had been lucky. It seemed like this trip had turned into one struggle after another. It was not so much a vacation on the great western river, but a struggle to survive from one day to the next. The date was December 14th, I had been on the river three days, and every day had been a close call. The enjoyment of the trip was disappearing rapidly. It had become a challenge just to keep going.

CHAPTER 21

"we landed a few minits to view a rapid . . . which was verry bad . . . at 16 miles the river passes into the range of high Countrey"

William Clark October 18, 1805

"This is a fickle, dangerous river . . . the H_2O was like glass . . . kept going and it really got rough."

Chris Bechtold December 15, 1999

I PILED INTO THE TRUCK, soaked from head to toe. Once again, I was forced to portage a portion of the river. I was getting disgusted with the whole process. We drove ahead to the next dam, or should I say damn. I think what I found so discomforting about the dams was the incessant hum they emitted. There was an undertone about them that never relented. A constant, unyielding hum, that in time became either unnoticeable, or unbearable. For me, it was the latter. I found the noise nerve wracking. Combined with the scale of the dams and the federal bureaucratic administration of them, the dams made me feel like a caged animal.

I never felt this way about the dams on the Missouri River, but then again, I never got too close to them if I could help it. Also, the dams on the Missouri were earthen dams for the most part. Here, the dams are large concrete walls; within them, enormous turbines spin, pouring forth electricity to the entire West. Maybe they bothered me because they make a person feel so small. We all like to feel big in our own way. Being out on the river, absorbing the feel of the water and the smells of the river, I tended to feel empowered, but on approaching the dams, all that was stripped away, and I was only left with the feeling of my own minuteness against these great walls of concrete and the policies of the government.

I was pleased to see that McNary Dam lay near the town of Umatilla, Oregon. We took advantage of that by stopping in at a truck stop and eating a big lunch with a hot cup of coffee. A marina lay just off the interstate on our way to the dam, so rather than cross the river to the dam to launch, we pulled in and put the boat in the water from the Oregon side. Surprisingly, by the time we got the boat back in the water, the surface of the river looked smooth as glass.

Seeing how smooth the river was, Dad decided that now might be the best time for him to join me. The small portion of river that Dad traveled with me proved to be the best traveling of the entire western trip. The river stayed smooth for twenty miles. All around us, geese and ducks rose off the water. Small islands dotted this portion of the river. Around them, waterfowl gathered by the hundreds. At every cove we flushed some species of fowl. Except for the cloudy sky, the fates seemed to be shining down upon us. This would not last.

After the first twenty miles the river began to rise and fall with swells. Soon enough, we started to see waves forming. Calvin had been hop-scotching ahead of us on the Washington shore. The next time we caught up with him, Dad decided to get out. Now it was back to Herschel and me. Once again, the waves battered us.

I was not so much worried about capsizing in the waves at this point, for the waves did not seem to be getting any larger nor the weather any worse. My largest concern was the tremendous beating the waves were giving my boat.

I picked a course that kept me tight against the rocky shore on the Washington side of the river. Here, twenty to fifty foot granite cliffs bordered the river. Against these, the waves crashed one after another, enough that they lost some strength in their own backwash. This afforded me some protection from the wind and waves combined.

I picked my way under these cliffs, battering the boat upon the waves. By the time I saw the John Day Dam ahead, I was ready to get off the river. It had beaten me up. My ribs and back ached from pounding on the metal seat of the boat. After pulling it ashore at the dam, I found the waves had cracked the boat's front support rib. Just my luck, it was also raining. It had been a long day and I was ready to call it quits for the evening. We portaged the boat around the dam, putting it back in for a quick run to the bridge at Marysville, Washington. I tied up under the bridge, deciding to sleep out of the rain underneath it.

Dad and Calvin headed across the river into Biggs, Oregon and got a motel room for the night. By this time Calvin was looking and feeling pretty sick. Dad also felt bad, possibly catching whatever it was that Calvin had. The two of them together looked like actors for a cold and flu medicine commercial. I tried not to get too close to either one of them. The last thing I needed was to get sick and still have a couple of days of river ahead of me.

I found it hard to keep my distance when we all piled into the pickup. I told them not to take it personally when I kept cracking the window on the truck and breathing the fresh air. It seemed that the damp cold air had taken its toll on both of them. I was constantly damp and wet, but I stayed warm in my wool clothes and the fresh air kept me invigorated.

I slept fitfully under the bridge that night. Every vehicle that crossed the bridge sent a deep rumbling echo amid the steel girders. My bed situation did not help me to sleep. The banks of the river under the bridge had been rip-rapped up to the bottom of the bridge. In order to get a spot to sleep I had to toss any rocks that I could lift out of the way. This left me with a sleeping area just big enough for my tired body to slip down into, though not comfortably. By no means did my little nest prove to be level either. The ground sloped over one foot from the top of my head to the bottom of my feet, which I had to curl underneath myself to fit into the rocks. But, I was dry. Throughout the night I fought with Herschel who continued to muscle his way into my little area. He had no soft spot to sleep either, so he would worm his way in tightly against me. The result was that neither one of us slept well.

The next morning, I got up early and boiled coffee. Dad and Calvin showed up about an hour later. I laid out the day's plans. The water looked smooth so I decided I would plan on meeting up with the two of them at the Dalles Dam. I looked forward to getting to the Dalles, it meant my entry into the mountains again, and one step closer to my final destination. With that, I pushed off into the slow current of the Columbia.

The morning proved to be idyllic for river travel, but also a little foreboding. Heavy clouds lay low in the western sky, forewarning of even more rain and bad weather. I kept the motor opened up wide trying to cover as many miles as possible before the weather changed which might force me to a halt. On each side of me the high desert land transformed to mountain foothills.

I noted that the riverbanks seemed to change also. The rocky shoreline increased in height, creating high, granite cliffs that loomed over the water. Above the cliffs I noticed steep grassy hillsides with a scattering of trees. In the distance, I could discern more trees on the hillsides. I knew the mountains were closing in.

How this land must have looked to Lewis and Clark. Much different than the land I was now seeing, that is for sure. From entries in the journals, I knew that in this area the river was fast and treacherous. Captain Clark wrote on October 21st, 1805 "we halted a fiew minits to examine the rapid before we entered it which was our Constant Custom, and all that was verry dangerous put out all who Could not Swim to walk around, after passing this rapid we proceeded on passed another rapid at 5 miles lower down . . . a little below is a bad rapid which is bad crowded with hugh rocks scattered in every Direction." One set of rapids after another confronted the men of the expedition. Add to this the number of natives that followed the Corp's progress down the river, and the difference between the landscapes in the last two centuries proved dramatic.

What must it have been like to speed down the river unhindered by dams, feeling the surge of the current around your boat? Imagine looking ahead and seeing the spray of rapids and the dull roar of water crashing amongst the rocks. How exhilarating it must have been. Especially knowing that the object of your journey was rapidly approaching. I am sure the men of the expedition must have felt invulnerable. How else to explain their repeated runs through the rapids of the Columbia? Runs that even the natives living along the river would not attempt.

Those must have been heady days for the Corps of Discovery. As for myself, I was not having as much fun. I felt torn between fulfilling my promise to myself of completing the entire voyage on the river, and my responsibilities of maintaining a schedule. Already, I was kicking myself for the loss of miles I already permitted. It seemed that the river was making me pay for every mile I gained.

While all of these thoughts ran through my head, I sped down the Columbia. Before me appeared The Dalles Dam, stretched across the river like a giant ribbon of concrete. The dams at this point on the river had decreased in height from the first dam I encountered on the Snake River. The Dalles Dam had a modest drop of 90 feet. I saw the guys pulled up at the boat launch next to the locks and pulled over to check in.

I decided to look over the locks, the smaller drop at the dam appealed to me a little more than the one hundred and five feet of drop at Lower Granite Dam. I thought I might lock through this dam rather than unload the boat once again. But, my apprehension around the dams got the best of me and I decided to portage once again. This proved a little more frustrating than I had hoped it would be.

After we loaded up the boat and piled into the front of the truck, we could not find a launch site below the dam. We crossed the river to look for an access point on the other side, but with no luck. I got more and more frustrated with the time we were wasting looking for a point to launch the boat. By now, I wished I had just locked through the dam. We found an access point downstream where I was able to get the boat back in the water on the Washington side. All the time we had been looking for a way to get on the river, the surface of the water had been smooth as silk. Knowing how fickle the river could be around here, I hated to waste even a minute of smooth water.

With the boat back on the river, I sped off upstream. I made a small loop under the dam then headed downstream. As I was making my loop, I could not help but notice the platforms, cobbled together with two by fours and plywood that hung from the rocky cliffs along the river. These scaffoldings were where the local Indians fished for salmon in their traditional manner. I admired their pluck for standing out on the spindly scaffolds above the river. Throughout that day, I passed numerous fishing platforms of every shape and construction, all clinging tenaciously to the stone faces above the river. I imagine that this tied my journey in a very small way to something that the Corp of Discovery may have seen. Everything else must have seemed so much different, of course, excluding the mountains.

From the Dalles to Hood River, Oregon, the river's surface remained glossy. Rounding the bend at Hood River (wind surfing capitol of the world), I noticed a light swell in the rivers surface, then another and another. Looking downstream, the mountains pulled together, allowing a narrow gap for the river to squeeze through. At the mouth of the canyon, I could see nothing but a wall of gray. I assumed I was entering a foggy area in the mountains with some rain. Meanwhile, the swells seemed to continue, nothing too large, just repeated rhythmic progressions.

CHAPTER 22

"accordingly I deturmined to pass through this placed not-
withstanding the horrid appearance of this agitated gut
swelling, boiling and whorling in every direction,"
William Clark October 24, 1805

"Then it got bad, REAL BAD. Waves came up out of
nowhere and 70 mph wind gusts."
Chris Bechtold December 16, 1999

WHAT HAPPENED NEXT proved to be the most dangerous experience I had on the river. I continued on towards the wall of clouds. Rain soon started to blow out of the gray wall ahead of me. Before I could react, the water's surface changed from light swells to waves. Rain fell from the sky in large drops and I could scarcely see the banks of the river. I started for the Oregon side of the river, but could find no place to put the boat ashore. High rock cliffs lined the bank. At every opening I looked for a place to find refuge on shore, but never with any luck.

The waves grew, becoming dangerous, whitecapped demons trying to smash the boat. I could not risk turning. To do so would have brought the sides of the boat open to the waves and I would have swamped. The waves continued to increase with the wind. At one point, the boat was being tossed completely out of the water. The whine of the engine sounded like a shrieking animal. The gear that I had placed at the front of the boat all bounced back towards the rear. I tried to kick it forward, but I could not risk taking my eyes from the river.

Waves punished the little boat, slamming it down time and again on the crests of the next wave. Wind shrieked across the water, carrying spray into my face and the sound of the motor away. I was afraid the wind would catch the front end of the boat and flip it end over end. I thought I could end up in the water at any moment. I tried to prepare myself for this event and how I would get to shore in the high waves.

Amidst all of this, I saw over the leaping front of the boat, a large rock standing out of the river. It stood about 20 feet above the water's surface and I estimated its width to be about 15 feet. The course I was on would bring me directly behind the rock, cutting the severity of the waves and sheltering me from the brunt of the wind. Off to my left, I saw a small cove in the high rock walls of the shore. If I could make it to that little cove, I could get out of this terrible predicament.

In the scant shelter of that lone rock, I made up my mind to try for the cove. I pointed the bow just a little off center to the wind and proceeded into the hellish waves. Letting the waves take hold of the boat, I kept my place in the water and between waves and poundings, I inched toward the cove. The waves subsided just enough that I knew I could make it. I pulled the boat into the cove and looked for a place to tie up.

There was only a little crack in the rocks along shore that I could fit the boat into. I headed into it. Now I had to get out of the boat without being flung back into the water and rocks. I screwed the motor down tight to keep it from turning and twisted the throttle up so the boat stayed pressed into the rocks; then I scurried across my gear, grabbing the lead rope before jumping to shore. In this way, I got the boat tied up amid the waves and rocks.

After wrapping my lead rope around the point of a rock, I leapt back into the boat and shut off the motor. The waves were battering the boat upon the rocks. I jumped ashore one last time with my essential gear and let some slack out of the lead rope so the boat could bob freely in the waves.

When I looked out over the river, wind and waves whipped by. I had been very lucky just to make it to wherever I was. The bottom of the boat had been smashed in leaving a three foot round dent. Rocks banged against the sides of the boat occasionally, but I didn't mind. I felt relieved just to be on terra firma. I had to find Calvin and Dad to let them know I was all right.

I headed up the bank towards Interstate 84 on the Oregon side. I must have been quite a sight crawling over the guardrail of the interstate wearing my hip boots and wool, soaked to the bone like a drowned cat. Looking back over at the river I saw a towboat going downstream. The waves hit the front of the barges washing over their bows. I could not believe I had been out on that water. I had been very lucky. I figured Dad and Calvin must have thought I was a goner.

Hiking along the interstate, I came to a small state park that was closed for the season. Just inside the front gate I spied a phone booth. Using my phone card I called Mom in Illinois. I knew that there would be no other way for me to get a hold of Dad. I also did not know his cell phone number, and knew that he was aware of this. Mom was the only contact that we both could count on communicating through.

When Mom answered the phone, she asked how things were going and if I was having fun. I told her I was not having fun, and on top of that Dad would probably be calling her soon. I told her to tell Dad I was OK and that I was at Viento State Park as well as which Interstate mile marker it was near. She immediately asked if I was OK which I assured her I was. I quickly said I would tell her more later and please relay the message to Dad as soon as she could. I knew he would be worried.

I was right about Dad. About forty-five minutes later he and Calvin pulled into the park. Dad's face still showed the worry he felt while Calvin looked like death warmed over. I think Calvin was too sick to worry. I filled Dad in on what happened while we all piled into the truck to head for the closest motel we could find. We ended up in the small town of Cascade Locks. I decided to leave the boat where it was and just hope it would be there in the morning. I didn't have any other option.

For once, I did not balk at getting a hotel room. I wanted nothing to do with sleeping out this night. Rain poured from the sky in buckets. Calvin looked and sounded terrible and Dad wasn't looking much better. My support crew didn't seem to be weathering the journey too well. I took a hot shower in the hotel and changed into dry clothes. After warming up, Dad and I went downtown for dinner. Calvin stayed behind being too sick to go. At dinner I told Dad I was beginning to think this trip crazy.

Every day brought some new danger. What was I getting out of this? Right then it appeared nothing. If anything, it cost me time off from work and money for all the fuel and supplies. I only continued because I swore to myself that I was going to do it. Now I wondered how much that really meant. I damned near killed myself earlier that day, Calvin looked terribly sick, and now Dad was coming down with the same thing. On top of all that, I had not even kept up my promise, but instead skipped about fifty miles of river. I asked Dad if he thought I should keep going.

He replied that it was all up to me. I was the one out there every day. It was my call to decide whether I should continue or not. I knew he was going to say that. All that did was put the ball back in my court. He said no matter what I chose, he would understand. Adding that I already had come this far and had nothing to be ashamed about. I knew he was trying to make it easy for me, should I decide to give up. Thing is, I just could not do it. I couldn't quit. Not now, not this close. I had to keep going, rain, shine, wind or waves, I had to at least try. Dad said he understood. I really think if anyone would, it was my Dad.

That night I slept on the floor of the motel room. Even with all the stress and weather tiring me, it was hard to sleep listening to Calvin and Dad hack and cough between snoring. I was glad to see morning arrive. Outside the rain had let up to a light drizzle. We ate a big breakfast before heading back to the boat. To my relief, it was still there. I climbed in and piloted it back to the park that I had made the phone call from. There, we slipped around the gates with the truck and got close enough to drag the boat up and load it.

We portaged to below the Bonneville Dam, the last dam on the Columbia, or first if you choose to look at it that way. Bonneville Dam was the first dam to be built on the Columbia back in 1937. In addition to being the first, it was also the lowest dam, with a drop of only 70 feet. I heaved a sigh of relief at being past all the dams. All the way up one side of he continent and down the other, I had run into dams; now they were all behind me.

The drizzle turned to rain before we got the boat back on the water. I entered the Cascade Mountains just the day before at Hood River. Now, I was leaving the mountains behind me, traveling into the broad valley of the Columbia between Portland, Oregon and Vancouver, Washington. The end was in sight, not physically, but I could feel I was getting close. The water had a smell about it that could only be ocean. My excitement began to increase with every mile I put behind me.

As I passed through the city of Portland, I took time to motor around the docks at Hayden Island. I needed fuel and wanted to get a closer look at all the floating homes. This was something completely novel to me. Beautiful homes, as nice as many in Choteau, were built on floats, forming communities on the water. I could scarcely believe it, being the landlubber I am. I circled around the island taking in the views and admiring the boats and homes. After fueling up, I headed across the river to Vancouver to make a phone call to the newspaper.

Word of my trip had gotten out the night before and a reporter called the hotel room to set up an interview in Vancouver. I called back and told the reporter I would meet her at one of the hotels overlooking the river. I waited for about a half hour, watching the river roll by. By then the reporter hadn't showed and with fog setting in, I decided I could wait no longer. I wanted to get past Portland and Vancouver before nightfall. From the maps, I planned to meet up with Dad and Calvin in St. Helens, Oregon for the night. I needed to get moving if I was going to make it by dark.

CHAPTER 23

"The Fog so thick this morning that we could not see a man 50 Steps off."

William Clark November 3, 1805

"Rain, Fog, . . . Lots of things to worry about in this river, wind, waves, big ships, logs."

Chris Bechtold December 16, 1999

LEAVING THE HOTEL, I started into the fog. I had become accustomed to being the only boat on the water, but things changed very quickly. Now I was not the only boat and definitely not the biggest. I passed several tugboats in the fog, dodging to stay out of their way. Angling toward the shore, imagine my surprise when the dark line I had thought was shore turned out to be a ship. My rule of thumb when out on the water is to yield the right of way to anything with a prop bigger than my boat. I reversed course as quickly as I could and tried to get my bearings.

I finally found the shoreline in the fog and stayed as close to it as I could. I needed to find the mouth of the Willamette River. From there I planned on turning into a small slough that would take me to St. Helens, thereby keeping me off the main river and out of traffic. I followed the shore until I found the mouth of the Willamette. I did not like what I saw.

The inky dark waters of the Columbia turned a muddy brown where the flooding waters of the Willamette joined. On top of the dangers I faced with large ships, fog, and other general hazards, now I had to keep an eye out in the fog for logs racing down the river. Easing along the shore, I kept alert to every possible danger and moved slowly trying to find the mouth of the slough I was looking for. About the time I found it, the Coast Guard came along, slowing to look me over. I sure hoped

Ship at Vancouver, WA

they didn't look too close. I was in no position to receive a marine inspection. I would have failed miserably.

The Coast Guard just gave me a wave and with that, I turned into the slough. Here, the current was more subdued and I didn't have all the dangers of the big river. I opened up the throttle trying to get as far as I could before nighttime caught me on the river. In the gloom of the impending darkness and fog, I raced down the little channel hoping I would know when I reached St. Helens.

The land I traveled in seemed the opposite end of the spectrum from that which I started out in on this leg of my journey. The high desert country of southeast Washington was but a distant memory. Here, the countryside was lush as a jungle. Heavy foliage lined the muddy banks of the river. Dampness pervaded everything. I still remained soaked to the bone, but relatively warm. A steady curtain of rain fell, obscuring my vision even more. I imagined that everything around here needed to be moved, painted, or run the risk of being overgrown with vegetation.

No wonder the leather clothing of the Expedition's men would rot. I felt like the Gore-tex coat I was wearing would fall apart at the seams in the incessant rain. I might as well have been wearing canvas for all the good my old coat was doing. I could not fathom how miserable the Corps of Discovery must have been in this damp, cold climate. It must have been near impossible to move around in the countryside, too. Thick vegetation crowded the river's edge making even a small excursion into the surrounding woods a trial.

At long last, I reached St. Helens. Darkness just about covered me in the fog. Passing along in the thick air and rain, I spotted the truck lights flashing above the city docks. I pulled in and tied up. Calvin and Dad had already rented a motel room for the night and now I need only dry and warm up before dinner. That sounded fine to me. I could not wait to shed my sodden woolens. That night, like every night, the heavy burden of worry fell from my shoulders like my wet clothing. I had made it through another day.

"Rained all the after part of last night, rain continues this morning," Captain Clark wrote. In two hundred years the weather seemed to change little. From what I looked at on the map, I thought just possibly I could make it to the ocean this day. I surely wanted to. To tell the truth, I just wanted to get there so I could be through with it all. The joy had left this trip long ago. It was instead a struggle to continue every day. I am sure that Lewis and Clark must have felt this way, too after having come to this wet coastal area. They had arrived around the same time I did; the cold, rainy, winter season.

I left St. Helens in the rain with river conditions fairly good. The water surface had a small chop to it, but nothing too bad. I had gone twenty miles when the river widened and the waves increased. Highway 30 skirts along the river at this point allowing Dad and Calvin to hop-scotch along with me and keep better tabs on my progress. Calvin felt even worse by now. I believe he was as ready for me to finish as I was. At Rainier, Oregon I started to pass a few large ships, inbound from the ocean. I marveled at their size. They made the barges I passed on the upper river look like toys.

The wind also picked up at Rainier. Here, the river makes a turn to the Northwest catching the winds blowing off the ocean. I pounded along on the waves, each one getting a little bit larger than the last until I reached Longview Bridge. There, I halted. I knew from now on, I would have little access to the highway and could not keep reliable contact with Dad in the truck. I also did not want to get caught on the water like I had two days earlier. It was at most thirty miles to the Pacific Ocean. I had to decide whether to keep going or turn in. The current of the river picked up considerably with the pull of the outgoing tide. A decision had to be made.

I watched another ship pass by and saw the waves breaking against its enormous bow. The waves did not even warrant a blink of the eye from the folks aboard that ship. For me, those waves were a persistent source of worry. The wind was increasing and with it, the rain. With a heaving sigh, I decided I had come far enough. I headed back to Rainier and pulled in to a loading ramp where Dad and Calvin could pick me up. I was done.

We loaded the boat back onto the truck. Soaked again, and cold, I told Dad that I didn't want to risk getting caught out there. I said if we found a good place to launch near Astoria, I would put back in and back track to make up for the lost mileage. But I did not want to stay out there today.

Seems I made the right choice. On our drive to Astoria, the radio reported a Pacific storm coming in and advised all boats to come to shore. High waves and heavy rain were forecast. The storm was to arrive by nightfall. I let out a sigh of relief. In Astoria, we drove straight through town on our way to Fort Clatsop National Park. The rain was coming down in sheets when we arrived. I was glad to see the storm.

At Fort Clatsop we were the only visitors. I toured the center and visited with the folks manning the desk. Dad puffed up with pride and told them about my trip. We all talked about the journey and my experiences. I took a few pictures inside the museum and at the fort. It seemed much smaller than I had imagined, similar to Fort Mandan.

Rain fell the whole time we were there. My mood reflected the weather. I felt a melancholy disappointment about the whole trip. Here I was, at the destination I had dreamt of reaching, but I felt I did not earn my passage here. I had skipped almost eighty miles of the passage. This made me feel like a cheat. Once again, I had reached an anticlimactic ending of the river. Like my final moments on the Missouri, I felt a lonely melancholy about the ending of my journey. I had traveled over 3,100 miles from St. Louis in a boat, and still I felt like there needed to be more.

We left Fort Clatsop Park just before it closed and headed back towards Astoria. On the way, the radio reported the Coast Guard was pulling vessels off the water in approach of the storm. Leaving the trees around Clatsop we looked over the water. High winds and driving rain buffeted the shoreline. I was sure glad I was not out there.

Calvin, by this time, had a terrible fever and hardly a voice. He consented finally to letting us take him to a hospital. At the emergency room, they diagnosed him with acute bronchitis and gave him a prescription. Lucky for him they did not bleed him like the members of the original Expedition. We found a room at a small hotel in Astoria. After we got Calvin settled in, Dad and I went out to dinner in celebration of my journey's conclusion. I think we celebrated the end of being out on the water every day more than the true end of the trip. We both admitted this had been no pleasure trip. I think we paid for our passage upon the Columbia with gray hairs.

That night in the motel room we enjoyed the end of the trail. I awoke early the next morning and slipped from the room for a walk with Herschel. The falling rain cast a gray, dreary outlook over the harbor. Sloshing through the puddles, I wandered down the streets of Astoria, taking in the sights of town and the ocean smells from the mouth of the river.

The sidewalk soon lead me to a small park under the bridge. I strolled down to the waters edge. The rain and heavy air obscured the far side of the river. Looking around I spied a monument behind me and ambled over to read it. The monument was in honor of all from this area who had died on the water. I scanned the dates and found that twenty-one people had lost their lives in 1998. To my dismay, nine souls had perished in 1999. These deaths occurred right close to this spot that I stood before. It was a sobering realization. I had been very lucky, this I knew. Just how lucky I now fully realized.

I gazed out over the dark waters. Somehow, luck had been on my side. I had taken on a river I knew very little about and survived. I looked back on the past few days and realized the chances I had taken. The last week had been no picnic, no fun journey; it had been a trial by water, and I had passed. I don't think my survival had much to do with innate skills, but more with just blind luck or divine intervention. How else to explain what I had done?

CHAPTER 24

*"Great joy in camp we are in view of the Ocian, this great
Pacific Octean which we have been so long anxious to See."*
William Clark November 7, 1805

*"Took . . . some pictures and . . . watched the waves on
the Pacific."*
Chris Bechtold December 18, 1999

ALMOST TWO HUNDRED YEARS PREVIOUS, the men of the Corps of
Discovery had accomplished so much more than I had. They had per-
severed through countless hardships, endured trials and tribulations that
today are unfathomable, and they did it all unscathed. I do not think
they had been lucky like me. I believe they accomplished their grand
feat with preparation and fortitude. I only wish I could claim the same.

What I marveled at during my few days along the coast was the
amount of rain that fell. In the last two days of my journey down the
Columbia, seven of inches of rain fell. To this day, I find it hard to
believe that so much rain could come in so short a period of time. I
admit this was unusual even for the coastal area. It was a lot of rain.

Now imagine being out in this cold rain with only leather clothing
on. The rain continuing to fall, leather becoming heavy and slick, and
you must continue on in these conditions with little or no shelter keeping tinder and gunpowder dry. That is how the men of the Corp of
Discovery did it. I wore a Gore-tex coat and woolens with rubber hip
boots and remained wet and miserable for days. I can only imagine
what it must have been like two hundred years ago.

Looking back at all I accomplished, I felt unimpressed. In perspective, I had only done what had already been accomplished two centuries

before. My ending to the trip had been anticlimactic. I simply finished traveling and prepared to go home. Now, from the comforts of my own home, I look back and wish that I had done things differently. I could have walked the banks of the river more, seen more of the country and visited with more of the people. I would not have taken the crazy chances just to meet a schedule that meant little.

The whole purpose of the trip was to see what Lewis and Clark had seen from the perspective of the river. I wanted to look at the land from the water, to experience the thrill of what lay around the next bend: smell the air, hear the birds and feel the wind on my face. I did this, but I will never be able to experience these things like the first white men who traveled this way. Not because of advances in technology or civilization, if that is what all this really is, but because the rivers Lewis and Clark traveled upon now exist only in short stretches.

These little stretches are connected like jewels on a strand of river, but the whole river no longer remains the same. How would early explorers view the large lakes of the Dakotas or the high dams of the Columbia? Would they look upon these things as advances in technology and living conditions? They certainly are that. Or would those early peoples look out over the landscape and lament the passing of the river? I don't claim to know. Who can?

For myself, I lament the loss. I traveled over 3,100 miles of river across our great land, reading The Journals of Lewis and Clark and others, I mourn the disappearance of the grand sights I read about. The rivers still flow, they still pass through outstanding areas, but we have tried to take the wildness out of the waters. For the most part we have succeeded. Yet, every now and then the old rivers, the wild ones, rear their mighty heads and remind us that they are not completely tamed.

Good for them. I hope that the old rivers push on, letting us know that they were once the great roads of a nation. I think they still are, but are little known. Maybe someday, more people will take the chance and travel down these rivers looking for something of the history of our nation. It is still there. The history is written in the landscape. It is in the names of towns and creeks, all standing idly along the river banks, all watching the waters flow by, wondering when the ever-changing rivers will change again. I know they will. But will we allow these changes to be in the right direction? Who decides? All of us, that's who. All of us must do our part to give voice to the river.

I spent the early morning walking the river's bank in the rain, wondering about the river, my journey, and all that has passed down the currents. The rain continued all morning. By nine o'clock; I arrived back to the motel to meet up with Calvin and Dad. My walk did little to calm my urge to be out on the water again. I told Dad if he was bored maybe we could go for one last spin on the water.

He readily agreed and we drove to a boat launch at the edge of town. I unloaded for the last time and put the boat on the water. The waves were light, but high enough to get my attention, yet not so bad that I would not go out. In the rain, I backed away from the dock and motored out into the big water of the bay. I did not intend to go far. I couldn't. I just needed to get the boat out in the bigger water to experience the salt air and slap of the bigger waves.

It didn't take much rough water to get my fill. I motored back to the dock to see if Dad wanted to go for a spin. The rain had picked up and he declined. With that, I pulled in to the boat ramp. For me, the trip now had reached its end. I drained the gas out of the motor before pulling it from the boat. I did not know if I would even use the boat again. I had fulfilled my promise to reach salt water with it, a promise that I made back in Illinois on the banks of the Mississippi River. I had now accomplished my goal. Dad and I loaded the boat on the truck and headed to the motel to get Calvin.

We decided to enjoy our last day on the coast and tour the area. We lolled away the day by driving down to Cannon Beach where Lewis and Clark encountered a beached whale. We did not find any whales, but I did find a small seal washed ashore. I looked over the little critter trying to find what had killed it, but could find no clues. The rest of the day we spent traveling along the coast. By nightfall, we found ourselves back near Portland.

After another motel stay that night, we started back to Spokane, Washington and the airport. I dropped Dad and Calvin off at the terminal that evening, much the worse for wear than when I picked them up ten days previous. Calvin still looked green around the gills and Dad had the beginnings of some sort of crud, not to mention the amount of worry I placed upon him. I thanked them all I could for the support they gave me. I truly could not have done this leg of my trip without them. After wishing each other safe voyages and Merry Christmas, I left them and drove back to Montana.

Late that night, I pulled into the snowy drive of my cabin. The next morning I unpacked my frozen gear from the truck. After putting everything away and dragging the boat across the snow, I settled down in front of the fire. With the entire journey behind me, I felt like nothing had ever happened. Even now, when I think back, I sometimes believe my entire journey was no more than a dream. How was it that I, some part-time cowboy, ended up making such a journey, and what was it that spurred me on? I don't know that I can answer that even to this day.

I am often asked why did you do it? The answer is so complex I have not the words to express it. Yet, sometimes I feel the answer deceivingly simple. Maybe the best answer I can give is simply that I knew I could.

"A fine morning we commenced wrighting &c."
William Clark September 26, 1806

Finally! At the confluence of the Columbia River and Pacific Ocean

AT THE TIME OF THIS WRITING, it has been over two years since I completed my journey at the mouth of the Columbia River. Since that time, I have been asked time and again if I would do it again. I never hesitate with my answer. Yes, an emphatic Yes, I would. Although, I might think twice about going down the Columbia and Snake Rivers again, I would not hesitate to float the Missouri River.

There is something magical and captivating about the grand, old, muddy Missouri. It grasps hold of your imagination and hangs on tight. It is a river of romance and adventure, history and conflict. The swirling waters at once take hold of a person, pulling one onward and downstream, luring one along for the trip of a lifetime.

My attraction with the Missouri became almost immediate the first time I put in upon its waters. I had seen both ends of the great river and knew I somehow must see what connected them. I will never regret that I did. From my first day upon the river, adventure loomed around every bend.

Where else in America can a person have an extended expedition and never leave the interior of our great nation? For years the Missouri River has been overlooked as an outlet for adventure. It has all the needed ingredients for a memorable journey. One can put in for a day or for months. Travel up stream or down, cover the upper river, the middle reservoirs or the lower river. The possibilities are endless. All a person needs is the gumption to do it and time.

I foresee the Missouri River being a new outlet of recreation for changing world. Threats of terrorism and an unsure economy have led many travelers to re-think their globe trotting plans for vacation and adventure. Why go thousands of miles away, when the great outdoors and the big skies of the West are waiting out the back door? The most wonderful aspect of the Missouri is that it is so easily accessible to millions of people.

Each year a handful of adventuresome folks put on the river in Montana and float downstream with the Mississippi their final destination. Some even choose further goals. It is not an impossible trip. It only requires some planning and fortitude, and a little bit of common sense.

Since the completion of my journey, several people have contacted me with plans to float the Missouri. I usually provide information on what hazards to watch out for and recommend certain items they take along. Many people want to see the river at certain sections and have no river experience. I often recommend outfitters in instances such as this. Many others want to be fully self-reliant. For this reason, I am providing a small list of things to consider before undertaking this two thousand plus mile trip.

BOAT: For upstream travel, I recommend a 14 foot or longer jon boat with a Modified V bow. Never use a boat narrower than a 48-inch bottom. For downstream travel, a canoe can be used, but a person must be aware that there is little or no current on the reservoirs of the Dakotas. It could mean a lot of paddling upon some very rough water or under a baking sun. For this reason, I recommend a canoe with a square stern that a small motor can be attached to. I would not recommend a raft due to the strong winds and possibility of debris damage. A jon boat would make a good downstream choice for a boat, also. When choosing a boat, look for welded construction. The abuse from high winds and waves tends to loosen riveted boats.

MOTOR: I chose a Mercury 9.9 hp two cycle outboard. My big concern was weight, and I wanted to be able to carry the motor if something went wrong and I needed to haul it for repairs or carry it into a town. Weight should be a factor if you plan to portage around the dams alone. Also consider the possibility of grounding out and having to push or pull your boat. A heavy motor could cause problems in this sort of situation. Many companies make a 15 hp motor that weighs about the same as the 9.9hp.

GASOLINE: There is no need to carry too much gas. Remember that there are towns scattered all along the lower river. At each reservoir there is at least one marina. So be able to pack gas, but don't go overboard. If you plan on traveling downstream, the current will always take you towards your destination. If you are going upstream, the longest stretch without fuel is in Montana, and you should be thinking of the motorized restriction dates if you plan to go through this section of river.

DAMS: Plan ahead for portage assistance if you are on a time frame. Each dam has a Corps of Engineers office that can direct you to a nearby marina. If time is not of the essence, I found people to be most helpful in giving me a ride. Have gear ready to go and in small bundles to make it easy for a good Samaritan to aid you. By calling ahead to the Corps of Engineers office, you can obtain maps and brochures of each reservoir you will encounter along with locations of campgrounds and boat access points.

TENT: I did not use a tent, but if I were to take one along think, about the change of seasons you will pass through from the most northern part of the river to the mouth of the river near St. Louis. A three-season tent would be the minimum. Be prepared for high winds on the prairie and mosquitoes at lower end of the river.

FOOD: Again, you will be passing many small towns along the way, so you need not pack too light. Groceries can be obtained all the way downriver. Think ahead about weight and how much your boat can safely handle and its optimum speed. During the summer, the sun can literally bake you out on the water. Plan on foods that need little or no refrigeration. Take a container to carry fresh water and fill it at small towns along the way. Also think about a purifier for days when you may have to lay over due to weather. I had problems purifying on the lower river. Too much mud clogged the filter.

MAPS: The US Geological Service and the Army Corps of Engineers have detailed maps of the river channel. However, a good road map will do the trick just fine. I used DeLorme Atlas and Gazetteers for many of the states I traveled through and was very pleased with them. They provide good detail of the river and some of the small access roads that lead to it.

GEAR: Everyone has their own opinions about this, so I won't go into the details, but instead just list some things to consider. For sleeping bags, think of the time of year you will be traveling. The northern states can spit some snow on you all the way into June. Likewise, the southern end of the river can be hot and humid. Plan a bag that will let you regulate temperature, or add a fleece liner to your regular bag. I cooked over a fire as much as I could, but I also carried a small back packer cook stove. I found it handy if I was in a hurry for a hot drink or quick meal. Try to get a small cook stove that will burn different fuels in case the small towns you stop in do not have what you need. Definitely use waterproof river bags. Carry a waterproof camera and keep your essentials in a bag that is handy to take with you on your forays into town. You will have to trust in the good of people and leave your often. Take the most important items with you. Use a good pair of hip boots or waders. I like hip boots because they are more comfortable and maneuverable. Bring along a spare paddle, some rope, and a prop for the motor.

BOOKS: Some books that I recommend reading;
- *The Journals of Lewis and Clark,* Bernard DeVoto
- *Floating the Missouri,* James Willard Schultz
- *The River and I,* John Niehardt
- *RiverHorse,* William Least Heat-Moon

For further information and consulting services, or to obtain equipment for an extended Missouri River Trip, please feel free to contact me.

Chris Bechtold
P.O. Box 543
Choteau, MT 59422

BIBLIOGRAPHY

DeVoto, Bernard. The Journals of Lewis and Clark. *Houghton Mifflin. 1953*

Duncan, Dayton, and Ken Burns. Lewis and Clark, The Journals of the Corps of Discovery. *Alfred A. Knopf, Inc. 1997*

MacGregor, Carol Lynn. The Journals of Patrick Gass. *Mountain Press Publishing. 1997*

You can order additional copies of this title by phone, email, or by sending in the order form below. Please include $4.95 per order for shipping and handling. Check or Money Order only.

ARNICA PUBLISHING
P. O. Box 543 • Choteau, MT 59422
PHONE: 406-466-3442
EMAIL: arnica@3rivers.net
WEB: arnicaventures.com

No. of Copies _____ @ $14.95 each   Subtotal _____

Shipping_____

TOTAL _____

Ship to:

Name:_____

Address:_____

City/State/Zip:_____

Phone:_____

Additional shipping address: (Please include additional $4.95 S/H per address)

Name:_____

Address:_____

City/State/Zip:_____

Phone:_____

☐ *Check here if you would like a gift card included:*

Message:_____

_____

_____